OXFO?
Harco
A fine
over(
(res'
H?
w

Teaching English
Texts 11–18

Also available from Continuum

Teaching Literature 11–18, M. Blocksidge

Learning to Teach Drama 11–18, A. Kempe and H. Nicholson

Teaching English Texts 11–18

Sue Dymoke

continuum

Continuum International Publishing Group

The Tower Building
11 York Road
London SE1 7NX

80 Maiden Lane
Suite 704
New York NY 10038

www.continuumbooks.com

© Sue Dymoke 2009

British Library Cataloguing-in-Publication Data
A catalogue record for this book is available from the British Library.

ISBN: 978-0-8264-9652-2 (paperback)
        978-0-8264-8358-4 (hardcover)

Library of Congress Cataloging-in-Publication Data
Dymoke, Sue, 1962–
Teaching English texts, 11–18 / Sue Dymoke.
        p. cm.   Includes bibliographical references and index.
    ISBN: 978-0-8264-8358-4
1. Reading (Middle school). 2. Reading (Secondary). 3. Young adult literature –
Study and teaching (Middle school). 4. Young adult literature – Study and teaching
(Secondary) I. Title. II. Title: Teaching English texts, eleven to eighteen.

LB1632.D96 2009
428.0071′241–dc22   2008047249

Typeset by Newgen Imaging Systems Pvt Ltd, Chennai, India
Printed and bound in Great Britain by the MPG Books Group

*This book is dedicated to Richard Wallace and
in memory of Bernard Harrison:
two inspiring teachers*

Contents

Acknowledgements

I would like to thank the following authors and publishers who have given their kind permission to reproduce the following work:

John Stuart Clark and David Belbin for an extract from 'If Shakespeare were alive today', published in 2007, *Tripod*, 3, 14–15; Ross Harrison for 'New Technologies and Digital Literacies: Exploring New Approaches to Narrative in Key Stage 3 English' (unpublished Masters assignment), University of Leicester; HMSO for 'Handout 4.4: A medium term planning template from the National Strategies Secondary subject leader development training' (2008: 00123-2008DOM-EN), reprinted with permission (PSI licence C2008001413); Sofie Khachik for 'Retrospective'; Laura Procter for 'Team Leader's Brief' and her accompanying description; Soriya and her teachers for 'Why Did I Do Nothing?'; NATE for the extract from (2006) *Group reading at Key Stage 3 – Year 8 extension pack, Theme: The Holocaust: Once*; Peter Lang Publishers for the extract from Thomas, A. (2007) 'Blurring and Breaking through the Boundaries of Narrative, Literacy and Identity in Adolescent Fan Fiction' in M. Knobel and C. Lankshear (eds) *A New Literacies Sampler*, pp. 139–40; C. Wyatt Smith, K. Kimber and NATE for 'Performance Terrain in Shaping Online, Multimodal Texts', published in Wyatt-Smith, C. and Kimber, K. (2005) 'Valuing and evaluating student-generated online multimodal texts: rethinking what counts', *English in Education*, 39(2), 22–43.

I would also like to thank David Almond, Taghi Amirani, Mike Atkinson, Michael Dymoke, Sandy Fagan, Anne Fairhall, Vicky Obied, and Andrew Parker for their help with interviews and other material; David Belbin, Anthony Haynes, Gill Murray and Megan Thirlaway for their advice and support during the writing of this book; the University of Leicester for granting a semester of study leave during which three chapters were drafted, and five fantastic cohorts of PGCE English/English with Media student teachers 2003 to 2008 for their questions and creativity.

List of Figures and Tables

Figures

Tables

Introduction

Teaching English Texts 11–18 is a book for all beginning secondary English teachers, including those on PGCE, GTTP or SCITT routes into the profession and those who have recently qualified. It is intended to support you in your professional development as reflective and critical readers, makers and teachers of texts. It engages you in debates about the current and future construction of the English curriculum.

Texts of many different kinds are at the heart of the English curriculum and debates about literacy occur on a daily basis in the media. This book offers you a variety of integrated text-focused approaches to teaching the subject of English across the 11–18 age and ability range. The term 'text', as used here, embraces a wide selection of texts including scripts and spoken texts, poetry, prose fiction, literary non-fiction, print media, moving image and multimodal texts. This book explores practical and inclusive approaches to teaching these many different text types and also asks you to think about the changing ways in which we make and interact with the texts around us. It draws on both creative practices and current research in the fields of literacy, English teaching pedagogy and ICT. The use of ICT and considerations for working both with lower ability and gifted and talented students feature throughout. In addition, it includes insights into the textual production processes of some professionals working in different textual fields.

In working with beginning teachers, both in school contexts and latterly as a PGCE English tutor, I am continually learning about the strengths and concerns of those entering (or re-entering) the profession. When confronted with the National Curriculum or an exam specification for the first time, beginning teachers are initially worried about their own subject knowledge.

> 'How will I teach any of these novels. I don't know them?'
> 'I avoided poetry modules at university and don't understand it!'
> 'I've only seen *Macbeth* on stage and that was fifteen years ago. Help!'
> 'I've never read any non-fiction. What do you recommend?'

Comments like those above are very common in the early stages of teaching. However, once you are in school on placement, you will find that you become increasingly concerned with the practicality of how you will survive in the classroom. A hunt for survival strategies or sure-fire winners is only to be expected. Nevertheless, if you *only* look for these you will place limitations on your experience of teaching texts at a time when you should be trying to broaden and deepen it. There is also a danger that by relying on someone else's successful lesson plan, you could neglect the pedagogy which underpins effective classroom practice. An understanding of this pedagogy and the research which has helped to shape it is vital if you, as a beginning teacher, are to lay down the foundations for a successful teaching career and create a repertoire of teaching strategies which can be used flexibly to suit both the students and the texts you are teaching.

This book aims to strike a balance between these different areas of potential concern and development need. It will help you to address aspects of your subject knowledge and point you to specific sources of support. It will encourage you to reflect on the nature of the texts you encounter and the ways in which you can begin to explore these with your students. Furthermore it will help you to engage critically with aspects of research in the field of English teaching. This could, in turn, stimulate your own further learning and research at Masters level. I hope it will also encourage you to become involved in critical debates about English through participation in subject associations.

The first chapter explores the changing place and nature of texts in the classroom and beyond. It introduces you to theoretical perspectives about reading and textual construction, which should inform and challenge your approach to teaching texts, and provides an overview of the changing place of texts within English curriculum frameworks. In considering how texts are positioned within the National Curriculum and the National Strategy, the chapter focuses on critical debates concerned with: the study of canonical and influential texts; the impact of the 'set' text; and the nature and location of texts from different cultures and traditions. This overview establishes a context for what follows in subsequent chapters, which engage with specific types of text and practical approaches to teaching them.

Chapter 2 moves on to consider the selection of texts for use in the classroom. It encourages you to ask questions about learners' prior textual knowledge in and beyond the classroom, their attitudes to texts and the particular influences that gender and linguistic background might have on choices and responses to texts. In addition, it considers how your classroom textual practices might be informed or challenged by your own previous experiences of texts. Long-, medium- and short-term planning are discussed with a view to developing your understanding of inclusive approaches that also take account of the resources available. Furthermore, this chapter highlights that one lesson, one learner and one text cannot be seen in a vacuum: school policies, course or examination criteria and assessment objectives also have a significant bearing on lesson shape, content (including text selection and approaches) and potential outcomes.

Chapter 3 explores the challenges and considerable pleasures of teaching different types of prose fiction. It considers approaches to teaching short stories and novels, including reading texts aloud; grouping short texts; managing lengthy examination texts; stretching high-achieving and less confident readers; 'boy friendly' texts; strategies with ICT for prose writing of collaborative texts; and a focus on the role of the schools' library service. The chapter also refers to an interview with the prize-winning children's author David Almond about his writing processes.

Chapter 4 argues for the centrality of poetry within the English curriculum and the pleasures of engaging with this dynamic, multimodal form of expression. It draws on research evidence to explore the subject knowledge issues and concerns which many beginning (and some experienced) teachers express about poetry and poetry teaching. Of all the forms of text explored in this book, poetry is the one which seems to present the most people with the most challenges. As teachers you will find a need to deal with these challenges while also allaying potential fears and prejudices about the genre. The chapter provides support, with key subject knowledge issues raised in the research, before going on to address the predominant pedagogic concerns identified. It asks what purposes poetry serves within English and our lives beyond the classroom and suggests activities which involve reading, writing, creating, listening to and performing poetry and using drama as ways in which to engage with the genre. The chapter explores the potential links between poetry and games as a way of conceptualizing poetry which can engage all learners (including boys). It also considers teaching poetry from different periods, poetry from different cultures and migrant voices in the English classroom together with the particular challenges of teaching poetry for examinations and using examination anthologies.

Chapter 5 begins by considering definitions of the broad term 'non-fiction'. It goes on to consider approaches to broadening the scope of students' reading alongside issues of gender and genre. The nature of literary non-fiction, including writers' diaries, journals and blogs, is investigated together with travel writing, reportage, print media and more ephemeral informational texts which serve very explicit or practical purposes. It continues with a look at issues of gender and genre. Strategies for analytical, comparative and creative work are also embedded throughout the chapter.

Chapter 6 explores ways into teaching texts that I have loosely grouped together as 'spoken texts and scripts'. This wide-ranging focus includes consideration of: our everyday speech as text; presentation skills and use of presentational tools; formal speeches; script composition; bringing drama texts off the page; the place of Shakespeare and other playwrights in the curriculum and approaches to teaching them. Once more I touch on issues of subject knowledge and point to sources of support for your further development in this rich and rewarding area for classroom study.

Chapter 7 begins by exploring definitions of multimodal texts and moving image texts – terms for types of texts which have rapidly taken a central role in young people's everyday lives beyond the classroom and which are slowly being acknowledged within school curricula, where more conventional print-based forms still hold sway. I then consider influential research into the reading and composition of these texts, together with teaching approaches for production, analysis and assessment. The chapter includes sections on the role of blogs and wikis, fan fiction and other social literacy practices and insights into the composition processes of Taghi Amirani, a documentary film-maker.

The book also contains two appendices: one which lists a range of recommended Children's and Young Adult print-based reading and a second which focuses on the opportunities for cross-curricular links between English, Media and Citizenship.

Becoming an English teacher is a challenging and exciting intertextual journey during which you should learn to take creative risks that will stimulate and engage your students in many aspects of their learning both in and outside the classroom. I hope, fellow traveller, that this text will help you on your way.

Sue Dymoke
October 2008

What is a Text? 1

1.1 Introduction

This chapter explores the changing place and nature of texts in the classroom and beyond. It introduces you to theoretical perspectives about reading and textual construction, which should inform and challenge your approach to teaching texts, and provides an overview of the changing place of texts within English curriculum frameworks. In considering how texts are positioned within the National Curriculum and the National Strategy, the chapter focuses on critical debates concerned with: the study of canonical and influential texts; the impact of the 'set' text; and the nature and location of texts from different cultures and traditions. This overview establishes a context for what follows in subsequent chapters, which engage with specific types of text and practical approaches to teaching them.

The word 'text' is derived from the Latin verb *texere*: to weave. In the medieval world, texts were almost exclusively Gospels or works of scripture with highly wrought pages illuminated by monks. Those writing and speaking in late Middle English would use the term 'text' to mean a saying or maxim which might, for example, appear in a copybook to be copied out by those practising their handwriting. By the time we get to the seventeenth century 'text' refers to a statement which might summarize an argument or initiate discussion. In the nineteenth century it acquired the meaning of textbook – a term which might now be all too familiar to any school student. In the twenty-first century 'text' has multiple meanings which reflect the variety of ways human beings communicate with each other and make meanings through words. Although we might conventionally think of texts as consisting of printed words on a page, texts can be purely visual. They can combine words with still or moving images or sounds or all three elements. Texts can be sacred manuscripts or canonical works which need to be preserved for posterity. They can be blogs, poems, graphic novels, speeches, collages, graffiti, libretti, film scripts, adverts, pages on YouTube, words scrawled in pencil, tapped into a PDA, typed on a computer screen, layered with sounds and images, digitally edited or texted by mobile and a lot more besides. They can be predictive text, parallel text (a translated version or version with additional notes running alongside), subtext, hypertext, body text on screen or tattoos written on the body.

This swift run-through of some of the extraordinary range of different text types, many of which you and your students will encounter every day, serves to highlight the complex, varied nature of texts. Thanks to a wealth of technological developments, texts can be kinetic, multimodal, easily manipulated, updated, forever changing and without closure. The varied forms and methods of production should, in turn, cause you to reflect on the location of such texts within the school curriculum and the pleasures and problems which might be encountered when trying to read, view, write, create, listen to or experience them. The English curriculum in schools is potentially an elastic and malleable curriculum within which there should be opportunities for studying and creating many text types as well as other newly emerging forms. Unfortunately, as those of you teaching in English schools will undoubtedly learn, this malleability is not always evident. There *are*, as is shown in Chapter 7, slowly improving opportunities for study of media/digital texts. However, a regime of testing at 11–14, 16 and Post-16 still creates barriers to fuller textual exploration and creation. One of the key messages I would like beginning English teachers to take from this book is the need for them to act creatively within the curriculum frameworks in which they are working. At the same time they should endeavour to ask difficult questions of policy-makers and contribute to debates about curriculum content through department meetings, online discussions, local training events and engagement with subject organizations.

1.2 Learning to read

No consideration of the use of texts in the classroom can take place without thinking about the act of reading itself: what happens when we read and what does it means to be literate? Reading is a very complex act. There is only space to provide a brief summary here of what this act involves. For Andrews, the process of becoming a competent reader involves 'gaining command of each of the levels at which the written code operates' (2001a: 61). These levels are:

1. Grapho-phonemic (relationships between letters and sounds in English)
2. Morphological (parts of words are known as morphemes)
3. Lexical (words)
4. Syntactic (the grammar of the language: how words combine to make phrases, clauses and sentences)
5. Sub-textual (paragraphs, stanzas, scenes – the blocks which create whole texts and through which whole texts can be analysed)
6. Textual (whole texts such as reports, poems, plays, novels)
7. Contextual (such as social, historical, cultural, moral, political, linguistic and generic contexts). (Adapted from Andrews 2001a)

Some of the above terms may already be familiar to you through your degree or Post-16 English Language studies. They represent the key building blocks in the reading process and are terms you will need to learn to use confidently when creating and analysing texts in the classroom. For well over thirty years there has been extensive (and often heated) debate among researchers about the most effective way to teach reading. The Bullock Report pointed to a false dichotomy between those who view reading as ostensibly a process of *decoding* print into sounds and those who place a greater emphasis on *reading for meaning* (DES 1975). Through a national survey of teachers of six-year-olds, Bullock revealed that a mixture of methods for teaching the mechanics of reading were used in many of the classrooms. These included: approaches based on whole word recognition ('Look and Say') and phonics-based approaches which concentrated on syllables or on letter sounds, digraphs and dipthongs. The practice of mixed methods has continued. Schemes which involve reading with real books, whole word recognition, synthetic phonics (where sounds or phonemes identified with letters are learned in isolation and blended together) or analytic phonics (where phonic elements are identified from a related set of words rather than sounds being pronounced in isolation) (Brooks 2003) have each found favour in different contexts and have been combined with other methods. No method is said to be more successful than another. In spite of this lack of consensus, following publication of the Rose Report (DfES 2006b), a review of the teaching of early reading, synthetic phonics was deemed the best method for developing young children's reading. This contentious conclusion led to the implementation of synthetic phonics-based approaches in primary schools and training for primary teachers.

Although you might think that the teaching of phonics will not directly impinge on your work in a secondary English classroom, you may well encounter learners who are not yet fluent readers and need to be supported in their reading and creation of texts. Discussion of the mechanics of reading is difficult to separate from consideration of the processes of reading. As young readers gain in fluency, they are also expected to become increasingly skilled and confident in their engagement with texts, both in and out of the seven different levels outlined above. They should become critical and discerning readers who can:

- infer and deduce meanings
- summarize arguments
- make judgements about (or appreciate) how meanings are constructed
- draw comparisons between texts.

These skills underpin assessment frameworks for reading in secondary schools which are often predicated on the assumption that all readers in a class are fluent. Clearly it is a challenge for hesitant readers to develop these skills and simultaneously learn how to decode print. As you think about the processes and skills of reading, try to discuss what you have observed with learning support staff and other adults working in your classroom. You will want to ensure you are not asking too much or too little of readers and that:

a) your textual choices are accessible but sufficiently challenging
b) your planning includes strategies to support reading and textual composition by less confident readers.

For more on planning and textual choices please refer to Chapter 2.

1.3 Theoretical perspectives on the reading of texts

1.3.1 Reader response theories

As has already been indicated, how we read a text and the interpretation(s) we develop of a text through reading are key elements of the reading process. Theories about reader response foreground the reader (and the plurality of meanings which they may bring to a text) rather than the author. Two key figures in this field with a major influence on the teaching of literature are Louise Rosenblatt and Wolfgang Iser. Rosenblatt's transactional theory of reader response is strongly allied to the 'personal growth' movement in English teaching, emphasizing 'the relationship between language and literature, and the role of literature in developing children's imaginative and aesthetic lives' (DES 1989: 2.21). It first came to prominence in the 1960s and continues to influence the teaching of English, particularly among experienced English teachers and teacher educators who have themselves been taught and trained within this tradition. D'Arcy (1999), Fleming and Stevens (2004), McGuinn (2005) all exemplify this focus on personal growth. Rosenblatt argues that a poem is created in the space between what the writer provides on the page and what the reader brings with them to the text, each text providing a 'blueprint' (1978: 88) which is made real by each new reader as they bring themselves, their associations, feelings and experiences to the page. Each text 'event' stimulates the reader's creativity. With an efferent, or non-aesthetic reading, the reader is primarily concerned with what they take away from the text, the information or instructions retrieved rather than how the words are written on the page or the rhythms and associations they might have for the reader. The reader's relationship with a text is impersonal and limited. However, with an aesthetic reading, the relationship with the text and what the reader brings to it in the event of reading are of central importance:

> In aesthetic reading the reader's attention is centred directly on what he is living through during his relationship with that particular text. (Rosenblatt 1978: 25)

Drawing on Rosenblatt's work, Dias and Hayhoe have observed that, during class reading of poetry, teachers 'unwittingly demand that pupils adopt an efferent stance' (1988: 22).

Iser's contribution to our understanding of reader response has had an even more significant impact than that of Rosenblatt. For Iser, reading is a dynamic, creative process with the reader's reception of the text as an act of composition (Iser 1978). A reader brings life experiences and knowledge of other texts to the reading. Interaction between text and experience results in an interpretation which develops gradually as the reader makes sense of the text. Although neither Iser's nor Rosenblatt's ideas were developed through empirical research, their perspectives are still debated. They asked key questions and offered new ways of thinking about the nature of reading which had a direct bearing on aspects of classroom pedagogy such as the use of reading journals and small group discussion (for example Benton *et al.* 1988). The positioning of reader and text within a reader response dynamic also influenced the framing of assessment tasks which, from the 1980s until the mid-1990s, focused predominantly on personal response to texts. At their best, these tasks led to original creative coursework responses (as exemplified in Harrison 1994). In placing the reader at the heart of the textual encounter, reader response theory can lay itself open to claims of subjectivism. When taken to extremes, a text could be perceived as being devoid of meanings except those imposed on the words on the page by its readers. Benton (1995) and others have observed that loosely interpreted reader response theory can lead to very open-ended, unstructured tasks in the classroom.

1.3.2 Critical literacy

Critical literacy, like genre theory which follows, emerged from a cultural analysis view of English that emphasized both 'the role of English in helping children towards critical understanding of the world and cultural environment in which they live' (DES 1989: 2.25) and the development of understanding about how meanings are conveyed and values carried by print and media texts. A critical literacy perspective concentrates on issues of the social construction of texts (rather than the technical aspects that are focused on in traditional school-based education). It is concerned with the literacy practices which occur in different social domains such as the schoolyard, the supermarket, the mosque, the doctor's surgery or the football commentary box. Key figures in this field include Paulo Freire, Shirley Brice Heath, Norman Fairclough and Brian Street. In his influential book, *Pedagogy of the Oppressed* (1970), Freire shows that reading is not just preparation for work: development of critical literacy can enable people to understand and transform their own and other people's lives in an often unjust, undemocratic world. Brice Heath (1983) focuses on the contrasting literacy events which occur in home and school contexts and the impact which these contexts can have on outcomes. Fairclough (1989) uses critical language study to explore the power relations which inform different forms of spoken and written discourse. Street (1993) views literacy as a flexible set of social practices, dependent on context and ideology rather than as a fixed set of skills which can be learned. His work concentrates on different sets of autonomous literacy practices. In contrast, those advocating a 'Multiliteracies' approach, such as the New London Group (1996), focus on the different media or channels through which meanings are communicated.

Reader response theories and those concerned with critical literacy offer different perspectives on the reading of texts. The former, being strongly focused on aesthetic reading of literary texts, is viewed by some as being in opposition to the more radical social justice agenda of critical literacy. In recent years there have been some attempts to reconcile these two positions (for example Misson and Morgan 2006).

1.3.3 Genre theory

Texts are traditionally categorized in genres. At their simplest, genres are particular types or styles of writing. The broader genres of Fiction and Non-Fiction or of Prose, Poetry and Drama should be familiar to anyone who has taken an English examination or ever been into a bookshop. Prose arguably dominates the assessment regime in England (see Dymoke 2003). In the 1980s genre theorists, particularly those working in Australia, such as Martin (1984) and Rothery (1984), initiated debates specifically about a need for the study of genre within English and the 'contexts for writing that different activities provide' (Czerniewska 1992: 145). Together with others based in the UK, such as Gunther Kress, they drew on influential work on systemic functional linguistic theory developed by Halliday (1985) and argued for the socially transformative power of genre mastery. In their view, students need to achieve an understanding of genres as part of their socialization: without this understanding they will be denied 'access to the subject' (Maybin 1994: 193). Coupled with this view, however, came a warning from Kress about the impact of genre mastery on a young writer's potential creativity: 'the child learns to control the genre but, in the process the genre comes to control the child' (Kress 1982: 11). Rothery and Martin, together with Derewianka (1990, 1996) had a major influence on the content and shape of the writing curriculum in England and Wales and, ultimately, on the *Framework for Teaching English* (DfEE 2001) itself.

The impact of genre theory on curriculum innovation highlighted an underexplored need for a close focus on relationships between language structures and issues of audience and purpose in writing (Czerniewska 1992). Opening an alternative perspective to 'personal growth', this focus on learning to 'control' genre(s) gave both 'empowerment through appropriation' (Morgan 1997: 59) to young language users and, perhaps, introduced a greater sense of realism to school-based literacy practices. The notion of 'real writing' within a school context is contentious, however. For Lankshear and Knobel, school learning remains just that – 'learning for school; school as it always has been' (2003: 31). In a similar vein, Myhill questions the nature of the 'school literacy' (2005a: 292) that has emerged as the result of heavy testing regimes that lack space for consideration of the prior knowledge or personal experiences that fall beyond the remit of a tight mark scheme.

1.4 Curriculum structures

1.4.1 National Curriculum and National Strategy

It is not the purpose of this book to pore over the history of the English curriculum with a microscope. However, it *is* important that you are aware of key developments which have shaped the current English curriculum and the research which informs understandings of young readers' interactions with texts and the place of textual work within English. If you have a grasp of this background you will be better placed to ask questions about the approaches to texts and textual selections which might suit the needs of your own students. You will also have a contextual overview to draw on for Masters assignment work you may be required to complete.

1.4.2 The National Curriculum: English

The National Curriculum: English lays down the statutory requirements for teaching English and the entitlements for all learners in state schools. Since its inception in 1990, it has gone through a number of revisions and different formats. Its genesis was in two reports: Kingman (DES 1988) and Cox (DES 1989). Kingman's remit was to produce a model of English teaching which would offer guidance in the teaching of English Language at a time when much concern had been expressed publicly about grammar. The Cox Report was more wide-ranging and underpinned the development of the National Curriculum. Its proposals were for a new assessment-driven curriculum in English and Welsh schools with five attainment targets: Speaking and Listening; Reading; Writing; Spelling; Handwriting and Presentation. This report also attempted to impose a linear model of subject development which mapped out progression for 5–16-year-olds across four Key Stages and ten levels of attainment. Cox recommended that the crucial link between language and literature should be consolidated through activities such as writing texts in different forms. Practical implementation of the first (1990) National Curriculum found favour with many English teachers since it was built on models of English teaching which were learner-centred while embracing aspects of cultural analysis and literary heritage (Protherough and King 1995).

From this period onwards the text itself came increasingly to the fore. The gradual shift of emphasis away from personal growth was clearly pointed up in the Language in the National Curriculum project (LINC). LINC was developed with the aim of providing professional development resources to offer guidance to teachers about the teaching of language in the light of Kingman and Cox and to support implementation of the National Curriculum (Carter 1990). Materials from this innovative, highly influential project were withheld from the full publication they deserved by a government which strove to maintain a more traditional approach to teaching grammar. Nevertheless, copies appeared in samizdat versions in English departments across the country. (They are now available for teacher education purposes at www.phon.ucl.ac.uk/home/dick/ec/linc.htm.)

Many other language-based publications, which placed individual texts at the centre, followed in their wake, as Burgess observes:

> In the centre now is text, flanked by producers and audiences. Text bobs like a cork upon the sea, driven by winds of the immediate context of situation, while out on the horizon lurk the vast influences of different ideological and institutional systems of society and culture. (2002: 33)

In 1993 a Conservative government attempted to revise the National Curriculum orders, driven by a desire to define 'basic skills' (DfE 1993: 71) and to reassert the place of English 'literary heritage'. The proposals recommended the insertion of lists of poetry and fiction so that students could access the 'richness of great literature' and the introduction of an anthology of 'high quality' poems and extracts for use in standard tests at the end of Key Stage 3 (DfE 1993: 72–3). The proposals provoked considerable controversy and led to a widespread boycott of the 1993 Key Stage 3 English SATs. The nature of the 'literary heritage' inferred from these lists of authors will be explored later in this chapter but their inclusion in the National Curriculum orders was to become an enduring feature and soon lists of pre-twentieth and twentieth-century authors were enshrined within the programmes of study. In other ways, the 1995 National Curriculum appeared to have some flexibility, slimming down from five to three attainment targets.

1999

The National Curriculum: English (published in 1999 and introduced into schools the following year as *Curriculum 2000*) was an even slimmer volume than its predecessor but had some similarities. The most significant changes concerned drama teaching and language study. Drama was included as a separate strand within Speaking and Listening for the first time. Explicit reference was made to the requirements for teaching sentence grammar and whole text cohesion (and these were detailed in full in National Strategy documentation).

Programmes of study for KS1–4 were still organized under three separate attainment targets for Reading, Writing, and Speaking and Listening. Each programme outlined the required *Knowledge, Skills and Understanding* (to be taught in each key stage) and *Breadth of Study* (the 'contexts, activities, areas of study and range of experiences through which Knowledge, Skills and Understanding should be taught' (DfEE/QCA 1999: 12). This version of the curriculum also listed the areas through which learning could be promoted across different subject curricula, namely spiritual, moral, social and cultural development, key skills and thinking skills.

The 1999 National Curriculum stressed, and endeavoured to preserve, the high status assigned to literary study in previous versions. From its opening pages, the publication refers to Literature (with a capital L) before mentioning any other text types or aspects of language study. It notes: 'Literature in English is rich and influential, reflecting the experience of people from many countries and times' (DfEE/QCA 1999: 14) and includes quotations from critically acclaimed authors (Anne Fine, Benjamin Zephaniah and Ian McEwan) and Professor Lisa Jardine about the potential power of English as a tool for life and the value of literary study.

Inherent within all four quotations, and the structure of the documentation itself, is an assumption that, by the time they reach Key Stages 3 and 4, students would be able to read the texts they are introduced to without difficulty. Not only this, but they will 'read a wide range of texts independently for pleasure and for study' (DfEE/QCA 1999: 34). Although it would be churlish to argue that these assumptions were not well intentioned, they sit uneasily alongside the realities faced by teachers in many secondary classrooms, where attainment levels in English are below the expected achievement of level 5 to 6 and where the inclusion of EAL learners, newly arrived refugee children and those with specific learning difficulties has to be carefully planned for.

1.4.3 National Curriculum English 2007

The latest version of the National Curriculum (published in 2007 and statutory from September 2008 with full implementation over a three-year period) is based on a statement of values concerned with valuing ourselves, our relationships with others, and the society and environment in which we live. The new curriculum's aims, shaped by the *Every Child Matters* (ECM) agenda, are:

> The curriculum should enable all young people to become:
>
> - successful learners who enjoy learning, make progress and achieve
> - confident individuals who are able to live safe, healthy and fulfilling lives
> - responsible citizens who make a positive contribution to society. (QCA 2007a: 5)

The National Curriculum also includes a series of dimensions: Global, Enterprise, Creativity, Cultural Understanding and Diversity. These are intended to provide a context/focus for work within and between subjects and across the whole curriculum. They should give students opportunities for engaging with ideas and issues that affect their lives and the world beyond school (QCA 2007a). For some examples of how these dimensions might enable you to forge links with Citizenship particularly, refer to Appendix 2. There is also a sharper focus on personalized learning. The new orders set out the admirable but challenging aim that curriculum and teaching methods should be tailored to individual learners' needs, interests and aptitudes to ensure they receive equality of opportunity (in terms of support) as they strive to achieve the highest standards possible in their subject-based learning (wherever they are placed on the ability spectrum) and to develop their Personal Learning and Thinking skills (PLTs). In spite of this new acronym and a page on personal development on the QCA website, the development of young people's spiritual, moral and emotional selves no longer appears to be the priority that it once was. It has been replaced by a pragmatic need to cultivate responsible citizens who are imbued with the spirit of enterprise and ready to take their place in a global economy.

In talking to experienced English teachers, at training events and in their own departments, it would seem that National Curriculum documents are rarely referred to on a day-to-day basis: it is the latest version of the *Framework for Teaching English*, together with the GCSE, A level and other examination specifications which are the most regularly consulted documents. These are often used as templates to inform departmental planning (and thus textual choices). Nevertheless, the National Curriculum document provides an overview of the whole curriculum and how English coheres with other subject areas. The current version must be essential reading if you are to gain an understanding of the place of textual study within the curriculum, the rationale which underpins the school subject of English and how teachers are guided to implement the orders across the curriculum within their schools.

1.4.4 The National Strategy

The National Literacy Strategy arrived in secondary schools in England and Wales two years after its implementation at primary level (in KS1 and KS2 in 1998) and at the same time as *Curriculum 2000*. At the heart of government policy, the Strategy was introduced to push up 'standards' and develop a more literate young workforce who would be equipped to 'enter a fulfilling adult life' (DfEE 1998: 1). It was initially implemented at KS3 as a pilot project in 2000 across 17 LEAs in England. However, midway through the pilot (and prior to completion of wide-scale evaluation) the Strategy document – the *Framework for Teaching English in Years 7, 8 and 9* – was 'recommended' (DfEE 2001) to all secondary schools. Although the *Framework* has never been a statutory document, the 'policing of Key Stage Three teaching' (Fleming and Stevens, 2004: 19) through Ofsted inspections and interventions by Strategy consultants has ensured its widespread adoption by schools. The Framework's link to the National Curriculum statutory requirements for English has been frequently debated. In its first incarnation in 2001, it offered a detailed outline of learning objectives, curriculum content and preferred pedagogical interventions for language analysis at word, sentence and text level.

Although many teachers welcomed the 2001 *Framework*'s clarification of certain aspects of the National Curriculum orders, they expressed concern about the speed of its implementation, the increased planning burden which accompanied it and the changing identity/content of the subject English (Furlong *et al.* 2001). Goodwyn's extensive survey of highly experienced English teachers also reports a concern about 'the encroachment of subject capital "L" Literacy' (2005: 194). In my own institution's yearly surveys of PGCE English students' views about the nature of English, only one person out of 244 students questioned in 2003–7 (prior to any critical discussion of the curriculum) expressed the desire to be known as a teacher of Literacy rather than a teacher of English. In the ensuing discussions, all those in the same cohort appeared to acknowledge the importance of literacy for adult life but perceived it as one element within the broader, richer subject of English.

The latest version of the *Framework for Secondary English* (DCSF 2008a) is intended for use across the 11–16 age range rather than just at KS3. It is structured along 'lines of progression' for each of the four main components: speaking and listening, reading, writing and language. Ten strands, 27 substrands and learning objectives for each year group emerge from the components. It presents an apparently clear-cut linear model of progression in English which, as any experienced English teacher would tell you, can never fully reflect the complex and often recursive ways in which students make progress in our subject. Word and sentence level work from the original 2001 *Framework*, together with functional skills, are embedded within the document. Essentially an online publication, published late in the school year in May 2008, it is too early to say what long-term impact this latest version will have on the teaching of texts. Used in conjunction with the National Curriculum, it does potentially offer a more coherent and yet flexible approach to teaching English. In its 'renewed not new' form, as the DCSF (2008a) is very keen to label it, the *Framework* focuses less specifically on aspects of grammar and linguistic analysis. As Gibbons (2008) remarks, it also appears to distance itself from the supposed theory which underpinned the original version.

The recommended pedagogic structure of the 2001 *Framework* was centred on a teaching sequence of five elements. The elements of this sequence are:

- Identification of prior knowledge
- Teacher demonstration of process
- Shared exploration through activity
- Scaffolded pupil application of new learning
- Consolidation through discussion/activity.

Harrison's (2002) DfES-commissioned review of the *Roots and Research* behind this sequence and the teaching approaches advocated in the Strategy places a very positive gloss on how these elements are supported by research findings. Harrison supports Flower (1994), who argued for both cognitive and social psychological perspectives within the field of literacy in order to understand the different ways in which novice and expert readers and writers interact with texts. He points to the sociolinguistic and cognitive theoretical underpinnings of the 'Extending Interactions with Texts' (EXIT) model (Wray and Lewis 1995) as a major influence on aspects of the *Framework* concerned with writing non-fiction and Literacy across the Curriculum (Harrison 2002). In his review, Harrison stresses the importance of providing poor readers with 'well organised, clearly sign-posted texts' (2002: 20) together with provision of scaffolded support and guided practice to enable all readers to cope with texts which may not be well organized. Strategies such as the EXIT model, writing frames and Directed Activities Related to Texts (DARTS) (outlined below) are perceived as vital elements of this support.

Interestingly, the teaching of grammar is the only area that Harrison appears to find difficulty in linking to the research. More recently, an EPPI review team, led by Richard Andrews, has found no high-quality evidence to support the view that teaching the principles of sentence grammar has any significant influence on the quality or accuracy of school-aged students' writing (Andrews *et al.* 2004).

1.4.5 The EXIT model

The EXIT model identifies ten elements of the complex process which occurs during the reading of information texts:

    i. Elicitation of previous knowledge
   ii. Establishing purposes
  iii. Locating information
   iv. Adopting an appropriate strategy
    v. Interacting with text
   vi. Monitoring understanding
  vii. Making a record
 viii. Evaluating information
   ix. Assisting memory
    x. Communicating information. (Wray and Lewis 1995: 4)

Although this well-received model is for informational texts, care must be exercised when applying it to literary texts to ensure that the affective nature of readers' responses to such texts is recognized.

1.4.6 Writing frames

Having established this model, Lewis, Wray and Mitchell (1995) began to investigate the use of writing frames to provide a scaffold for primary school children's interactions with texts and an integrated approach to their development of reading, writing, speaking and listening and social skills. Writing frames are now widely used in many subject areas in both primary and secondary schools. Forests of worksheets have sprung up as a result. Writing frames can provide invaluable support to less confident communicators by giving them a loose structure for their ideas, which can be dismantled as the writer becomes more confident. The structure might include:

- sentence stems
- sentence shells with blank phrases
- paragraph openings
- paragraph endings
- word banks.

Unless used with care, writing frames can become straitjackets which reduce the level of challenge offered by a text and opportunities for high-level individual responses to it. When used to support essay writing at examination level especially, the frames can spawn clumsy identikit essays (Fones 2001). Therefore, students need to be given the choice to break out of the frame or reject it altogether, especially when they are drafting potentially much freer forms such as poems or scripts. For more about writing frames refer to Chapter 5.

1.4.7   DARTs

Coming from an earlier period, Directed Activities Related to Texts (DARTs) grew out of *The Effective Use of Reading* project (Lunzer and Gardner 1979). This uncovered the limited interactions with texts and/or with other readers that took place during reading in school. DARTs (Lunzer and Gardner 1984) are activities that create opportunities for shared exploration of texts. These opportunities will provide feedback which is especially needed by weaker readers if they are to develop their comprehension of texts.

DARTs include:

- Prediction (of next lines, chapters, events)
- Cloze (a type of prediction where words, phrases, line endings or rhymes are blanked out and readers use contextual clues to 'make' the text)
- Sequencing (of lines, sentences, stanzas, images, etc.)
- Highlighting, underlining or text marking
- Labelling
- Card sorting and statement games
- Diagramming
- Re-creative activities (such as storyboarding, rewriting the text in a different genre or from a different point of view).

DARTs are very prevalent in the teaching of humanities and science as well as in English. They are also used to promote the development of thinking skills across the curriculum. Like any activity, they should be used sparingly and only where appropriate: DARTs are about textual interaction and reflection, *not* about finding the right answers. Texts, especially poetry, can be killed stone dead if they are constantly introduced via cloze and sequencing or if students are given limited opportunities to compare their own version of a text with the original (Dymoke 2003).

1.5 Implications for your teaching of texts

1.5.1 Grammar knowledge

On a practical level, the 2001 *Framework* required English teachers to have a much greater knowledge of the way language works than previously so that they would be able to use its metalanguage when they modelled the writing of texts, analysed how these texts are constructed with a class and supported the development of students' own use of language (especially their writing). This requirement led to 'delivery' of training packages on Grammar for Writing and Grammar for Reading, which were given a very mixed reception by the profession (Cajkler and Dymoke 2005). The 2008 *Framework* is much less explicit in its references to grammar. It will be interesting to see how English departments respond to this change of emphasis. Whatever the curriculum states, you should have a good grasp of grammar. If you are concerned about your own grammar subject knowledge or simply want to brush up on key terms then you might find it useful to try out activities recommended in Chapter 6.

1.5.2 Lesson structures

A four-part lesson is a common structure used in many English lessons. The structure and content of these lessons embrace the five pedagogic elements (outlined earlier in this section) which underpin the Strategy. Four-part lessons usually include:

- a starter activity focusing on an aspect of language work and/or thinking skills (ideally this activity should be linked to what follows)
- an introduction to the lesson topic and objectives which draws on prior learning and involves direct teaching, modelling by the teacher, paired or shared work
- a development stage involving scaffolded active engagement with texts – reading and/or creating texts in small groups (sometimes guided by a teacher) and independent work
- a plenary where the learning is reflected on and summarized in an interactive way and which leads the students on to the next stage.

Contrary to popular belief, this four-part structure is *not* sacrosanct. Confident English teachers should be able to make their own decisions about the structure, pace and content that are appropriate for their own classes. Successful lessons do not have to be compart-mentalized, nor do they have to include all of the elements listed above. Variety is a key feature of any successful lesson sequence so that all learners can be engaged and included in the learning in different ways. Chapters 2 to 7 explore a range of teaching and learning strategies for creative work with texts of many kinds and learners at different stages in their learning, both in and outside of the classroom.

1.5.3   Personal response and enjoyment

Prior to the arrival of the National Strategy, D'Arcy questioned the increasing prevalence of a 'mechanistic framework . . . bound by a paradigm, which focuses on writing largely as a matter of construction and correctness' without regard to specific meaning, over a 'contrast-ing paradigm' (1999: 3) with its focus on the thoughts and feelings of both writer and reader in textual construction and interpretation. Explicit references to a reader's relationship with a text (in terms of values, feelings or issues of critical literacy) are not very apparent in the Strategy model of English. They are not completely excluded, as Fleming and Stevens (2004) observe, but the contrast between mechanistic and reader-centred approaches to reading and writing has concerned many teacher educators including Marshall (2004) and Stevens and McGuinn (2004) and has been reported by Ofsted (2005).

Part of a reader's relationship with a text involves enjoyment (even though a QCA officer tried to convince me recently that enjoyment could not be measured and therefore could not be included as a learning/assessment objective within the *Framework*). One could argue that enjoyment cannot directly be linked to learning and that it is impossible to 'enjoy' every text one reads (gas bills, detention forms and speeding fines are just three examples that spring to mind). Nevertheless, if young people are to be switched on to reading for life, they need to be given opportunities in and out of school to enjoy at least some of their encounters with texts. Reading for pleasure enables readers to develop their criticality about a range of texts and refine their reading preferences, whether these be for computer games, televi-sion programmes, lyrics, 'zines or young adult fiction. Furthermore, becoming an enthu-siastic reader can have an impact on a person's future job prospects. The Programme for International Student Assessment (PISA) report states that 'being more enthusiastic about reading, and a frequent reader, was more of an advantage on its own than having well-educated parents in good jobs'. It concludes that 'finding ways to engage students in reading may be one of the most effective ways to leverage social change' (as cited by Ofsted 2005). The radical educator Paulo Freire phrased this more succinctly: we must 'read the world through the word' (1970: 69).

In its review of inspections 2000 to 2005, Ofsted indicates that, although standards of reading have improved:

> Too few schools have given sufficient time and thought to promoting pupils' independent reading and there is evidence that many pupils are reading for pleasure less widely than previously. (2005: 9)

This observation should come as no surprise to anyone: a pressure to study a much wider range of non-fiction texts in English has led to a diminution in the time devoted to library visits, private reading and (especially in KS2 and KS3) shared stories. Some schools do have a policy of five or ten minutes' quiet reading at the beginning of English lessons. However, this does not always appear to be meaningful reading time: it often seems to be used solely as a behaviour management strategy. Ofsted refers to teachers' concerns that teaching reading is no longer a 'fun' activity in classrooms. Where once the reading of whole texts was a shared experience involving personal response and engagement, now the text appears to be treated as 'a kind of manual' (Ofsted 2005: 26) selected with reference to its purpose rather than its quality. The review also states that, as interest in reading declines, secondary-age students find it increasingly hard to find books they enjoy reading. It identifies a need for teachers to adopt a balanced approach to the teaching of reading, by using a variety of appropriate strategies and keeping up to date with their own reading of good-quality contemporary fiction for children and young adults. As an English teacher you will need to model yourself as a reader and writer of texts and the rest of this book offers a variety of suggestions about how you could achieve this in order to support your own students' reading and textual composition.

1.5.4 Creative text making

At the time of its introduction in 2001, fears were raised about the *Framework*'s impact on creative classroom approaches and opportunities for development of sustained writing, and arguments about a creative curriculum have continued ever since. It has also been argued that the increasing managerialism of schooling has resulted in a decreased autonomy for teachers (Jones 2003). In some schools learners are 'hustled from one skills based task to another' (Marsh and Millard 2000: 61) and given dwindling opportunities for risk-taking or creativity by their teachers, who are trying to meet targets, climb value-added league tables and not displease their management teams. Operating within an education marketplace, English teachers increasingly deal in knowledge rather than meaning making (Kress *et al.* 2004) and are expected to 'deliver' the goods rather than to teach young people to engage in deep learning. Ofsted have written of the text as being used as a 'manual' (2005: 26). To take this analogy further, I suggest that this utilitarian approach to texts has opened the door to an IKEA-style English in which flat-packed (specification compliant) framework responses to texts are reassembled and transformed into 'personalized' learning outcomes.

Fortunately, however, this bleak picture does not reflect the situation in every classroom. Creative teachers have continued to find ways to teach imaginatively and to inspire young readers by using active approaches. Support for these creative approaches is also at hand as increasingly intense debates about the need for flexibility and creativity have had an influence on some aspects of curriculum development. A statement by the English poet laureate

Andrew Motion as part of QCA's *English 21* consultations highlighted issues of creative entitlement. He wrote: 'Every child has the right to read and write creatively and we believe that creativity should become a central part of formal education' (QCA 2005a: 1). This paper provoked other productive discussions between artists, educators, subject associations and researchers, including a conference at Keele University and proposals for a Creative Writing AS (Advanced Supplementary) exam specification.[1] Subsequent *Playback* and *Taking English Forward* publications (QCA 2005b, 2005c) reinforced a desire from many quarters for creative curriculum opportunities. To some extent the revised content of the Primary Strategy documentation (DfES 2006a) and the National Curriculum (QCA 2007a) both aim to reflect this new mood.

Innovative schemes including *Writing Together*, *Poetry Places*, *Poetryclass*, *Creative Partnerships* and *We're Writers* have also established stronger links between creative practitioners and learning communities. Such initiatives began to emerge in the late 1990s with the now defunct 'Writers in Schools' projects. However, there now appears to be a greater emphasis on teacher development to ensure that creative work is carefully planned for and has a lasting impact on the participants. When such projects succeed they can be a powerful force for creative renewal in a school and for professional development across a department team (Arts Council 2003, Grainger, Goouch and Lambirth 2005).

1.5.5 Assessment

In spite of these developments, students' achievements in English at the end of KS3 were assessed, until October 2008, through increasingly unreliable externally marked tests. Although the format of these tests had changed almost beyond recognition since their much maligned introduction in 1993, the data gleaned from test results still had a major impact on how a school's achievements were 'measured' by an Ofsted team. It will be very interesting to see how data gleaned from the teacher assessments (which replace SATs) will be used in school inspections from now on. Thus the overarching assessment framework continues, unsurprisingly, to influence English departments' practices with regard to their interpretation and use of the *Framework*.

Without doubt, assessment demands will be a central focus of your planning, teaching and reporting but it will be crucial for you to keep these demands in perspective. Myhill has shown that preparation for assessment draws on a narrow range of students' prior knowledge, namely 'what they *should* know' (Myhill 2005a: 291) and understandings that they have previously gleaned *in the classroom* rather than in other contexts, outside of school. Furthermore, she also suggests that the emphasis on *written* genres within the testing regime privileges those learners whose home backgrounds have, in sociocultural terms, prepared them for the production of such texts (Myhill 2005b). The influence of the world beyond the classroom is a key issue for Chapter 2, which considers how prior learning experiences could and should inform classroom practice.

There is a very strong link between reading and writing in the English curriculum: Hull (1988), Barrs and Cork (2001) and others have stated that writers should be readers. They should be able to browse in literature-rich environments and think about potential audiences as they write. Writing is frequently used to assess students' reading of and response to texts. However, the National Curriculum reinforces this relationship strongly by requiring teachers to provide opportunities for learners to 'meet and talk with other readers and writers' (QCA 2007a, 2007b). An understanding that the terms reader and writer embrace viewer and maker of multimodal texts is more explicitly stated in some sections of the programmes of study than others (see Chapter 7).

1.5.6 Lists of authors

One of the most contentious aspects of the National Curriculum has always been the lists of 'major writers' and 'major poets' whose works *should* be selected for study in KS3 and KS4. These lists first appeared in proposed revisions in 1993. They caused controversy even among those 17 writers who were listed (Harrison 1994). The 1995 curriculum stipulated that works studied were all to have been published before 1900. In 1999 this cut-off date was extended to 1914. Three revisions later, named authors remain a central element of the 'Range and Content' of Reading. In both the KS3 and KS4 programmes of study there are lists of pre-twentieth-century writers from the English literary heritage, some of whom should be included in the range of literature to be studied. For the first time the explanatory notes accompanying each programme of study attempt to justify the inclusion of the writers by emphasizing their transcendent and enduring appeal and pointing to the reinterpretation of their works both in print and on screen for contemporary audiences. The programmes stipulate that study should be 'based on whole texts and presented in ways that will engage students (e.g. supported by the use of film resources and drama activities)' (QCA 2007a, 2007b). The requirement for study of *whole texts* is important to remember when you are planning your own schemes of work. Chapter 3 contains advice on the practicalities of working with lengthy whole texts.

The latest lists of English literary heritage writers indicate some differences in expectation about who should be studied at each key stage (see Figure 1.1).

The majority of these names featured in previous versions of the programmes of study. However, some prose and poetry writers (Masefield, Chopin and Dorothy Wordsworth) have been elevated in stature and the list also features a number of key dramatists (Congreve, Goldsmith, Marlowe, Sheridan and Wilde) who had previously just been named as 'examples of major playwrights'. The lists embrace prose writers, poets and dramatists. The inclusion of the latter can be seen as a consolidation of the position of drama within the orders and an attempt to streamline the view of the English literary heritage being presented here. William Shakespeare remains the exception to this rule. His sonnets are listed in KS3 and the stipulation that at least one of his plays should be studied both in KS3 and KS4 means that he is the only named author whose work

KS3 and KS4	KS3 only	KS4 only
Jane Austen	Elizabeth Barrett Browning	Matthew Arnold
William Blake	Robert Burns	Emily Brontë
Charlotte Brontë	Kate Chopin	Robert Browning
Geoffrey Chaucer	Arthur Conan Doyle	John Bunyan
John Clare	Thomas Gray	Lord Byron
Samuel Taylor Coleridge	John Masefield	Wilkie Collins
Charles Dickens	Christina Rossetti	William Congreve
George Eliot	William Shakespeare (sonnets)	Joseph Conrad
Thomas Hardy	Dorothy Wordsworth	Daniel Defoe
John Keats		John Donne
Mary Shelley		John Dryden
Robert Louis Stevenson		Henry Fielding
Jonathan Swift		Elizabeth Gaskell
Alfred, Lord Tennyson		Oliver Goldsmith
H.G. Wells		Robert Herrick
Oscar Wilde		Gerard Manley Hopkins
William Wordsworth		Henry James
		Christopher Marlowe
		Andrew Marvell
		John Milton
		Alexander Pope
		Percy Bysshe Shelley
		R.B. Sheridan
		Edmund Spenser
		Anthony Trollope
		Henry Vaughan
		Sir Thomas Wyatt

Figure 1.1 Writers from the English Literary Heritage named in the National Curriculum

must be read by all students. (For more on Shakespeare refer to Chapter 6.) The English literary heritage as defined by QCA remains very much the stronghold of dead white male authors. Only one female author (Kate Chopin, an American) has been added to its ranks at KS3 and there is no place for Aphra Behn, Charlotte Mew or Edith Wharton. Teachers working in other anglophone nations do not have to concern themselves with such tightly structured lists.

1.5.7 Texts from different cultures and traditions

Writers of non-fiction and non-literary texts such as reportage and travel writing are not exemplified separately in the 2007 orders. However, a variety of writers deemed 'appropriate' for study are listed in the supporting guidance. They are examples of: 'contemporary writers; those 'from the English literary heritage during the twentieth century'; and authors 'from different cultures and traditions' (QCA 2007a, 2007b). The crossover between the three categories presents a potential challenge and perhaps an increased flexibility both for teachers and for those setting assessment tasks. For example, contemporary writers such as American novelists Robert Cormier and Louis Sachar could also be defined as writers 'from different cultures and traditions'. British Asian writers Bali Rai and Meera Syal, named as 'from different cultures and traditions', would arguably be better located among examples of contemporary writers. The study of texts 'from different cultures and traditions' has been a feature of the National Curriculum since its inception. The name for this category of texts has fluctuated from 'different cultures and traditions' (1989) to 'other cultures and traditions' (1995) and back to 'different cultures and traditions' again (1999, 2007). Rose and Scafe consider that 'Poems from other cultures and traditions' emphasize 'difference and . . . distance students from the experiences and cultures that are being described' (1997: 129). The changes of terminology seem to reflect an uncertainty about how this artificially constructed group of texts and writers is constituted or located in relation to other groups.

In selecting texts from different cultures and traditions, teachers are guided to look for high-quality texts written by 'authors who are so familiar with a particular culture or country that they represent it sensitively and with understanding. The texts should help students learn about literature of another culture, as well as reflect on their own experiences' (QCA 2007a, 2007b). The authors listed as appropriate include a variety of voices originally from Africa, Australia, the Caribbean, China, India, Pakistan, Poland, Turkey, the USA and different ethnic communities within the UK.

I hope that, in reading and enjoying these texts, students will explore how experiences are represented within them, and how these experiences might lead them to a greater understanding of the diverse cultures that they live and work among as well as the ways in which other people shape and reflect on their own identities through language. Much will depend on how these texts are taught in schools and how students' responses to them are assessed. Interpretations of the term 'different cultures and traditions' are most readily apparent in the content of GCSE examination board anthologies. For example, the AQA Anthology (for examination in 2008) features poets who originate from Scotland, Africa, the Caribbean, North America, India, Pakistan and Africa. A number of these writers live in Europe and the poems selected deal with concerns of identity and origin, the natural world, dislocation, social responsibility and injustice. English teachers interviewed during case study research on poetry teaching in secondary schools were divided on the merits of such anthologies and the perspectives they offered on cultural issues. One questioned why they could not include cultures and perspectives which were relevant to the communities the student readers were from. Another welcomed the opportunity for engagement with multicultural issues for students who had previously lacked exposure to the cultures represented in the poems (Dymoke 2002).

1.5.8 Set texts

As this book goes to press, the relationship between the programmes of study for reading and assessment remains unclear. Nevertheless, the 2007 lists have attracted extensive newspaper coverage. Some reports reveal a misunderstanding of how the lists should be used or what they previously contained. A report in the *Guardian* stated that W.B. Yeats was 'no longer considered to be a must-read for 11–14 year olds' (Wignall 2007: 2). In fact Yeats was *never* listed as a *required* major author for any Key Stage but was included as an example of a major poet writing after 1914 who could be studied. Meera Syal, a newly listed writer from a different culture and tradition whose works include *Anita and Me* and film script *Bhaji on the Beach*, was interviewed about her inclusion as a 'set text'. She recognizes the potential dangers of being labelled in this way: 'studying a book can kill off any affection you have for it. I suppose it depends on how it's taught. My books are in the hands of teachers now!' (Wignall 2007: 2).

The use of set texts is problematic. The National Curriculum does not in fact stipulate specific set texts: examination boards and their paper setters select set texts on the basis of their own interpretations of the National Curriculum and the QCA criteria for each specific examination. Set texts can dominate examination preparation and teaching time in ways that are disproportionate to their weighting within a scheme of assessment. In writing about text selection at Post-16 level, Gary Snapper observes: 'too much emphasis on set texts can encourage spoon-feeding, transmissive approaches, and does not effectively develop independent, transferable reading skills' (Snapper 2006: 30). He highlights a concern, expressed by university lecturers, that students have limited knowledge of wider contexts or interpretation processes as a result of their explicit focus on set texts. In spite of frequent changes to the content and structure of public examinations, teachers will still turn to set text lists when they consider adopting a new specification. Their text choices have huge implications for the examination business and it is little surprise that the boards monitor centres' text choices in an effort to keep customers happy and discourage them from registering with another examination board.

1.6 Conclusion

This chapter has introduced you to theoretical perspectives and curriculum documents which help to shape the nature of classroom English in the twenty-first century and, more specifically, the teaching of texts. It has shown that English teachers (in England at least) have to respond to frequent challenges to their classroom practice and to their choice of texts. Many of the issues introduced here are returned to in greater depth and with a more practical focus in the chapters that follow.

Note

1. For more details go to www.nawe.co.uk (accessed 9 October 2008).

Prior Textual Knowledge, Text Selection and Planning

2

Chapter Outline

2.1   Introduction

This chapter explores the selection of texts for use in the classroom. It encourages you to ask questions about learners' prior textual knowledge in and beyond the classroom, their attitudes to texts and the particular influences that gender and linguistic background might have on choices and responses to texts. In addition, it considers how your classroom textual practices might be informed or challenged by your own previous experiences of texts. Long-, medium- and short-term planning are discussed with a view to developing your understanding of inclusive approaches that also take account of the resources available. Furthermore, this chapter highlights that one lesson, one learner and one text cannot be seen in a vacuum: school policies, course or examination criteria and assessment objectives also have a significant bearing on lesson shape, content (including text selection and approaches) and potential outcomes. Although 'high-stakes testing', especially in England, can have a major (and sometimes crippling) influence on textual selection and teaching practices, you are encouraged to look beyond these restraints to consider how you can build in flexible practices that promote opportunities for wider reading. In doing so you will enable your students to engage creatively and thoughtfully with texts they have chosen independently and with those chosen by others.

2.2 Students' prior textual knowledge

To begin to understand students' prior experience and knowledge of texts you should try to find out:

    i. what the students learned/are learning about texts outside of school
    ii. what they have learned previously in school about texts before you began teaching them
    iii. what previous records or assessments indicate about their knowledge and understanding
    iv. how they are demonstrating their understanding about texts now
    v. what might be the potential for further development of their understanding.

2.2.1 Texts outside school

The first point above is the most neglected and difficult to ascertain but also the most crucial. Too often school-based work with texts becomes a self-referential activity which draws entirely on previous school-based experiences. One result of such an insular approach is that mainstream texts (i.e. those within the established literary canon, those included in examination lists of set texts and anthologies, the winners of establishment awards like the Carnegie)[1] are privileged over others. Texts such as comics, graphic novels, gaming and other multimodal texts lurk on the fringes of acceptability. They appear to merit limited reference in the classroom and then only for specific purposes. Such texts are judged as being lower down the cline of literariness (Carter and Nash 1990). Their absence from so many classrooms arguably makes them more attractive to readers and, as is explored in Chapter 7, they have become the locus of much powerful out-of-school literacy activity.

2.2.2 Reading surveys

Taking stock of the range of texts your students engage with or compose outside of the classroom can be difficult. Surveys of young people's reading habits over the last 40 years in the UK include wide-ranging surveys such as those of Whitehead *et al.* (1977) and Hall and Coles (1998) and those with a smaller focus such as Benton (1995) and Millard (1997). These provide some interesting analyses of their reading preferences. Whitehead *et al.*'s influential survey noted a decline in adolescent reading, particularly among boys, that has continued to be remarked on by researchers ever since. Although the design of the Whitehead survey has been replicated by others, the sample readers they questioned and the reading material commented on in the seventies is very different from that available to readers in 2008. In *Children's Reading Choices* (1998), Hall and Coles reported that the range and diversity of children's reading among 10-, 12- and 14-year-olds increased as they grew older, possibly to reflect more adult reading preferences. At the same time, however, they began to read less. Although reading remained a significant leisure activity, gender differences in genre choices and attitudes to reading were uncovered: girls were said to share a 'canon of series books and periodicals as they grow older' (Hall and Coles 1998: 84) with the result that they were able to share more common ground in their discussions of texts. The readers questioned were more likely to be influenced by siblings, friends and peers in their reading choices than by adults. Although this finding is perhaps unsurprising, it could inform how you promote and share reading recommendations in your classroom.

Hall and Coles' research also explored periodicals: texts such as tabloid newspapers were read regularly and in significant volume (five titles) by over a quarter of their sample. How these titles were read was noticeably different from other texts:

> Children see the periodical reading process as provisional and different to book reading. They read in a non-linear manner in ways which sometimes approximate more to reading screens than to traditional ways of reading books. (Hall and Coles 1998: 66)

The non-linear paths that readers take through multimodal texts have subsequently been examined by Kress and van Leeuwen (1996, 2001, 2006), Kress (2003) and others and this research is explored in Chapter 7.

Both Benton (1995) and Millard (1997) recognize a widely held view that it is better for a child to be reading something than nothing at all: engagement should be the primary objective, with a view to moving on to 'better' texts later. But who makes the decision about what is better, and what influence will this have on the actual reading diet? Whitehead's 1977 survey categorized texts into what now seem very simplistic 'quality' and 'non-quality' groupings. Subsequent surveys have been slightly more circumspect in their judgements, recognizing the demanding, complex nature of some text types that young people read. In his survey of Year 8 students' reading habits (aged 12–13), Benton reflects on a fear that children's fiction has lost ground to the instant gratification offered by other less demanding texts, including television programmes, video and gaming texts. He questions the quality of 'easy reads' (Benton 1995: 105) such as titles from the *Point Horror* series. In his view, readers succumb to these titles through peer pressure, and he questions the role that such texts play in young readers' emotional growth. He notes the likely continued fading 'cultural capital' of canonical children's literature in the face of media developments/convergence and the displacement of modern children's fiction by the assessment imperative to study Shakespeare and pre-twentieth-century fiction. Benton could not have foreseen the impact that the publication of J.K. Rowling's *Harry Potter and the Philosopher's Stone* in 1997 would have on children's reading habits just two years after his survey was published. Nevertheless, twelve years later, many of his concerns remain pertinent today.

Millard's survey focused on the 'choice of narrative pleasures' (Millard 1997: 49) made by students aged 11 to 12 in their first year of secondary schooling. Although it drew on a smaller sample, Millard's work embraced a wider scope of literacy practices than other surveys discussed here in that she explored young people's reading histories and habits in both home and school contexts, including their interests in reading comics and magazines, viewing television programmes and playing computer games. (Interestingly, viewing and playing are perceived as separate activities from reading.) Like Benton, she notes marked differences between male and female readers' narrative pleasures and their approaches to reading. She observes a downward shift (first noted by Whitehead *et al.* 1977 with a 14+ age group) in young boys' reading of fictional narrative comics in favour of non-narrative periodicals such as computer or other hobby-related magazines and links this to a male preference for non-narrative television programmes. Millard concludes that girls in her survey tended to be the more sustained readers and viewers of narrative but their reading matter (primarily emotional and relationship-based texts) can be repetitive and undemanding. The boys she questioned read comics more regularly than girls (sometimes to the exclusion of all other texts). They much preferred computer games and seemed to resent class reading sessions. Millard notes a declining interest in fiction read voluntarily outside of the classroom: for many male *and* female students reading has become 'a chore imposed on them by others, mainly their English teachers' (1997: 97). Her conclusion should serve as a warning about how your students might perceive the classroom-based reading activities they are obliged to be involved in.

24 hours of reading

It is worth taking time to explore how your students view reading and what their reading preferences are. A quick survey of their reading in the last 24 hours can be a good starting point for this discussion. Not only should it shift the focus from a school-centred approach to literacy but it could also open up broad and challenging questions about the nature of reading.

For example, look at the list of items below:

cd cover	football match reports	*Cineworld* film times leaflet
shopping list	address book	junk mail
bus ticket	newspaper TV pages	recipe
easyJet website	friend's blog	seed packet
Sky Plus menu	online library catalogue	episode of *Doctor Who*
Match of the Day	credit card statement	chapter of *The River King*
poster	poems by Helen Dunmore	sell by date on milk carton
e-mails	mobile phone call list	gardening magazine
iPod menu	clothing catalogue	microwave instructions
train timetable	calendar	episode of *The Wire*
BBC1 *News at Ten*	to do list	*The Guardian Review*

Think about the different ways these items could be grouped. What do they reveal about the person's reading habits? The items could be listed on an interactive whiteboard (IWB) page or on separate cards. Students could use inductive processes to rearrange the items, define their categories and reach conclusions. By using your students' own lists (or providing them with a skeleton list which they can adapt) you could open up discussion about perceptions of:

- what constitutes a text
- who makes texts (and how/if this authorship is acknowledged)
- why they read (and for what purposes)
- who influences what they read
- the kinds of texts they prefer
- how they read (and what strategies they use)
- where they read
- how long they read for and how often
- differences between their preferences and habits and those of readers of different ages, genders and ethnicities.

2.2.3   Reading histories

Having established a snapshot of a day's reading you might then want to move on to a more in-depth investigation of their reading. Millard (1997) explored aspects of students' reading histories. She investigated 11-year-olds' memories of learning to read, first books, whether the students were read to at school, the place of reading and readers in their homes. Depending on the nature of your class, these aspects could be shaped into a stimulating set of questions for students to investigate and reflect on. When I was teaching in schools I completed a reading histories project every year with my Year 9 classes in the summer term. It often resulted in the most successful, analytical and personal piece of work the students produced. Many of the students seemed to relish the opportunities that such a negotiated project presented. Areas of interest included: revisiting their primary school reading books: rediscovering old (and frequently abhorred) reading schemes; talking to parents and carers about picture books they had loved as young children; reminding themselves of favourite sections of *The Guinness Book of Records*; analysing collections of comics, computer game instructions or football stickers. One student completed an entire project on his reading of texts and free gifts from cereal packets! Another, after rereading the *Billy Blue Hat* reading scheme, began to develop her own critique of gendered representations within the scheme. The exact nature of the topic (and modes of presentation) can be negotiated with individual students to ensure that everyone has an appropriately challenging and interesting focus. However, rereading childhood texts will not necessarily invoke warm memories. Furthermore, not every child will come from a home where reading of any kind has been a priority. Research indicates that many 'looked after' children own very few (if any) of their own books. When given the chance to do so, they not only relish the opportunity to read and share texts with others but this ownership can have a significant social impact (Dymoke and Griffiths 2008).

2.2.4 Opening the book

Another approach to exploring reading habits and the development of tastes stems from the work of Van Riel and Fowler, whose *Opening the Book* (1996) identifies different ways in which readers experience books and their reasons for doing so. This text focuses on fiction. It is predicated on the notion that you do *want* to read and is aimed at the adult reader. However, the ideas can be easily adapted to suit the readers you are teaching. Readers are first asked to reflect on their 'reading personality' (Van Riel and Fowler 1996: 13). They are given a series of descriptive outlines of different types of readers to match themselves against:

> the thrill seeker
> the stressed out reader
> the avid reader
> the self-protective reader
> the ambitious reader
> the indulgent reader. (Van Riel and Fowler 1996: 14–15)

Labelling oneself as a particular type of reader provides a good starting point for discussion with many different age groups. I have used these activities with Year 9 and Post-16 students as well as beginning teachers. The labels they gave themselves have included 'Non-fiction Junkie', 'Re-reader' and, perhaps most memorably, 'Reading Tart'. The labelling activity leads into a second focus on reading habits and consideration of the place of fiction in every day life. It explores:

- where and when reading takes place
- how you read
- whether you ever cheat at reading (i.e. look at the end of a book before starting to read)
- whether you read several books at once or just single texts
- whether you reread
- books you want to read (but never get round to)
- a book that recalls a specific time and place of reading
- books remembered from childhood
- how reading fits in with other aspects of your life.

Issues such as strategies for risk-taking in reading; the reader's relationship with the writer; and suggested ways into reading different fiction genres (and moving from one genre to another) are also included. The authors discuss the idea of charting your own 'reading curve' (Van Riel and Fowler 1996: 24) with a view to helping you to approach your next read with a more open mind and gaining a deeper understanding of personal patterns of reading (for example your expectations and predictions or why you might enjoy or abandon particular types of books).

2.2.5 The rights of the reader

Daniel Pennac's fascinating book *Reads Like a Novel* (1994) (republished in 2006 as *The Rights of the Reader*) raises many questions about how young readers perceive the act of reading and their relationships with texts (particularly within the French examination system). Like Van Riel and Fowler, Pennac explores readers' descriptions of themselves, albeit with more surprising results. He recalls asking students to describe a reader and realizing that, among their images of godlike figures, eccentrics and characters who have refrained from all the good things in life in order to read, 'not a single one of them describes himself, or a member of his family or one of the innumerable readers he crosses everyday in the metro' (Pennac 1994: 138). He views the teacher as a matchmaker in the reader–text relationship: a teacher's narrative can help a reader to discover (or rediscover) the intimacy which can exist between author and reader. However, this should be achieved discreetly and in a non-pressurized way so that literature is not turned into a research problem. In Pennac's view, readers have rights and the last section of his book is devoted to exploring these.

1. *The right not to read*
2. *The right to skip pages*
3. *The right not to finish a book*
4. *The right to re-read*
5. *The right to read anything*
6. *The right to 'bovarysme' (a textually transmissible disease)*
7. *The right to read anywhere*
8. *The right to browse*
9. *The right to read aloud*
10. *The right to remain silent.* (Pennac 1994: 145–6)

With the republication of the book, these readers' rights have been reproduced as a chart illustrated by Quentin Blake.[2] They would make an interesting focus for discussion and might also lead you (and your students) to question whether non-readers have rights too.

In Pennac's view, real readers relish the silences of reading which form part of the intimate relationship between reader and text. These silences enable them to escape into another world, where they want to remain long after a good book is finished. The love of reading as an escape is also described by Spufford (2002). In his case he escapes from an oppressive atmosphere brought about by a young sister's lengthy illness. Both books are written by avid readers – not a label which you will be able to give to all those you teach. English teachers predominantly have this 'love of reading' of novels (Goodwyn 2002) which can make it difficult for us to comprehend a student's lack of enthusiasm. (Poetry is another matter, as is shown in Chapter 4.)

Once discussed and explored, shared knowledge of students' reading preferences, rights and habits beyond the classroom should be built on. Students should be given opportunities to bring their experiences and understandings of how their preferred texts work into classroom discussions of all kinds of other texts. In this way they will be able to use their prior knowledge to negotiate and inform their own compositions and develop their understanding of aspects of intertextuality.

2.2.6   Private reading records, logs and journals

Students can come to view their school-based private reading (as it is often termed) as a 'chore' (Millard 1997: 97). Private reading is hardly that if it is taking place at a time desig-nated by someone else, in an uncomfortable classroom space with thirty other people close by. In some schools 'private' has been replaced by the control mechanism of five minutes' 'silent' reading at the beginning of lessons while a teacher completes an electronic register. In lessons I have observed, this 'reading' time often ends abruptly without any discussion of what has been read or enjoyed and then the real business of learning begins. In her observa-tions of school literacy events in primary schools, Moss (2007) also notes the lack of reading that occurs and the varying extent to which students can exercise free choice over the texts they read at such times.

Asking students to make a record of their 'private reading' could be construed as putting a private act under surveillance: it becomes public reading and therefore something less special or individual. On the plus side, creating a record may give students the chance to reflect critically on their reading choices. It could also provide you with the opportunity to intervene in or guide their reading and introduce them to new text types or specific titles that they might enjoy. With this in mind, reading logs can be a useful method of supporting gifted and talented students in their independent reading. Younger students may be famil-iar with the reading logs or diaries used in primary schools. Used ostensibly as a means of dialogue between parents, carers and teachers about reading completed at school and home, these logs seem to record progress in learning to read rather than a child's engagement with the texts. They can even become a source of parental rivalry and competition (Chambers 1991). The idea of introducing a parental contribution to a secondary school reading record would horrify many students.

In secondary schools, many different formats are used to record 'private reading', includ-ing print and web-based formats. Each English department, and, in some cases, each teacher, may have their own and you should find out what these are and whether you are free to adapt them to suit your own purposes and your students' needs. Ideally each student would use the same record throughout their school life but this is rare. If your purpose is simply to keep track of what is being read by each student then perhaps, as Chambers (1991) suggests, a bibliographic record would suffice. However, you might well ask what would be achieved by overseeing such a list of books? How will you actually know if they have been read or what impact these texts have had on the reader? If you want to encourage students to share reading preferences, extend and deepen both their reading and critical reflection, then the last thing you may want them to do is to spend too much of their precious (and increas-ingly limited) private reading time on writing activities. The best types of record are easy to complete and flexible. They can include reading trails or pathways and reading journals. In Figures 2.1 and 2.2 a recently qualified English teacher, Laura Procter, demonstrates her use of a reading log approach with groups of gifted and talented students.

I am currently teaching a very able Year 8 group (most with reading ages of 15:03+) and was asked to study *The Snake Stone* [by Berlie Doherty] with them . . . I have grouped my Year 8s into five reading ability groups so they can work at their own pace but with the support of other students. Every lesson each group nominates a team leader (see 'Team Leader Brief sheet' below). They are in charge (it is a bit like *The Apprentice*). They must decide how much of the novel they will read that lesson, how they will read it and answer the questions. They are also in charge of guiding the discussion. The theory is that G&T students need to bounce ideas off each other and feel more comfortable doing so in smaller groups, rather than whole-class discussion; it also allows more students to contribute. The questions I provide them with are challenging (hopefully) and act as a support to guide them through the text. They are comprised of comprehension questions, predictions and language. It is a reading log of sorts but it does not require them to log which pages they have read. Each member of the group must take a turn to be team leader and at the end of the scheme each student will evaluate how successfully they fulfilled this role. Hopefully it encourages them to take responsibility for their own learning too.

Figure 2.1 Using a reading log: an approach to challenge gifted and talented students described by English teacher Laura Procter

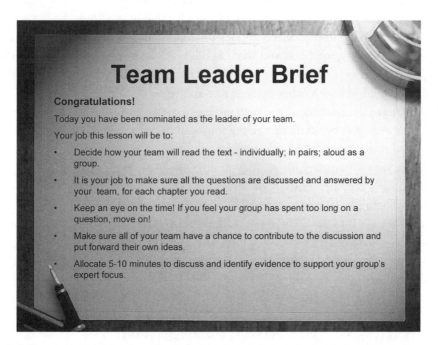

Figure 2.2 Team leader brief for use with gifted and talented students devised by Laura Procter

2.2.7 Reading journals

Reading or response journals provide a semi-private place for written formative dialogue between student and text (and teacher or other reader) about the ongoing processes of independent reading. Discussions might include: predictions and initial reactions to a text; developing questions, allegiances and suspicions; fears, hopes and other feelings evoked along the reading journey; the betrayal, satisfaction or uncertainty caused by the impact of an ending; questions about what to read next. Journals can also be used for texts studied in class. Time permitting, they can be an invaluable means of shaping sustained responses to examination texts. I have used journals with GCSE classes to help students record initial impressions of poems and to revisit these first thoughts at later stages in their study (Dymoke 2003). Although a teacher might comment on journal responses, in my view the journal should remain an assessment-free zone: it is a place for structuring thoughts, trying out ideas before they are ready for more public consumption. It can also be a very suitable location for Vygotsky's 'zone of proximal development' (1978) as Bearne and Cliff Hodges (2000) indicate: the teacher can both review a reader's developing understanding and establish what his or her potential capabilities might be.

The litblog is similar to the reading journal in that it can include snippets of reflective (and subjective) exploratory dialogue about books. Litblogs are a rapidly developing feature of the blogosphere as Storie (2007) and a quick trawl of the 'from the blogs' column (in the *Guardian*) both testify. Some litblogs provide a readers' advisory service to help readers find their next good book and more besides. For example, www.librarything.com enables members to catalogue their own books; tag books with key words; converse and share recommendations with other readers; rate and review books; and 'unsuggest' books, i.e. books that are the least likely to be attractive to readers who have enjoyed a particular book. The Amazon bookseller's website (amazon.co.uk) features *Listmania!* – lists of recommended reads compiled by other readers. Students could also use these sites and, if they take care with cybersafety issues, they could make their own contributions.

Private reading records, journals or litblogs provide some, albeit partial, evidence of students' developing tastes and responses to texts. However, these might give you a much more limited insight into the texts young readers *compose* for themselves outside the classroom, such as songs, novels, podcasts, blogs and Massively Multiplayer Online Gaming (MMOG) narratives. For more on the relationship between reading and composition in digital environments, please refer to Chapter 7.

2.3 Finding out about in-school prior reading

Clearly you will want to gain a picture of previous opportunities your students have had to engage with texts at school. If the English team devise and use agreed schemes of work then these should give you a broad picture of the types of texts used/read over a given period and how these texts have been taught. In looking at these schemes you should remember that effective and creative English teachers adapt other people's plans and resources to keep the material fresh and stimulating and to ensure that they are suitable for the specific needs of their students. If possible, you should discuss any department schemes and resources with teachers who have previously taught your classes. Also try to carry out a review of students' exercise books, work samples or portfolios of written and other outcomes. Wherever appropriate, these processes should be supplemented by a discussion with the students themselves to find out what official records can never tell you: what they think about the texts they have read, written or rejected and how they have been asked to study them.

2.3.1   Assessment records

Departmental assessment records should indicate what students have achieved in major pieces of assessed work, baseline test results, end of year teacher assessments and externally marked SATs. Some will also include evidence of formative, peer and self-assessment. Well-maintained records should give you a fair picture of students' achievements together with the school's expectations and agreed targets for their potential progress, at least in future test situations. An increasing emphasis on personalized learning in English schools in the next decade could result in much more detailed (and potentially relevant) information becoming available. Nevertheless, test results can only reflect the nature of the tests and what has been tested. Like any other form of evidence, they do not provide a completed picture. They indicate how well students can respond to or compose texts in a test situation *at a given time within a given set of parameters*. Tests are biased towards writing: students are required to demonstrate and express knowledge and understanding of their reading *in written form*. Spoken responses to texts (whether in the form of presentations, in-role or thought-tracking activities or small-group discussion) remain a peripheral element of assessment. In public examinations in England they are given much less weight than written responses. Visual responses are even rarer and are only likely to form an examinable element of a student's work if accompanied by a written commentary. Nevertheless, they can be an extremely powerful form of response, as is shown, for example, in the masks made by American twelfth grade students (UK Year 13) during a project on literature and personal identity described by Smagorinsky *et al.* (2005). Developments in assessment of student-created multimodal texts are taking place in the UK and Australia (see Chapter 7). These could eventually have an impact on current assessment processes.

2.3.2   Progression

In 2006, as an element of work on Assessing Pupils' Progress (APP), the DfES launched a series of web-based 'Progression maps' for use by English and Maths teachers (refer to www.standards.dfes.gov.uk/progressionmaps/). The 'maps' aim to help teachers plan the 'learning journeys' of students who are achieving 'below expectations and need to make better progress' (DfES 2006c). They offer a diagnostic approach to assessment intended to enable teachers to arrive at more accurate summative level judgements for students aged 11 to 14. Teachers are first required to match students to descriptors which define their current level of achievement. The site includes exemplars and possible targets to move students on. The targets are linked to suggested teaching approaches, potential texts for study, resources, literacy progress units and other support material. The maps are available for 'readers' and 'writers' but, interestingly, not speakers or listeners. They are aligned to assessment focuses used in Key Stage 3 testing. A reader is said to move through the following categories and must 'secure' alignment to a particular descriptor before moving on:

- Developing Reader: Reads with increasing fluency and accuracy and uses a range of strategies to construct meaning.
- Competent Reader: Reads between the lines, seeing meaning that isn't stated directly. Deploys a wide range of active strategies to find and read texts for different purposes.
- Active Reader: Has a sense of the writer at work behind a text, and can explain something about how a text is constructed, based on plenty of prior reading experience.
- Reflective Reader: Can make a considered response to a range of texts and use information from a range of sources.
- Versatile Reader: Is a critical and thoughtful reader across a wide range of texts: selecting, sifting, summarizing, comparing and contrasting. (From: http://nationalstrategies.standards.dcsf.gov.uk/node/42856 [accessed 14/1/09])

Although these headings appear to provide a helpful structure for teachers and learners (and also for parents, carers and mentors who can click on their own support guidance), the underlying assumption of one final destination for all in the reading journey is problematic and potentially misleading. Reading and writing development are complex, often recursive processes which do not occur in a straightforward linear fashion. In his poem, 'A Course in Creative Writing', William Stafford asks just how much direction a teacher should give and how much should writing (and I would add reading) texts be a journey of discovery. These questions seem particularly pertinent within a system in which high-stakes testing inevitably influences classroom approaches.

2.4   A model reader and writer of texts

One of the challenges for you as a beginning teacher is the expectation that you should actively model yourself as a reader and writer of texts in order to motivate your students (within the terms reader and writer I would also include viewer and maker). This apprenticeship model of teaching was embedded within the *Framework for Teaching English* (DfEE 2001) but was established long before the Strategy. When taught without due care, apprenticeship can simply mean teacher transmission of genre structures, leading to uncritical or faithful reproduction of text types and limited development of a student's individual voice within the writing process rather than creative experimentation and discovery through composition (Morgan 1997). However, role models can be very important in fuelling 'the will to learn' and enabling young readers to imitate reading behaviours and participate in day-to-day interactions about reading (Bruner 1966, as cited in Bearne and Cliff Hodges 2000: 9). Becoming a role model could seem to be a daunting prospect but you should see it as an aspect of your developing professionalism. All beginning teachers arrive in the classroom from different degree routes and life experiences. Therefore, although you may have had a rich experience of literature and/or media texts in your degree courses and in your own schooling, you may have had little experience of composing these texts for yourselves. My own research on beginning teachers' poetry subject knowledge (conducted through questionnaire and semi-structured interviews with students from three PGCE English courses) indicates that very few of them had previous experience of writing poetry or working with published writers in workshop situations prior to their training (Dymoke 2007). Although you could be an avid reader of canonical pre-twentieth-century prose you might have far less familiarity with, for example, texts from other cultures and traditions, literary non-fiction or graphic novels. You might have carefully selected your degree module to avoid poetry study at all costs or, alternatively, written a dissertation on Blake. In the early stages of your initial teacher education, you should cast a critical eye over your prior experiences of texts in order to identify your current strengths and to map out new textual encounters you might need to broaden and deepen these. Opportunities for self-review could arise at your course interview (or in your preparation for it). In many ITT courses, your textual knowledge and preparation for the classroom will be mapped through a staged process of subject and pedagogic knowledge auditing and development. I am not suggesting that you should be expected to know every text by the end of your training! Far from it. However, you will need to develop the skills to respond flexibly and apply your knowledge to the different texts you will be teaching. Furthermore, if working with texts is going to be an enjoyable and enriching experience for you and your students then your reading/creative journey should be a lifelong adventure which, in part, needs planning for. Even at this early stage in your career you should aim to read and write beyond the prescription of exam specifications and set text lists. In this way you can begin to extend the textual diet served in your classroom rather than simply replicate a predictable menu. You can also begin to exert influence on those who select the texts for examination study.

The Arts Council consultation document, *From looking glass to spyglass* (2003), highlighted concerns about the lack of statutory requirement for initial teacher education courses to familiarize beginning teachers with children's literature during their training. Although the findings were refuted in some quarters, one of the report's outcomes was *Literature Matters*. This two-year national programme (extended in some areas) was designed with the aim of developing 'knowledge, enjoyment and confidence in children's books' (MLA 2003: 3) among trainees and to raise awareness about the roles of school libraries and library support services. Although it is difficult to judge the long-term impact on beginning teachers' pedagogy, the project did have a variety of successful outcomes (Edwards 2006, Bailey *et al.* 2007). The University of Leicester Secondary PGCE English course was involved in this programme. Our focus was on how teachers could promote and share enjoyment of reading beyond the English classroom. Some of the strategies used in this project are outlined in Chapter 3. If you would like to develop your own knowledge of children's literature then you may also want to refer to the titles suggested in Appendix 1.

2.5   Planning

2.5.1   Long-, medium- and short-term planning

'There can be no single formula for teaching a text. The "best" approach may be dictated by the uniqueness of the book itself and the distinctive character of each group of young readers; and of each teacher' (Benton and Fox 1985: 108). In spite of all the curriculum changes which have occurred (in England at least) since Benton and Fox wrote these words, their advice still holds true. Much of what follows in this section, and throughout this book, is predicated on the understanding that beginning teachers must plan and develop classroom approaches that are appropriate, stimulating and challenging for all their students and the contexts in which they are working.

Fleming and Stevens suggest that planning can 'be akin to a military operation with very precise targets, rigid structures and exact timings; the semblance of order may conceal lack of involvement and ownership by those involved' (Fleming and Stevens 2004: 93). Planning approaches currently used in schools in England are increasingly objectives-led: the choice of text is made to suit the stated objectives of a scheme of work. This is in contrast to approaches used previously where a text or theme would provide the starting point for planning. Strategy training has emphasized a need to share objectives and intended learning outcomes with students (couched in student-friendly language) at the beginning of a lesson. It is also considered desirable that the outcomes are differentiated to cater for the ability range and to offer a sufficient level of 'stretch and challenge' for gifted and talented learners (DCSF 2008b: 7). In many classrooms these intended outcomes for the lessons are shared with the students in terms of what they 'must, should and could' achieve. There is, however, no single way to plan for teaching texts. As was shown in Chapter 1, certain lesson structures and planning/teaching strategies are strongly advocated in government training materials and reflected in exemplar plans provided in official documentation. Advice offered here focuses on broad principles. These are followed up with more specific details in subsequent chapters.

You will need to think in terms of planning *individual lesson plans* for each lesson that you teach. Each institution has its own format for these but, whichever you use, they should give a clear outline of the lesson structure, your objectives, resources, activities, support needs and intended student learning outcomes. You should identify any differentiated approaches or materials that might be needed and pay close attention to how you are planning to assess what has been learned. Try to be realistic about what you and your students can achieve in one lesson and remember that, due to the nature of the subject, what students learn in English will not always be what you have planned for. When you begin teaching you might also find it useful to supplement the plans with lesson notes. At first these might look like a script but they can provide a valuable lifeline in your early days in the classroom. They could include questions, page references, examples and reminders to yourself about students or points you want to emphasize. As you become more confident you will rely on them less heavily. However, they will still provide a useful addition to your lesson plans.

When grouped together, your lesson plans will form a series of *short-term* plans or *schemes of work*. Each of these will consist of a short sequence of lessons (for example five or six lessons, reflecting the number of English lessons taught over one timetable cycle). A short-term plan provides lesson by lesson detail and is usually based on a unit of work with a specific focus such as ballads, persuasive speech writing or analysis of a film trailer. You would normally expect to find that a short-term plan states which Framework or examination objectives are addressed. You will want to share these explicitly with students (in student-friendly language rather than strategy speak). A *medium-term plan* sets out goals and expectations over a longer period of time (for example half a term, a term or even specific weeks within the term). It outlines the coverage of a particular aspect of the subject or a skill throughout the given time period and shows how these relate to the curriculum (see Figure 2.3). Finally, you will also expect to see a *long-term plan* for each class. These give a broad overview of curriculum coverage over a whole year so that, at a glance, you can see, for example, when a class will be working on writing and performing drama scripts or when they will be devising and marketing their own computer games. Most departments begin their planning with the long-term plan for each year. This enables them to ensure that each class is covering the agreed curriculum for that year group and enables the subject leader to keep an eye on resourcing issues. Medium-term plans are usually developed (and frequently revised) by teams within the department. In most schools, short-term planning and individual lesson plans are the responsibility of the class teacher. Even within a highly directed structure, this is where you, the individual teacher, should be able to use your creativity to shape lessons which are appropriate for the individuals in your classes. Make sure you seek guidance from your school mentor about department policy and preferred planning formats before you begin to draft them.

Whatever approach to planning you adopt or adapt, you should think critically about your responsibilities as an English teacher. Your planning will have a direct influence on your students' learning and, potentially, their expectations for subsequent English lessons. To help you to think further about planning, consider your responses to the following

Handout 4.4: Medium-term planning template

Title of unit:	Year:	Term:	Duration:
Overview of unit:			
Cross-curricular/extracurricular links:			
Key concepts:			
Competence			
Creativity			
Cultural understanding			
Critical understanding			
Progression substrands:			
Speaking and listening		Reading	
Writing		Language	
Texts and resources:			
Teaching strategies and activities:		**Assessment outcomes and criteria:**	

00123-2008DOM-EN

Figure 2.3 A medium-term planning template (From the National Strategies Secondary subject leader development training (2008: 00123-2008DOM-EN). Reprinted with permission.)

scenarios. You might like to discuss them with your subject mentor.

- If you decide to adhere to a tightly structured objectives-led lesson format, what would you do if a text provokes a response you have not planned for and which causes the class to go off at a tangent?

- What happens if an unexpected major news event occurs in the middle of your short-term plan? Should you pull the class back to focus on the designated text and your desired learning outcomes or should you change direction midstream and enable students to reflect on what has happened?
- If your subject leader prefers you to outline the lesson structure and learning outcomes at the beginning of each lesson, should you deviate from this script when a text demands to be experienced without prior comment? (Two examples would be a short prose text like 'Boo' by Kevin Crossley-Holland or the opening sequence of Alejandro Amenábar's film *The Others*.)
- Should students always be expected to summarize what they have learned in a whole-class plenary at the end of the lesson? Is it appropriate to reflect on all learning in this way? When and how could plenaries be used most effectively?
- If you were being observed by an inspector during any of the above scenarios, would this make a difference to your response?

Much of what happens in English classrooms can and should be dependent on the individuals in the group. This does *not* mean you should leave students' learning to chance: you should of course plan carefully and be very well prepared. However, be prepared to be flexible. Students should be active agents in their own learning, rather than experts in the construction of 'schooled responses' to texts (Misson and Morgan 2006: 107). If you ensure that they are not strapped into an objective straitjacket and are given opportunities for individual choice or negotiation of tasks then you will help them to remain so.

2.5.2   What influences planning and choice of texts?

Any planning activity must be inclusive and take account of the teaching support and other resources available. Your plans cannot be fully realized unless you draw on your awareness of each student's specific learning needs and prior attainment, their physical and mental capabilities, their gender, ethnicity, social and cultural background. Much of the essential information should be made available to you through:

- class records from the previous teacher
- the school's confidential special needs register
- students' Individual Education Plans (for those who have an IEP)
- copies of school reports
- transfer data (from primary or other previous school)
- baseline test and other assessment records.

To gain a more complete picture you will need to get to know the students for yourself by looking at previous work in their exercise books and portfolios and, most importantly, making time to talk to them individually. Until you begin to develop a rapport with them, you will never be able to gauge what students are capable of, interested in and what might motivate each of them to learn.

Developing your awareness of your students' social and cultural backgrounds should be an important part of this process. This information could have a direct bearing on your choice of texts and when and how you use them. For example:

- A unit on the narrative voices in *The Other Side of Truth* by Beverly Naidoo and *Refugee Boy* by Benjamin Zephaniah could help refugee children to explore their feelings of loss or disorientation and others to understand what they might have experienced. Alternatively, it could provoke distress and misunderstanding.
- A themed unit on food involving instructional writing of recipes, analysis of arguments presented in the C4 programme *Jamie's School Dinners* and designing an advertisement for a new health drink could be a very insensitive unit to introduce during Ramadan but might be very successful after Eid el-Fitr.
- Listening to *The Adoption Papers* by Jackie Kay and writing poetry which combines different voices could help students to explore feelings about parentage or expose them to issues they are not ready to deal with yet.

You cannot be expected to be aware of everything that has happened in every student's life but you do need to be sensitive and able to adapt plans and text choices at short notice if necessary. You will also need to ensure that the texts you read and view together (as well as the ones you will ask your students to compose) are accessible to them. You could try out a simple SMOG (simplified measure of gobbledygook) test on potential texts to give you an idea of their readability.[3]

If you have students in the early stages of learning English as an additional language (EAL) it will be essential to check any potential linguistic ambiguities or difficulties they may encounter. In their everyday and literary forms, spoken and written English are rich in metaphor and idiomatic language. This can present problems for EAL learners as well as those on the autistic spectrum, whose understanding will tend towards literal interpretations of what they have heard or read. For example think about how you might explain the phrases in Figure 2.4 to someone who was not a confident English speaker.

Visual material such as photographs, film clips, drawings and simple diagrams can be extremely helpful in bridging the gap between word and understanding. Nora McWilliam's *What's in a Word?* (1998) provides extensive food for thought in this area together with practical advice and key questions to consider when planning. Other extremely useful sources of information and support include:

- the NALDIC website at www.naldic.org.uk/ITTSEAL2/teaching/index.cfm (accessed 9 October 2008)
- *Access and Engagement in English* (DfES 2002), available at www.standards.dcsf.gov.uk/secondary/keystage3/all/respub/englishpubs/en_eal. This includes an appendix focusing on activities with texts and the potential difficulties that EAL learners may encounter when they participate in them.

All these resources emphasize a need for clarity of instruction, use of visual support materials and creation of opportunities for speaking and listening activities. In many ways they exemplify good practice for working with *all* students.

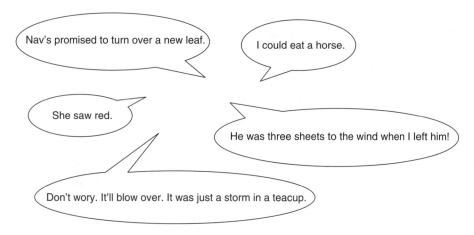

Figure 2.4 Examples of idiomatic phrases which could present difficulties for EAL learners

2.5.3 Gender and texts

The section on reading surveys (section 2.2.2) earlier in this chapter demonstrates that researchers have frequently highlighted differences in male and female reading preferences and habits. Much has also been written in the last 15 years about perceived problems with boys' underachievement in English. Boys' lack of interest in reading is seen in some quarters as a key element of this problem. The publication of the report *Boys and English* (Ofsted 1993) confirmed what many educators have long suspected – that, although the reasons for poor achievements in English were hard to identify, there was a difference in the attitudes of boys and girls towards reading and writing: 'girls are more likely than boys to be enthusiastic about these aspects of their work' (Ofsted 1993: 27). In her seminal work *Differently Literate* (1997), Elaine Millard argues that the increasing feminization of the teaching profession has caused boys from a very early age to perceive reading and writing as female activities. She believes it is their need 'to establish a masculine identity in relation to these activities that presents the greatest barrier to literacy' (Millard 1997: 29). Influenced by an agenda to drive up standards, a raft of policy initiatives and government-sponsored campaigns focused on boys and reading have been launched in the last decade. These include *Reading Champions*[4] (featuring Premier League footballers, wrestling stars, dads and other male reader role models) and *Riveting Reads*.[5] These campaigns aim to dispel myths about reading by showing it as a cool and enjoyable activity with something for everyone. Meek's perception that if readers can see the point of reading they are more likely to benefit from it (Meek 1990) is pertinent to *Riveting Reads*, a campaign which focuses solely on books. It is underpinned by conclusions from unidentified research findings which have found that:

- Boys often prefer non-fiction; illustrated books; and 'fun facts' material
- Boys frequently choose books 'because they feel they have to', but may be more susceptible than girls to recommendations from librarians and teachers

- Boys are drawn to fiction related to out of school interests – sport, computers, music
- Boys enjoy fast-paced stories, with plenty of action
- Boys often have crazes for the subject of the moment, and switch to new ones fast
- Boys may have more difficulty identifying themselves in stories
- Children can seem like 'grazers rather than diners' in their reading, and boys in particular will dip into books, lacking reading stamina
- Boys visit libraries, but to meet, browse, and play games. Far fewer of them take books out. (Williams 2007: 11)

This publication introduces practical approaches and questions to reflect on. It could provide a useful basis for discussion with your school librarian. It also lists popular titles, grouped in categories including 'Boggle . . . Go Wild . . . Play . . . Survive . . . Train'. In his introduction, Williams acknowledges the danger of pigeon-holing boys into set library or reading behaviours. Nevertheless, in consulting targeted lists you should tread warily. The boy-friendly categories used here and in other publications such as *The Dangerous Book for Boys* (Iggulden and Iggulden 2007) endorse gender identities based on a fixed set of attributes. Each of your students is an individual and, as Moss so eloquently reminds us, 'there is no single way of being a boy or being a girl' (Moss 2007: 35). Every student will respond to (and create) texts in their own way, depending on their previous experiences, the context they are in and the resources available. Who is to say that the listed titles will not appeal to girls too or that, as they go through their schooling, what it means for students to be male or female and to be readers or writers will not change?

2.6   Teaching examination texts

Ultimately your choice of printed texts may be limited to those stipulated in the examination specifications you will be teaching. An additional limitation is what is actually available in your department's stock cupboard (or what the department can afford to buy). When you are in your first teaching post you should have some leverage about being given first choice of the texts available. You might be able to encourage the department to invest in some new titles and other resources as part of its investment in you as a Newly Qualified Teacher.

During your training year it is essential to read (and view) as widely as possible in order to familiarize yourself with titles that you might be expected to teach. Wherever possible, try to move beyond the tried (and frequently tested) titles and below/beyond the age ranges that you will be teaching: seek out newly published texts and those presenting fresh perspectives that your students will want to respond to. Refer to Appendix 1 for ideas. This includes lists of poetry, prose, graphic novels, picture books, non-fiction and scripts for 11–14 year olds, examination set texts and other printed texts for use in the classroom. Many other texts are recommended throughout this book.

You will also need to look closely at the lists of set texts in examination specifications and those recommended for use in KS3. These can be found as follows (all websites were accessed on 27 October 2008):

- for information on KS3 teacher assessments, keep an eye on new developments at www.naa.org.uk
- GCSE English, English Literature, Drama and Media Studies examination specifications at:

  - www.aqa.org.uk
  - www.ocr.org.uk
  - www.edexcel.org.uk (also includes English Studies pilot)
  - www.wjec.co.uk

- AS and A2 English Language, English Language and Literature, English Literature, Drama, Theatre Studies, Media Studies Communication and Culture and Film Studies: at the sites above
- Advanced Extension Award: www.qca.org.uk/qca_4115.aspx or www.direct.gov.uk/en/Education AndLearning/QualificationsExplained/DG_10039019
- Standard Grade, Higher and Advanced Higher English: www.sqa.org.uk
- IB (International Baccalaureate): www.ibo.org – this site provides a general introduction and guidance about the structure of the three programmes. You can also purchase a PDF of the English A1 prescribed text list.

2.7   Evaluation

When teachers first begin working with classes they can be tempted to cram too much into a single lesson. They might ask students to read or view too much or simply to cover too many different activities. In their anxiety to 'get through' a lesson they might not give space for rereading, reflection or the students' own questions and find themselves closing down discussion too quickly. Once you have begun working with a group, your forward planning should be informed by evaluation of previous lessons you have planned and taught. Successful teachers are reflective teachers who are able to look critically at their practice and to review it regularly in the light of experience, student response and feedback from others. Lesson evaluations should enable you to replay your lessons, pause and review them from many different angles in order to:

- reassess students' spoken, written and non-verbal responses to texts they are reading or producing. Were the students curious and engaged? Were they enjoying their work, taking creative risks or challenging themselves?
- review the personal experiences and perspectives the students have brought to the classroom. Were these viewpoints acknowledged? How did they contribute to understanding?
- consider whether the text/activity offers sufficient challenge for very able learners
- pinpoint those students who are finding texts too difficult and the reasons for this
- explore linguistic issues which have arisen
- reflect on the pace of the lesson
- think over your instructions and questioning

- explore alternative ways of structuring the learning
- think again about your resources and use of the physical space. Were the written resources readable? Were there too many? Were other materials such as visual or auditory aids needed? Did you deploy the teaching assistants effectively? Was the classroom layout conducive to learning?
- decide whether your intentions for your next lesson and the whole short-term plan are still appropriate.

Critical evaluation will help you to get over the anxious early stages, revise your expectations about what can be realistically achieved and plan with confidence. Increasingly you will be able to focus on individual learners in your classes.

2.8   Conclusion

When done well, careful planning informed by evaluation is one of most creative, enjoyable and rewarding aspects of English teaching. It is also a vital element in successful teaching of any type of text. The next chapter concentrates specifically on one of these types – prose – in all its rich variety and builds on the contextual and practical aspects explored here.

Notes

1. The Carnegie Medal is awarded annually by UK children's librarians for an outstanding children's book. Many school groups participate in shadowing activities and voting.
2. The poster can be downloaded from http://www.walker.co.uk/The-Rights-of-the-Reader-9781406300918.aspx (accessed 27 October 2008).
3. To try this out go to www.literacytrust.org.uk/campaign/SMOG.html (accessed 9 October 2008).
4. Reading Champions website at www.literacytrust.org.uk/campaign/Champions/About.html (accessed 9 October 2008).
5. www.sla.org.uk (accessed 9 October 2008).

Prose Fiction 3

3.1 Introduction

Definitions of 'prose' concern themselves with ordinariness, lack of distinctive metrical structure and even dullness – terms which do the sparkling prose of Dickens, Atwood, McEwan, Pullman and so many others a disservice. Prose fiction is defined as 'the genre of fictional narratives written in prose' in the *New Shorter Oxford English Dictionary* (Brown 1993: 2384) and, as such, encompasses a wide range of texts. This chapter explores the challenges and considerable pleasures of teaching the reading and writing of some of these. It focuses on approaches to teaching short stories and novels including: the place of the class reader; reading texts aloud; grouping short texts; planning to teach a lengthy prose text for the first time; stretching high-achieving and less confident readers; drafting and ICT-based strategies for collaborative prose writing and the role of the Schools' Library Service. It also refers to an interview with award-winning novelist and playwright David Almond.

3.2   The class reader

For many English teachers, the experience of reading a class reader with a whole class can be a pleasurable event, a daunting prospect and a major planning exercise (and not necessarily in that order). For students, the class reader (usually a novel or sometimes a selection of short stories) can provide a comforting structure to their English work, a sense of continuity and shared experience. However, if they do not like the book or do not understand it, if they are frequently absent or have already read it for themselves, it turns the text either into an insurmountable challenge or a dull chore. The increased use of extracts rather than whole texts, coupled with other factors outlined below, means that students now have fewer in-class opportunities to read lengthy prose texts together than they would have done 15 years ago. At that time, English teaching (in lower secondary especially) was predominantly centred around half-termly class readers. Stock cupboards were filled with class sets of novels and little else. These texts would provide a springboard for thematic or genre-based work or re-creative writing activities which enabled students to explore aspects of character or predict events in forthcoming chapters (such as writing a diary entry, an extra scene or the script of a conversation between two characters). Typically, a Year 8 student's school diet of prose might consist of *The Machine Gunners*, *The Demon Headmaster*, *Flour Babies*, *Buddy* and *Goodnight Mister Tom*.[1] Teachers would select class readers for the whole year (sometimes before they had encountered the individual students in their classes). This is not to say that the texts mentioned above are no longer worth reading or that aspects of the teaching did not exemplify good practice. However, an increased emphasis on inclusive and differentiated approaches to learning has had an impact on the teaching of class readers. In addition, the National Curriculum requirement that students should be given opportunities to experience a wide range of text types means that the whole-class reader places less of a stranglehold on English curriculum time than previously. In spite of these changes, the shared experience of reading a prose text can be very memorable. In my view, it should be something that all students experience at least once a year, whether in a small group or as a whole class.

3.3   Factors influencing text selection

As you have seen in Chapter 2, one of your first challenges will be to select text(s) that are appropriate for the individuals in your class. In making this decision you might find it helpful to think about the following questions:

i)   What have they learned previously and what do I want them to learn now? Should I use prose to help me fulfil this aim?

    ii) What have they read before as a group? As individuals?

   iii) Which text(s) might interest and engage them?

   iv) If applicable: what choices are offered by the exam specification?

    v) Who will actually choose the text(s)?

   vi) How will I manage the reading of the text?

  vii) How much time can I allocate for reading and responding?

 viii) Will they be able to take the text(s) home?

   ix) How will this reading experience be built on/developed in the next unit?

All of these questions could also apply to students' reading of other text types. Questions (i) to (iv) require you to draw on your knowledge of the students' tastes and previous reading (as explored in Chapter 2). They also require you to think about your intentions for the unit. What kind of outcomes are you hoping for, both in terms of fulfilling any specific curriculum or examination requirements and, more broadly, in terms of the students' developing awareness and responses to the texts they read?

Questions (ii) to (v) ask you to think about the place of negotiation in your classroom and, inevitably, lead to another set of questions. For example, is it fair for you to always make the choices? If students vote for a text, will they be more motivated to study it? What happens to those who didn't vote for it? Is there literally only *Hobson's Choice* open to you because of what is left in the stock cupboard or what the examination specifies? What happens if you choose a text which *no one* appears to like? Should you abandon it? Should you bring in other texts to complement it or switch the focus? Does everyone have to read the same book at the same time? There are no hard and fast answers to these questions but beginning teachers always seem to think there are. The short answer is to say that so much depends on your group, the individuals within it, other contextual aspects and the approaches or activities that you choose to use in relation to the text(s). As is shown later in this chapter, small-group reading activities centred on a group of texts can open up opportunities for much more independent work.

Questions (vi) to (viii) are concerned with planning for and managing the actual reading. This should include opportunities for reading aloud, but what strategies could you use for achieving this? Figure 3.1 outlines some of the most commonly observed strategies. All have their advantages but some of these are heavily outweighed by disadvantages. You might like to reflect on those you have observed and those you might use. You could also think about any new ideas that you could devise and try out for yourself.

3.4   Reading aloud

As a teacher you will be expected to read texts aloud. This is something that beginning teachers can find very daunting at first. If you feel this way then remember that you should give yourself a chance to practise reading, whether it be in front of the bathroom mirror or your housemates or by volunteering to read in your training course subject sessions. If the reading is to be a genuinely shared experience rather than a chance for you to show off

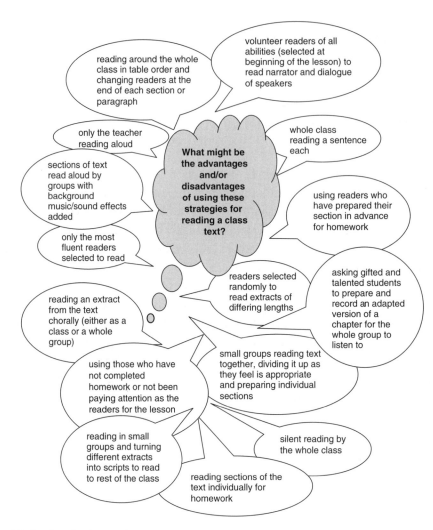

Figure 3.1 Reading aloud strategies

your oratory skills then it will be important to create a supportive atmosphere in your class-room where everyone will feel able to participate in the reading in some way or other. Your reading might be the first reading of a text that the students hear, but wherever possible it should not be the *only* reading. This will be particularly important with poetry texts, where the sounds of the words and their cadences will be such a key part of the experience. With lengthy prose texts it is clearly much more difficult to reread the whole more than once. However, film extracts, extracts from talking books, play or radio adaptations and the students' own performances of certain passages can provide contrasting ways of hearing a key revelation or description, which will help to bring the words off the page, offer alternative interpretations and make a text memorable.

When considering question (vii) above (how much time can I allocate to reading and responding?) there are many factors to consider. It is easy to underestimate how long it will take to get through the first reading of a text. The text length and a practice read-through should give you some idea and your observations of experienced teachers will give you further indications. However, the level of difficulty can make a short text long or a long text short. There are no hard and fast rules.

3.5 Planning for teaching a prose text

Beginning teachers can find that texts take considerably longer to read than they had planned for, with the result that they have to compromise their plans and race to complete the reading of the text before the books are passed on to another class. Once you have chosen which text you are going to use, give yourself plenty of time *before* you begin using it with a class, to think through your intentions and desired outcomes for the whole unit in broad terms. Try reading a section aloud. How long did it take you? Next, discuss your ideas with a colleague *before* you go on to break the unit down into a sequence of lessons and homeworks. In most cases, s/he will know the group much better than you and will know what could be realistically achieved (and by whom) and what would be desirable within the time allocated. As soon as you are fully familiar with the text yourself, you should map out where the key moments in the text occur and where the key events are, together with the features of style or form that you will want to devote time to. This is especially important for lengthy prose works where you will not have the time to devote an equal amount of attention to every word in class. Try asking yourself:

- Which are the sections I will want to linger over?
- Are there sections which seem essential for us to explore together as a whole group?
- How long are each of these sections?
- What challenges could these sections present for my students? What reading skills will they need?
- Are there moments in the book which are perhaps better suited to individual reflection?
- Which of the strategies outlined in Figure 3.1 might be best to use at each stage in the reading (including rereading)?
- What else is there about the text which is less obvious but which is intriguing or thought-provoking?
- Is there the potential for students to go 'off-piste', encounter the unexpected, experiment, raise their own questions and respond in creative ways? If so, how much time should I allow for that?

While you are doing this essential preparatory work, you must of course also keep firmly in your head:

1) why you have chosen this particular text in the first place
2) what you want students to experience and learn in the course of their engagement with it
3) what else the text might offer them or lead to.

In asking these questions, and attempting to judge what is manageable within your given time frame, you are beginning the process of blocking the text. In these early stages I hope you will feel a bit like a leader beginning to map out an expedition of the whole text rather than someone planning a whistle-stop tour of its highlights. You should be thinking through the time constraints, the logistics, the potentially rough terrain, the high points and moments of beauty, the uncharted or as yet unknown opportunities which might present themselves. You are not aiming to scour every surface but you must try to build in enough opportunities to ensure everyone has a coherent, thought-provoking experience of the text. You will of course have a destination in mind as well as some idea of what might happen on the way but, if the expedition has been planned with a sufficient degree of flexibility, then both journey and destination will be different experiences for each reader. Some students may be able to make connections with past schooled and unschooled experiences of other texts. Some may need greater guidance than others and may feel unsure of their footing at points along the way. Most (ideally all) should make new discoveries. If the text and approaches are well chosen, all will be changed in some way by the individual and group journeys they have made.

When teaching the text you will inevitably have to make some sacrifices about what you want the students to experience. However, it is also a good idea to have some extra/replacement activities up your sleeve in case of unforeseen problems. In planning any unit of work you will need to take into account whether your students are permitted to take their texts home with them. Due to mounting replacement costs or lack of availability of texts, some schools simply cannot allow this. This is a sad state of affairs. Once you are a more experienced teacher you may have the opportunity to influence this decision. In the meantime, you should take it into account when choosing the text, allocating class reading time and deciding on the range/ number of activities (including homework tasks) that students will be able to engage with.

A final question to think about is question (ix) – how will this reading experience be built on or developed in the next unit? Although there might not be a direct textual link between the different units within the long-term plan for each teaching group, you and your more experienced colleagues should ensure that, during the course of the year, each class (and each individual learner) is given a balanced diet of texts which present them with a range of opportunities to help them develop their creativity, competence, critical thinking and cultural awareness. Where appropriate, references back and forward to prior and intended future learning should be built into your planning.

3.6   Teaching short stories

Short stories have always been a popular prose form for use in the classroom. Many are a manageable length to enable a first reading and at least an initial response to a complete text within a typical hour-long English lesson. They can provide rich opportunities for comparative work either by author, theme or subgenre. They can easily be used alongside other types of texts in a scheme of work and serve as useful models for the students' own writing or for adaptation activities for short film or podcast formats. Educational publishers have long recognized the attractiveness of the short-story form. There are many collections available, including collections specifically prepared for the GCSE examination boards. The most inventive short-story collections are those which arrive at fresh and interesting combinations, including stories which are not all readily available elsewhere. As with poetry anthologies, the least exciting collections substantially repeat the contents of others on the market and, as such, offer nothing new in terms of combinations and contrasts of texts. Some collections contain teaching activities but others just include comprehension-style questions at the back of the book. Although these might seem like a time saver and could be invaluable in a sudden emergency like a staff illness, these books (or indeed any school textbook resource) are not written with your specific students in mind. Ideally you should always use your own ideas when teaching a text, borrowing and adapting from a wide range of other sources if need be and where appropriate.

Below are some suggestions of short-story groupings and starting points for potential units of work with different year groups:

3.6.1 Sinister or unexpected twists for Year 7

A selection of short stories with sinister or unexpected twists could provide an ideal focus for a Year 7 unit. Stories such as 'Boo' (Crossley-Holland), 'The Pond' (Kneale), 'Journey by Night' (Giuseppi), 'Mystery Train' (Belbin), 'The Fly-Paper' (Taylor), 'Lamb to the Slaughter' (Dahl) and 'The Scarlatti Tilt' (Brautigan) provide a variety of resolutions, reward several rereadings and provoke plenty of discussion. They are all very atmospheric pieces with contrasting settings. Some appear to be rooted in the real world (the Crossley-Holland, Giuseppi, Taylor, and Dahl stories) while the others (Kneale and Belbin) move between reality and fantastical or ghostly worlds. All would serve as useful models for students' own writing as well as stimulus for further reading of whole collections.

'Boo' is a great story to use first as it is very short, clearly written and should be accessible to almost all readers. It has a simple but creepy ending that will open up discussion about how an author can engage a reader in so few words. You might want to follow this up with 'The Scarlatti Tilt' which, in a mere 34 words, demonstrates superb economy of language. This could lead to further research and perhaps writing of the shortest stories in the world. From time to time, very short stories are the subject of competitions. In 2007 the *Guardian* newspaper ran a feature called 'To cut a long story short' in which it challenged well-known contemporary authors to tell a new tale in a mere six words. Examples of the stories can be found at www.guardian.co.uk/books/2007/mar/24/fiction.originalwriting (accessed 10 October 2008). You might not consider all the stories suitable for use with this age group, so be prepared to be selective and devise new examples yourself.

The other stories with twists listed above could all be read by the whole class. Because of their varying lengths and levels of challenge, you may prefer to divide the class up and allot a different story to each small group. Each group could present their work, including a dramatic reading or recording of their story, to the rest of the class. Several of the stories involve strange encounters between people and other beings. All have moments of tension. Students could explore how these encounters and moments are signalled by their writers through a mapping activity. You might also want them to think about how these tense moments would be indicated in a dramatic reading or through use of music or other sound effects. Many of the stories lend themselves to prediction work. After discussion of the openings, students could be given a variety of endings. After using skills of deduction and in-depth discussion of language and structure, they could vote on which one seems the most effective ending and justify their choice. Alternatively, the students could write their own ending either as a group or individually. In teaching this unit you would be able to focus on the following substrands from the Framework:

Speaking and Listening: substrands 3.1, 3.2
Reading: substrands 5.2, 5.3, 6.3
Writing: substrands 8.4, 8.5

3.6.2 Science fiction stories

From Year 7 onwards students should focus increasingly on comparisons between texts and authors, including thematic and stylistic aspects of their work. Comparative work can be approached through exploration of a small group of stories which adhere to similar conventions such as crime, war, gothic horror, science fiction, fantasy or some other hybrid form. Stories such as Bradbury's 'The Golden Apples of the Sun', 'All Summer in a Day' and 'A Sound of Thunder'; Staig's 'Close Circuit'; Westall's 'The Vacancy' and Asimov's 'The Fun they Had' all fit loosely into the science fiction category. They present contrasting (and often sinister) pictures of alternative/future worlds and are ideal for high-achieving Year 8 students or a Year 9 class. (You might want to add Wells's 'The Time Machine' to this list to stretch your very able students.) In creating their vision of the future each author explores concerns which arguably reflect the times in which they were writing.

It would be interesting to explore the extent to which each story relates to the social, historical and cultural contexts in which they were written (Reading substrand 6.1) and how the writers' use of linguistic and literary features shapes and influences meaning (6.2) along with consideration of how each story adheres to or deviates from established conventions. However, any such exploration should not turn literary study into a trawl through texts to find salient features and points of comparison: the stories have so much more to offer than that and should primarily be enjoyed and discussed rather than filleted. With the return of *Doctor Who* and the arrival of *Heroes* on television screens, the growing fascination with tourist space travel, glimpses of the not-too-distant future in films like *Minority Report* (set in 2054) and alternative worlds like *Second Life*, there seems no better time to introduce students to the potential riches of science fiction and to exploit its connections with the multimodal texts like those above. ('A Sound of Thunder', concerned with a time-travel dinosaur hunt and the impact that this has on the future, would link particularly well with *Doctor Who*.) Discussion of the issues raised in these texts could also be enhanced by the use of role-play and other drama strategies (for more on drama strategies refer to Chapter 6).

3.6.3   Social and cultural contexts

From Year 8 onwards, students are expected to pay increasing attention to the social and cultural contexts of the literature that they read, particularly in terms of how the texts refer to and reflect the culture and times in which they were written. Clustering texts by theme rather than genre can, as the National Curriculum notes, facilitate an integrated teaching approach. The KS3 programme of study also advises that choices of texts 'should be informed by the cultural context of the school and experiences of the pupils. It could include texts that: help pupils explore their sense of identity and reflect on their own values, attitudes and assumptions about other people, times and places, either through continuity or contrast with their own experiences [and] explore common experiences in different and unfamiliar contexts (time, place, culture)' (QCA 2007a). With this guidance in mind, short stories can provide snapshots of a wide variety of characters living in other times and cultures. For example pre-twentieth-century stories such as 'Story of an Hour' (Chopin) and 'The Grave by the Handpost' (Hardy) and more contemporary tales like 'Enemies' (Gordimer) and 'The Flowers' (Walker) could provide useful starting points for consideration of how authors construct characters' identities through their language and their response to a single incident (in each case an unexpected death). A short scheme of work for using these stories with a Year 9 class could encompass:

> Speaking and Listening substrands: 3.2, 4.1
> Reading substrands: 5.2, 5.3 6.1
> Writing substrands: 7.1, 8.1, 8.4, 8.5
> Language substrands: 10.1, 10.2

3.7   Teaching novels – what should I read and how should I prepare?

When applicants first come for a PGCE course interview some already seem preoccupied by what they will need to read for their teaching placements. Although it is good to plan ahead, there can be a danger in focusing too quickly on those texts someone else (or an examination board) has chosen. The golden period, before you begin teaching full time, may be the last time in a long while when you are truly able to read for pleasure. Use it to the full: reading widely and being able to apply what you have learned and experienced of texts to a range of titles will ultimately make you a much more adaptable, creative teacher and not the one who always teaches *Of Mice and Men* every year. Not that there is anything wrong with *Of Mice and Men* – it is just that there are a lot of other good texts out there which you should want to introduce your own students to (and learn about from them). Having said this, there are a number of novels, canonical and otherwise, which are regularly found in school stock cupboards and on examination specifications and you would be foolish not to be aware of these. Refer to Appendix 1 for suggestions for further reading. You might find many of the GCSE texts listed are already very familiar to you.

All of the short stories referred to in this chapter are crafted, whole texts. They could provide a bridge to the study of full collections of stories or novels by the same authors or on similar themes. Teaching a sequence of short stories over a series of lessons may seem manageable but handling a lengthier text like a whole novel over a month or half a term can seem much more challenging. Once you have read your selected novel for the first time (preferably not before), you should begin to address how you are going to teach it. Everyone has their own method for this: effective planning is a creative process which takes time but it should be time well spent. Some people mind-map their ideas: others jot down the oppositions which appear to exist within the text and develop their plans from there. Many teachers focus on what seem to be the crucial episodes, chapters, events, quotations or language features in a novel and start to structure their scheme around these. They begin to block the text according to how much class and homework time they have to cover these features, the nature/needs of their students and what they hope the final outcome(s) of engaging with the text might be. This process can be quite tentative at first. For me, it has much in common with how a theatre director works when she comes together with actors and script in a performance space for the first time. You will need to make numerous changes before you are satisfied you have a manageable scheme (and when you teach it a second time you will inevitably change the scheme again). Once you are at this point you might want to remind yourself of the guidelines earlier in this chapter and also explore what kinds of resources are available to support your preparation. The texts and sites listed below can provide helpful ideas but, as has already been stated, you will need to think about what is most appropriate for *your own students* and make your plans accordingly.

3.8   Examples of print and web resources to support your teaching of prose texts

Some of the best and most flexible resources for teaching novels are published by The English and Media Centre and by the National Association for the Teaching of English (NATE).

English Allsorts (2008), published by The English and Media Centre, is a splendid compendium of strategies to use with all sorts of texts. It comes with a CD-ROM. The

Centre also produces a wide variety of photocopiable resources (often with accompanying DVDs and interactive whiteboard software) on many texts commonly taught at GCSE and A level including Sherlock Holmes stories, *Of Mice and Men* and *Lord of the Flies*. Their books on different text types at KS3 are also well worth looking at. For more information go to: www.englishandmedia.co.uk.

The Full English (Julie Blake, 2006), published by NATE/Teachit, features a wide range of lively and creative DARTs which you could adapt to use with many different texts.

The Critical Reading at Post 16 series (ed. Sue Dymoke) published by NATE includes resources on teaching the novels *Wuthering Heights*, *Beloved* and *The Handmaid's Tale* as well as drama texts by Friel, Stoppard, Williams and Webster.

The Classic Reading Series (ed. Robert Protherough) (published by NATE) focuses on short pre-twentieth-century texts including *Doctor Jeykll and Mr Hyde*, *The Adventures of Sherlock Holmes*, Hardy's *Wessex Tales* and poetry by Clare, Chaucer, Keats and Shakespeare.

For further details on NATE publications go to www.nate.org.uk and while you are there find out about the advantages of becoming a member.

Teachit at www.teachit.co.uk contains extensive commentary on many topical aspects of English teaching as well as lesson materials devised and shared by practising teachers. You should think about contributing your own ideas to this site too.

Universalteacher: Perhaps the most helpful website for specification-specific teaching ideas for examination texts is that originally set up by the late Andrew Moore: www.universalteacher.org.uk.

If you do download lesson resources from any website and use them wholesale (which is not advised) you should take care to acknowledge your sources. As with any resource, quality can be very variable: cast a critical eye over the material and tailor it to your students' needs.

3.9   Scheme of work

Once you have begun to think about your potential approach to teaching the text and your students' needs, you will want to draw up a scheme of work (see also Chapter 2). Overleaf (in Figure 3.2) is a sample extract from an AS scheme of work for teaching the post-1990 novel *Wise Children* by Angela Carter.

This extract demonstrates just one of the ways you could organize your planning. For further examples you should consult colleagues in your school or college, refer to teacher support material on examination board, NATE and National Curriculum websites and investigate the downloadable planning tool on the Strategy website (www.standards.dcsf.gov.uk/secondary/framework/english/fwse.)

In Figure 3.2 you can begin to see how the novel has been blocked into manageable sections (in this case these reflect its five-part structure). You will also notice the focus on assessment objectives. These have been embedded in the plan at an early stage and would

	Learning Objectives	Activities	Resources	Differentiation
WEEK ONE: PRE-READING LESSONS 1–3				
1	– Introduction to the novel – Consideration of expectations/Predictions about the text (AO1) – Understanding of prose subgenres (AO2) – Consideration of different interpretations of the novel (AO3) – Beginning to research the time period (AO4)	Consider 'statements about the novel' handout. Highlight sections of statements that give a clue about different elements of the modern novel, e.g. mixing genres, tale of love, real life, etc. – Do you disagree/agree with any of these statements? – Are these elements what you would expect from *Wise Children*? Do these statements agree with Handout 2: what makes a novel 'modern'? Discussion of genre(s) in the modern novel: novel v. play, magic realism. Link to intertextuality discussion. Clarify understanding of these terms. Prepare presentation on chosen focus in time. HW: Finish timeline for chosen focus and prepare presentation with handout. DUE LESSON 2	Handout 1: Statements about the novel Handout 2: What makes a novel modern? Handout 3: Timelines with sectioned periods and focuses	Be prepared with definitions of genre and intertextuality for those students who are less well informed.
2	– Understanding of the time period – Being aware of context (AO4)	Groups feedback their information through presentation on chosen topic. Each student fills in timeline with notes from other presentations. Discuss the context the novel is set in compared to the context in which it was written (early 1900s compared to late 1980s).	Handout 3: Timeline for focused topics	Activity suited for small groups and individual learning.
3	– Exploration of denotation and connotation (AO1) – Exploration of 5-part structure (AO2) and connections with different literary texts (AO3)	Look at front cover. What responses are evoked? Why? Discuss denotation and connotation. Discuss 5-part structure – link back to genre and intertextuality. Shakespearean plays always written in 5 acts. Shakespeare comes in later. Is there anything else in the novel which suggests it is mixed with elements from a play? (Dramatis personae at back.)	Handout 4: Copies of different front covers Handout 5: 5-part structure information	Extension task: research *Wise Children* in relation to Shakespeare and be prepared to contribute in a fuller or more active manner in future lessons (probably lessons 5 and 8).
From WEEK THREE				
9	– Recap events of Part One – Developing independent opinions (AO1) – Thematic understanding (AO2)	Consider the events in Part One. How does Carter mix the comic and the tragic? Consider: – Character of Wheelchair – Abandonment of Nora and Dora – Life of Nora and Dora at this point – Tristram and Tiffany – Tristram and Saskia – What we learn about Melchior Hazard Work in pairs or small groups and create a mind map in the form of a poster that can be put up as a wall display for Part 1.	Sugar paper Pens Blu-tack/pins Display headings: comedy and tragedy in Part One	Activity to benefit visual learners. Also can be referred to over a period of time as revision aid.

Figure 3.2 Adaption from an AS level scheme for teaching *Wise Children* by Angela Carter (originally devised by Herbert, Ingham, Judge, Quirk and McDougall 2005)

be used explicitly with students. This scheme refers to the 2009 AS assessment objectives for English Literature and begins with a week of pre-reading activities. These provide opportunities to: explore expectations about the novel; foreground terminology that students need to begin to understand; and place the novel in a context of other novels. Devoting time to these activities may seem like a luxury but this is time well spent. As a whole, the scheme builds in opportunities for a range of activities to stimulate different types of response, including whole-class and individual reflection, paired reading and discussion. Throughout it the beginning teachers who originally devised it have an eye to differentiation. However, as is stated in the notes accompanying the original scheme, there is also an expectation that when reading does take place in class, students should read ahead so they can contribute fully to class discussion and be able to clarify their understanding during lesson time.

These are admirable intentions which might seem very reasonable for Post-16 students. Unfortunately, some of the students you teach may find these difficult to achieve. Even though students might have obtained C grades or above in their GCSEs, or equivalent qualification, Post-16 English classes do not consist entirely of students who love reading, want to study English at university or even want to be in Post-16 education. In the UK, the provision of an Educational Maintenance Allowance (EMA) can be the reason for their attendance. New pathways in the 14–19 curriculum in England and Wales came into effect from 2008 with the result that this picture may begin to change. These should provide greater opportunities for a variety of work-based learning options as well as increased access to International Baccalaureate (IB) diploma courses and revised A level courses. From first examination in 2009, A level courses have been slimmed down from six to four assessment units. This means that teachers should have more time to establish the vital foundations for Post-16 study and enable students to make a smoother transition from their previous courses. Whatever the make-up of your Post-16 classes or the content of the examination courses that you are teaching, you will be teaching texts to mixed ability groups. You will need to ensure that your teaching methods and strategies are suitably varied and differentiated to stimulate learning by all.

3.10   Using extracts

In teaching a novel, you may at first feel a huge pressure to get through the text as quickly as possible in order to move the class on to the activities you have planned. It is important to remember that the reading is an *essential part of the learning experience* and not a precursor to it. The move straight to an activity is arguably exacerbated by the extensive use of extracts in some classrooms and study of scenes from Shakespeare rather than whole plays (for more on this see Chapter 6). We live in an age where text is frequently divided into small gobbets such as text message, half-sentence email replies or short web summaries (with hyperlinks for additional information). The result is that the experience of reading a lengthy whole text from a book could become a distant memory for some readers (and perhaps an alien experience for the youngest). The use of photocopied extracts and those on IWBs and OHTs in classrooms can deny students physical contact with/experience of a complete text and also remove the language under discussion from its all-important surrounding context. Clearly there is a place for using extracts: they can powerfully place a text under the microscope and draw the class together on a discussion about a particular stylistic or structural feature. However, extracts should not replace the experience of reading *whole* texts as is stipulated in the National Curriculum programmes of study (QCA 2007a) and required for GCSE and A level study.

3.11   Group and guided reading

In choosing to use a novel with your class you may feel it is not appropriate for the whole group to be reading the same text or that groups within the class require structured support at certain stages in their reading. If this is the case then guided reading is a strategy worth considering. Originally an element of the first version of the National Strategy, guided reading focuses on the development of a set of reading strategies through structured small-group work. This is led by the teacher, who works with each group in turn (and ideally the whole class over a period of three or four weeks). The reading strategies outlined in the Framework and associated training materials are:

- highlighting
- skimming
- scanning
- those concerned with inference and deduction such as: seeing images, hearing a voice through the text, predicting what might happen, speculating about characters and events, summarizing what has been deduced
- those concerned with response such as asking questions, empathizing, relating to experiences, passing comments
- those concerned with reflection such as rationalizing what is happening, rereading, re-interpreting, making judgements, interpreting patterns (theme, language, structure), relating to previous reading experiences, establishing a relationship with the author/narrator, relating a text to context (DfES and NATE 2003)

You might have already seen guided reading in action in some form in your preliminary visits to primary school classes. Usually the class teacher (or a teaching assistant) supports each small group for approximately 20 minutes. Students will then spend some time reading independently. Follow-up tasks and target-setting are also key elements of this approach. The groups usually consist of students of a similar reading ability, need or focus. Every group could be reading the same text, in which case group sessions are interspersed with periods of whole-class work including reading. Alternatively, you could select a different text for each group, linking them by theme, period or author. Schemes of work, lesson plans and resources for group and guided reading on 15 challenging novels and play texts such as *Chinese Cinderella* (Adeline Yen Mah), *Holes* (Louis Sachar) and *The Wind Singer* (William Nicholson) and on a set of thematically linked 'Holocaust' novels: *Friedrich* (Hans Peter Richter), *Last Train from Kummersdorf* (Leslie Wilson), *The Boy in the Striped Pyjamas* (John Boyne) and *Once* (Morris Gleitzman) are available for free download in PDF format on the NATE website at www.nate. org.uk. For an example of the materials see Figure 3.3. These 'Holocaust' novels could also be

Once	Morris Gleitzman
Lesson 4	Group card O4

Objectives: R4 Versatile reading
R12 Independent reading

Resources: None

As a whole group we have:
• revised the range of reading strategies you have available to you;
• explored narrative hooks;
• explored the developing relationships between character and place.

Now you are going to:
• explore the characterization in more depth.

Group reading
Read together pages 57–65.

Group task
In these pages we learn more about Felix and see his understanding grow.
On page 64 he tells Zelda that the old lady who could not go on was, '…just having a rest'.
Imagine that a minute later Zelda and Felix heard the rattle of machine gun fire where the elderly lady had been resting.

1. In pairs, decide who will play the role of being Felix and who will become Zelda.

2. Improvise an imaginary conversation that takes place between them as the sound of gunfire fades away.

3. Select one pair to repeat their improvisation for the rest of the group.

4. As a group, discuss how Felix has changed since he met Zelda:

    i. Why do you think that the author shows us this character growing up in these pages?
    ii. What does this suggest about how Felix might behave in the future?
    iii. How does Zelda feel about her protector, Felix?
    iv. Why does Felix feel so protective towards her?
    v. Why are these changes in Felix's manner significant?

5. Discuss the reading strategies you have used during the lesson so far.

6. Select one member of the group to feed back on the reading strategies you have used today, during the plenary.

7. Read pages 66–73 before the plenary.

© NATE 2006   Group reading at Key Stage 3 - Extension Pack: Year 8   Theme: The Holocaust

Figure 3.3 Extract from *Group Reading at KS3 Materials: Extension Pack Year 8. Theme: the Holocaust* (published with permission from NATE)

used in cross-curricular work with History and Citizenship. For further ideas about cross-curricular activities, please refer to Appendix 2.

At secondary school level, the take-up of guided reading has been patchy for a number of reasons, including the time and staff resources required. An emphasis on reading strategies (and the mantra-like recall of these strategies shown in some training materials) can become too skills-focused and detrimental to students' engagement with the texts they are reading. Nevertheless, you might find the suggested guided approaches beneficial in helping EAL students or those with specific learning difficulties to develop their confidence in discussing aspects of texts. In addition, the use of linked small-group readers could enable you to steer gifted and talented students towards independent work and reflection on a range of challenging texts.

3.12   Schools' Library Service

The Schools' Library Service offers teachers extensive support with reading recommendations, access to class sets and book boxes of assorted titles, including all titles recommended throughout this book. The *Literature Matters* project outlined in Chapter 2 gave beginning teachers many practical ideas for how to talk about and share a range of literature beyond the confines of the classroom and the set text. Beginning teachers on the PGCE course at Leicester in 2005 to 2007 were quick to try out the ideas and (in true English teacher fashion) to adapt them to suit their own students. Popular strategies included:

- belly bands – students design and write the wrapper which goes round favourite or new books on display in the library (this seemed to be hugely successful with one group of boys especially)
- post-it note-sized reviews with emoticons – students make very quick judgements on whether the look of a book, its blurb and opening page will appeal and share these with others in their group
- speed dating a book – one minute for each person in a pair to say what they thought of a book (before the whistle blows) and another minute to ask questions
- email shared class correspondences – two classes in different schools email each other throughout a term with book recommendations and updates.

For more information about the Schools' Library Service go to www.sla.org.uk.

3.13   Writing prose fiction

So far this chapter has concentrated primarily on reading and responding to prose texts, albeit in some cases using these texts as models for students' own writing. However, we should not ignore the challenges and pleasures of writing prose fiction of all kinds. Writing prose fiction is one of the more common secondary English classroom activities and stories are first on the list of written forms that they should experience in Key Stage 3 (QCA 2007a).

By the end of Year 9, students should have learned how to 'establish and sustain distinctive character, point of view and voice in their fiction writing by choosing from a wide range of techniques and devices used by writers' as well as to plan and develop their ideas effectively, drawing on established conventions and with a clear sense of purpose and audience in mind (DCSF 2008a). Increasingly, they should be making links between their reading and the choices they make as writers.

Despite the references to story writing in the National Curriculum, this does not mean that students are always writing stories or being given the freedom to write in other forms that they would wish. A frequent complaint from both primary and secondary English specialists is that time for students to write at length in any genre is at a premium. The inception of a revised curriculum with greater emphasis on freedom for creative experiment in a wide range of forms extending 'beyond narrative and poetry' (QCA 2007a and b) could answer these complaints. However, a crammed and assessment-led curriculum does not allow space for extended work and the elephant of assessment will need to vacate the room before the environment can really change.

These aspects of prose fiction detailed above should not be viewed in isolation. The techniques that students develop in writing prose fiction should inform their writing in other genres, enabling them to experiment with different ways of telling, to break down perceived genre conventions and to become increasingly experimental and creative in their writing. An awareness and increased use of drafting processes (planning, drafting, editing, proofreading and self-evaluation) are central to the students' continued development as writers of prose fiction. The acknowledgement of these crafting and shaping processes within the English curriculum represents, Hilton argues, 'a hard-won victory for educationists who maintained steadily for several years that children, like all writers, learn to write most effectively through deploying a series of complex recursive stages as the work progresses' (2001: 8). Some argue that the English classroom is not the place for learning such processes. They think it is inappropriate to formalize processes which they perceive as being more fluid or whimsical and reliant on happenstance rather than forward planning. When she was interviewed as the UK's Children's Laureate, Anne Fine, author of *Flour Babies*, publicly stated her dislike of drafting in schools. Philip Pullman, highly celebrated for the *His Dark Materials* trilogy, does not approve of the preoccupation with planning and drafting in the English curriculum. He views each of his texts as 'final versions' rather than drafts (Carter 1999: 184).

In contrast, prize-winning author David Almond describes different processes for the different types of texts he writes. These include picture books, short stories, plays and, most recently, the libretto for an opera of *Skellig*, the children's novel for which he is best known. I interviewed him for ongoing research on writers' text-making processes in different genres. He talks of 'writing down pages, getting into the rhythm' of a novel that might run to a number of drafts on the computer, many of which get lost in the ether. This is in contrast to short stories which arrive with their own shape, albeit overlong at first, and picture books which come 'instantaneously'. When he first wrote, Almond was essentially a short-story writer. He thought he 'couldn't write long' but began to approach the novel through his short-story writing and gradually learned how to link scenes together. Almond sees a change in his composition process since he began writing: he acknowledges his growing confidence about what to throw away and feels he has become braver about taking risks. He also believes in the need to trust one's imagination when writing. He is concerned by the compartmentalization of texts in primary school – a fact which is reflected in the questions asked when he is on school visits: 'What genre do you write in, Mr Almond?' Almond likes to write in many forms and feels he is 'not crossing boundaries, just telling stories'.

If you would like to know more about the composition processes of leading children's writers and poets, please refer to Carter 1999 and Dymoke 2003.

3.14   Writers and readers working together

3.14.1   Barrington Stoke

Barrington Stoke is a small Scottish company with a fast-growing reputation for publishing high-quality short prose fiction for children and young adult readers who are reluctant to pick up a book or who have reading difficulties. Not only are their books beautifully produced, on cream-coloured paper with font styles and layouts which are much easier for dyslexic students to read, but also the publisher involves young readers much more fully in the writing process than conventional publishing houses do. Authors' draft manuscripts are sent out to school groups and teachers for review. Students (of the appropriate reading age for the book) are asked to comment extensively on vocabulary choices, plot lines and other details. Their responses are taken very seriously and fed back in a lengthy discussion between editor and author. For more information about Barrington Stoke go to www.barringtonstoke.co.uk.

3.14.2   Donald Graves

Graves's investigation of young children's writing in New Hampshire, USA had a great influence on the emergence of a process model of writing and informed the Writing programmes of study in the first National Curriculum orders for English. His book, *Writing: Teachers and Children at Work* (1983) concentrates primarily on writing prose texts. It remains an essential and energizing text for those who face the day-to-day reality of trying to teach writing. For Graves, the teaching of writing was the teaching of a craft consisting of a number of stages from rehearsal through drafting and revision (which involved conferencing) to publication. To support students' developing drafts, he described 'scaffolding conferences'

(Graves 1983: 280) held between teacher and student-writer(s). These focused on any element of the writing (including punctuation and selection for publication). Providing space for young writers to reflect on their work in the certainty that, given this space, they will have something to say about it, is a central principle of the conference approach. In describing these conferences Graves acknowledged the leap from conversation to composition which young writers needed to make (Bereiter and Scardamalia 1987). He urged teachers to use simple, straightforward approaches involving active listening and demonstration, which would enable young writers to make sense of the unpredictable and often complex nature of their writing (Graves 1983). In his view, the conferences worked best when the children were able to ask their own questions. Like Baldwin (1959), Stibbs (1981), and others before him, he also believed that teachers had a kind of moral obligation to write themselves. The empowerment of young writers to ask their own questions and make their own choices and the role of teacher as writer were all very much in the minds of those who led and participated in the *We're Writers* project (Grainger *et al.* 2005). This project gave both teachers and students the opportunity to develop their awareness of what it means to write and to take creative risks beyond the confines of a highly restrictive, extract-focused curriculum. It highlighted a need for new and more experienced teachers to be given opportunities to learn more 'about themselves, about writing and about the art of teaching writing' (Grainger *et al.* 2005: 177). Some INSET opportunities do exist but they are rarely given a high priority. If you can obtain funding, then I would strongly recommend that you attend an Arvon writing course or a Poetryclass event for teachers.[2] Both of these would help to build your confidence in your own writing and in talking about writing with others.

If your students are to fully understand and utilize the recursive processes which many professional writers engage in at different stages in the production of their work, then it seems appropriate they should be given opportunities to engage collaboratively in aspects of the writing.

This could mean that they:

- take on the roles of editors or publishers' readers for each other's texts
- work as an editorial group to hold conferences to consider the potential of work in progress or of completed individual stories for presentation, podcasting or publication on the school's website
- team up as pairs of visual artists and writers working together to make picture books or graphic novels
- compose a real or virtual group story – either by each taking responsibility for a chapter or by drafting the whole story together using either pen and paper or different technological means such as IWB flipchart screens (and a tablet or wireless keyboard passed round the group) or via email exchange, MSN or synchronous online discussion.

If carefully planned and implemented, these strategies can lead to a greater sense of student involvement (by boys and girls) in composition processes as well as an excitement about what is being created which can motivate the least confident writers in a class.

3.14.3 Collaborative story writing using wireless keyboards

The benefits of group composition were made clear to me during a qualitative research project on using wireless keyboards in secondary English classrooms carried out in 2004 to 2005 (for a fuller report see Dymoke 2005). The project explored some of the potential uses of wireless keyboards and mice for teaching and learning in English lessons. It was based in six secondary schools, using an opportunity sample of eight beginning teachers, their mentors and students from one or more English classes in each school. Collaborative writing strategies were used by all the pilot schools. Writing included story openings, endings and complete stories by pupils in Years 7, 8 and 10. In one school, a Year 10 special needs class of 12 pupils worked together in three of their project lessons to draft 'The Footsteps', a horror story. Expectations for collaborative work were established by Amy (trainee teacher) and her mentor and students were reminded of them at the beginning of each lesson. Rules for use of the equipment were also devised and shared with other schools via the project's VLE discussion board. During their collaborative writing, one keyboard and one mouse were passed around the group. The emerging text was projected onto an ordinary whiteboard at the front of the room. Students volunteered to take turns with the equipment when they either:

a) suggested a plot development or descriptive phrase for the story that had been approved for inclusion by the others in the group; or
b) drew attention to punctuation, spelling or an aspect of grammar they wanted to correct.

During one session the story was restructured and an extra paragraph about the main character inserted. Observation notes on the second of these sessions reveal the students' eagerness to participate, their patience and willingness to listen to each other's ideas. They made frequent and constructive suggestions based on close reading of their shared draft. These included the following typical exchanges and contributions:

> *Student A: We need a different word . . .*
> *Student B: We've already used 'terrified' . . .*
> *. . .*
> *Student C: . . . she can't adjust to light in darkness. Can she?*
> *. . .*
> *Student B: Run?*
> *Student D: Scarper.*
> *Student E: Flee.*
> *Student A: Use the word 'scram'!*
> *. . .*
> *Amy: What could happen next?*
> *Student B: . . . the door turns and locks or . . .*
> *. . .*
> *Student F: Squeal or scream?*

Student C: She's stunned . . .
Student D: Yeah! Stunned.

. . .

Amy: How could we start the sentence to get the reader's attention?
Student A: Turning towards the window?

. . .

Student G: How do you spell 'realizes'?

Although Amy occasionally prompted students for suggestions, both she and their usual class teacher were delighted by the whole group's ownership of their text and their willingness to participate voluntarily. The use of a carefully structured but flexible approach placed value on exploratory talk and promoted reflection leading to further understanding. Both teachers thought the students were motivated by the equipment: it seemed to give them a confidence to experiment and support each other with language choices which had not been evident in their previous English work. It also reinforced in the students an understanding that all their views on the developing text were of equal value. At the end of the project the equipment was retained for further use with the Year 10s and other groups for collaborative writing and textual analysis activities. Amy thought her students relished the fact that they were the only class in the school involved in the research: it gave them kudos and made them feel that their opinions were valued. One needs to be aware of the 'Hawthorne effect' here: it can be argued that this 'special treatment' made the class more predisposed to praise the hardware. However, when they were observed, individuals wanted to talk about how and what they were writing together. They wanted to comment critically on the effectiveness and limitations of the equipment. One girl said she liked the equipment as it gave her opportunities to be involved in the work, while one boy said he had enjoyed story writing more as a result of using it. Several students said that the group had gradually become accustomed to the small size of the keys but they had all used the wireless mouse without problems if it was on a table top. They had noticed an occasional delay between typing words and their appearance on screen. They also thought that the keyboard seemed to respond more slowly in certain parts of the room. One boy wrote in his final evaluation that he wanted to try out the keyboards with PowerPoint and other software while another stated that 'this type of equipment would be useful in all schools. It has been a pleasure to help in this project.'

Use of the wireless equipment for supporting collaborative writing in a classroom would seem to have some potential. The affordances offered to learning (among sample groups in this study) are such that individuals can be given an increased stake in the written draft and a sense of ownership. Young writers are able to intervene in the drafting process and share their ideas visibly on screen for others to discuss, develop further or delete wherever they are seated in the classroom. Similarly the wireless mouse frees up engagement and can be used by teachers and students to focus or initiate discussion on features of their drafts. The wireless equipment appears to engender a mutually supportive atmosphere in some situations where students previously lacked confidence in commenting on their peers' use of written language or exposing their own writing to public criticism.

Further examples of collaboration and of exploring composition processes used by real writers are explored in Chapter 4 (Poetry) and Chapter 7 (Multimodal texts).

3.15   Conclusion

This chapter has explored a number of questions about the choices you will make and some of the approaches you will take when reading, responding to and making prose texts with your students. For many teachers, teaching prose represents safe ground compared with the deep and choppy waters they confront when teaching poetry. Poetry is the focus of the next chapter. I hope you are ready to take the plunge.

Notes

1. Novels by Robert Westall, Gillian Cross, Anne Fine, Nigel Hinton and Michelle Magorian.
2. The Arvon Foundation runs residential writing courses led by professional writers at a number of venues around the UK. Some grants are available for teachers. For further information go to www.arvonfoundation.org. Poetryclass, run by The Poetry Society, organizes INSET events for teachers, provides advice on working with poets in your classroom and ideas for poetry activities. See www.poetryclass.net (both websites accessed 10 October 2008).

Poetry 4

Chapter Outline

4.1 Introduction

Of all the text types explored in this book, poetry is the one which seems to present the most people with the most challenges. As teachers you will need to confront these challenges and also allay potential fears and prejudices about the genre by engaging your students in stimulating approaches to reading, writing, listening to and performing poetry. This chapter argues for the centrality of poetry within the English curriculum and the pleasures of this dynamic, multimodal form of expression. It draws on research evidence to explore the subject knowledge issues and concerns which many beginning (and some experienced) teachers express about poetry and poetry teaching. It provides support for these subject knowledge issues before going on to address the predominant pedagogic concerns identified. In this chapter I ask what purposes poetry serves within English and our lives beyond the classroom and explore potential links between poetry and games, conceptualizing poetry in a way that can engage all learners (including boys). The chapter also considers: teaching poetry from different periods; poetry from different cultures and migrant voices in the English classroom; and teaching poetry for examinations.

4.2   Research on beginning teachers and poetry

This chapter draws on evidence from a study of the developing poetry subject and pedagogic knowledge of beginning English teachers (carried out in 2005 to 2006) and involving a sample of 70 student teachers enrolled on three PGCE (Postgraduate Certificate of Education) English Secondary courses in England. Its purpose was to gain a clearer understanding (at both pre- and post-course stage) of student teachers':

- previous poetry experiences (both in education and beyond)
- their subject knowledge
- the use and transformation of their subject knowledge into pedagogic knowledge as they develop their classroom expertise
- their views about poetry and the place of poetry within the school curriculum.

The research findings were intended to inform the future support and development of trainee English teachers. Data was collected using qualitative methods. This consisted of pre- and post-course semi-structured questionnaires, recorded and transcribed telephone interviews and some work samples at key points during the PGCE year. The pre-course questionnaire explored:

a) previous experiences of reading, writing, listening to and speaking/performing poetry during compulsory and post-compulsory education and outside the classroom
b) prior study, reading and listening to poets listed in the National Curriculum and the student teachers' reactions to these lists
c) interpretations of the term poetry 'from different cultures and traditions'
d) observations and experiences of poetry teaching prior to PGCE
e) expectations for their own poetry teaching
f) support needs with aspects of poetry or poetry teaching
g) personal tastes in poetry
h) awareness of living poets they might want to work with in a classroom.

In devising the questions, I decided *not* to ask directly about different poetic forms which the teachers might already be familiar with: it was important to see what, without undue influence, the teachers would recall of their previous poetic experiences and/or highlight as potential support needs. I also did not want to present poetry as a checklist of terms and 101 forms (Hull 2001) to be ticked off or to alarm the beginning teachers with a bank of terms which might (especially in the case of the graduates without English degrees) be very

Table 4.1 Poetry subject knowledge research questions

The beginning English teachers were asked the following questions:

a) How would you describe your own school/university experiences of poetry?

b) Did you have opportunities to write poems at school? Yes/No

c) Have you written any poetry since leaving school? Yes/No

d) Have you had any experience of working with a visiting writer in a writing workshop (either at school or elsewhere)? Yes/No

e) If yes, please give brief details.

f) Which poets (from any century, culture or tradition) do you enjoy reading or listening to? Please list below:

g) Do you participate in any of the following? (please circle appropriate answers)
Attending poetry readings/slams?   Regularly/Sometimes/Rarely/Never
Reading poetry for pleasure?   Regularly/Sometimes/Rarely/Never
Listening to/viewing poetry programmes?   Regularly/Sometimes/Rarely/Never
Visiting poetry websites?   Regularly/Sometimes/Rarely/Never
Performing your poems to an audience?   Regularly/Sometimes/Rarely/Never
Discussing poetry with friends/book group?   Regularly/Sometimes/Rarely/Never

h) Have you observed or taken part in any poetry teaching prior to beginning your PGCE? Yes/No

i) If yes, please give brief details:

j) What are you looking forward to about your poetry teaching?

k) What would you like pupils to learn in your poetry lessons?

l) Are there any aspects of poetry/poetry teaching which you would like support with during your PGCE course? Yes/No (If yes, please outline below.)

m) If you could invite any living poet in to work with you during your PGCE year, who would it be? Why?

n) – r) asked them to tick the poets named or exemplified in the National Curriculum KS3 and KS4 lists (1999–2007 version) whom they had previously studied or read.

s) Please list any poets (other than those listed in the four tables above) whom you have previously studied or read:

t) What were your initial reactions to these National Curriculum lists of writers?

u) What is your understanding of the term poetry 'from different cultures and traditions'?

v) How do you think you might want to prepare yourself to teach poetry 'from different cultures and traditions'?

unfamiliar to them and require explanation in the questionnaire. You might like to reflect on some of specific questions I asked them (see Table 4.1). In doing so, think about your own responses and the implications which these responses might have for your own professional development needs.

In reviewing the beginning teachers' responses, a number of common threads began to emerge, some of which may echo your own. At the beginning of their courses 79 per cent of those questioned identified poetry subject knowledge support needs either related to their own subject knowledge or to transforming aspects of their knowledge for classroom use. Their concerns were linked to personal development and a growing awareness about what would be required of them in schools.

4.3 Subject knowledge support

Subject knowledge support needs were connected with:

a) Extending knowledge of specific poets, periods, groupings of poets (such as contemporary or children's poetry) and moving beyond canonical texts. (These responses were probably partially influenced by the lists of National Curriculum poets in the questionnaire.)
b) Technical aspects such as improving understanding of structure, poetic terminology, stressed and unstressed syllables and forms (including ballads and sonnets).
c) Analysis and appreciation of poetry texts.

If the subject knowledge needs above overlap with your own then I hope you will find the development suggestions in Table 4.2 helpful.

Aspects of poetry-teaching pedagogy that the beginning teachers wanted help with were sometimes couched in broad terms such as 'ways into teaching poetry': at this stage in the research, they did not know about the exact nature of the classes and schools they would be working with. Nevertheless, three significant areas of pedagogical need were emerging:

a) finding ways into teaching poetry which would support specific groups of learners (such as boys or those within a particular ability range) and choosing approaches linked to teaching and assessment objectives
b) selecting appropriate poems for specific age groups/abilities
c) support with teaching poetry writing.

Other issues included: 'positive' assessment of students' work; availability of contextual material; poetry performance skills; being enthusiastic about poetry. Area a) was notably the most pressing concern and was expressed by 38 per cent of the subgroup. Implicit within these responses is both an awareness of differentiation (even though the term 'differentiation' was not used by *anyone* who completed the questionnaire), and a sensitivity towards how they might, as beginning teachers, engage with learners. The predominance of area a) indicates that *beginning teachers appear to be more concerned with what might be effective classroom practice than with their own subject knowledge.* They are already starting to think as teachers, working in an assessment-focused environment where teaching and learning must be appropriately packaged to ensure 'delivery' of a quality outcome in assessment terms. Because the questionnaire focused specifically on poetry, it is not possible to ascertain whether the expressed support needs are entirely genre-specific or if they would be

Table 4.2 Supporting poetry subject knowledge development

Area of need	Suggested activities	Resources
Extending knowledge of specific poets, periods, groupings of poets (such as contemporary or children's poetry) and moving beyond canonical texts	Develop your confidence and tastes by reading a wide range of poetry from single collections, anthologies and poetry magazines. Use guidance about what to read from themed library lists, poetry reviews, poetry texts included in exam specifications, specialist guides. Talk to your local librarian about popular texts and ask children about their favourite poems. Listen to poetry on internet, radio, CD. Go to poetry slams, readings and other performances. Browse poetry sites on internet for historical information, critical readings and links. Reading introductory guides to poets' works and literary periods.	Poetry library: www.poetrylibrary.org.uk Scottish poetry library: www.spl.org.uk (These fantastic libraries are well worth visiting and also have excellent online resources) Reviews in professional journals like *Books for Keeps, English Drama Media, NATE Classroom, Secondary English Magazine* *Universal Verse: Poetry for children* (guide edited by Hallford and Zaghini 2006) www.poetryarchive.org www.poets.org Radio 4's *Poetry Please* and Radio 3's *The Verb* CD recordings borrowed from libraries Look at local listings for events in your area www.applesandsnakes.org Find out about GCSE *Poetry Live* events www.thepoetryhouse.org www.contemporarywriters.com *Lives of the Poets* (Schmidt 1998) *Strong Words: Modern poets on modern poetry* (Herbert and Hollis 2000) *The Deregulated Muse* (O'Brien 1998)
Technical aspects of poetry such as improving understanding of structure, poetic terminology, stressed and unstressed syllables and forms (including ballads and sonnets)	Make links between reading aloud, listening to poetry and experimenting with writing. Experiencing poetry in these varied ways will help to develop understanding. Consult a well-written guide to poetic forms. Try out a writing workshop.	*Poetry in the Making* (Hughes 1967) – observing and writing *Writing Poems* (Sansom 1994) – excellent writing activities *Jumpstart* (Yates 1999) – writing in the classroom *The Poet's Craft* (Brownjohn 2002) – very helpful glossary *The Forms of Poetry: A practical study guide* (Abbs and Richardson 1990) *Poetry: the Basics* (Wainwright 2004) *Metre, Rhythm and Verse Form* (Hobsbaum 1996) Try local arts listings or online workshops. The Arvon Foundation and The Poetry Business run courses pitched at different levels of experience
Analysis and appreciation of poetry texts	Read aloud one new poem a week. Reflect on how it is written. Analysis of *how* its language works should link with *why* the language has been chosen and the impact this has on you and other readers. Develop confidence and your tastes in poetry by trying out activities listed. Share knowledge and identify ways to support each other in all three areas.	*52 ways of looking at a poem* (Padel 2004) – an accessible collection of short critical readings of contemporary poems *Poem for the Day One* (Albery and Ratcliffe 1994) – a varied and interesting selection each with a brief commentary. Subsequent volumes are also worth a look

replicated in questions about teaching other genres/other aspects of the English curriculum. In reviewing your own responses (to the questions in Table 4.1), think about this balance between subject knowledge and pedagogy. It would also be enlightening for you to explore potential overlaps between your support needs for teaching poetry and those for other types of texts. The pedagogic needs identified above inform much of the rest of this chapter and you will find ideas throughout to support your development.

The beginning teachers were asked a very similar set of questions at the end of their PGCE year, when they also provided details of the poetry lessons they had taught, reflected on further professional development needs in teaching poetry and their views about why poetry should appear in the curriculum. These views are explored later in this chapter.

4.4   What is poetry?

There is a fundamental uncertainty underpinning debates about poetry's place in the curriculum (and how poetry might be most effectively taught), which is concerned with its nature. What is poetry? Is it actually that special or different from other forms of writing? Attempting to define poetry may be like 'trying to pin down vapour' (Andrews 1991: 13) but it is important to consider definitions in order to arrive at some understanding of learners' potential reactions to the genre. Poetry's distinctiveness is primarily derived from poets' uses of language – poetic language which is like no other: on the 'frontiers' (DES 1987: 1); precise 'as geometry' (Flaubert 1853) or 'like a microscope' (Andrews 1991: 42); pared down, showing 'a pressure of language on meaning' (Prynne 1999); enigmatic 'like a wild animal' (Stafford 1986: 99); imbued with magical power (Heaney 1989); uncompromising like a 'tough old bird' (Horner 1999: 59) and demanding of its readership a 'new effort of attention' (Lawrence 1929: 255). Poetry has frequently been seen as a problem to be solved, a 'jigsaw puzzle' (Baldwin 1959: 187), a 'crossword' (Woodhead 1980: 42), an enigma, a 'verbal contraption' (Auden 1968: 50), 'a knit of words' (Steiner 1978: 21). It has been most famously described as 'the best words in the best order' (Coleridge 1827: 90). This definition asserts poetry's superiority over other forms of expression and has perhaps done the genre no favours by placing it on so high a pedestal.

Andrews devotes a lengthy chapter to consideration of rhythm, concluding that 'the notion of the line as the defining characteristic of poetry is a central one' (1991: 58). For others, including Frost (1930) and Harrison and Gordon (1983), it is metaphor which sets poetry apart. Miroslav Holub wrote a fine example of this metaphoric activity in *Poem Technology* (1987). In celebrating the potentially explosive (while at the same time very individual) power of poetry, he demonstrates many of the qualities which differentiate poetry from other language forms. The poem's argument centres on the extended metaphor of the creation of a poem as the lighting of 'a fuse'. The 'fuse'/poem can be written or spoken in any location and, in speeding along, gaining momentum (or alternatively pursuing a more fragile existence) and eventually exploding/reaching its fruition somebody somewhere will be provoked into a reaction of some kind. The compressed words, packed in like explosive, jagged edgy structure (mirroring the lit fuse path), uneven rhythm and excited tone of this poem all set it apart from prose. This is not to say that these elements could not be found separately in other forms but that only poetry presents them in this striking combination.

You may wish to use some of these definitions with your own students – particularly as an introduction to poetry at the beginning of Post-16, IB or AS level courses. (For an A level version of this activity refer to Dymoke *et al.* 2008: 8–9.) At this level students should reflect on and draw on their previous experiences of literature as they learn to articulate critical understanding of how structure, form and language shape meanings in literary texts and the impact these will have on readers (see for example Higher level objectives for the IB Language 1 and AO2 for AS English Literature).

4.5   Who is poetry for?

The definitions of poetry above give some indication of the nature of poetic language and what it might look like on the page. However, this is a text which you will be required to teach in an inclusive and supportive way, therefore you will also need to think further about the potential audiences for and purposes of poetry and how individual learners might respond to the linguistic and other demands which poetry might pose for them.

Some potential readers of poetry appear to be alienated by the language, imagery and diction of poetry (Benton 1986). These are the very elements which, others would argue, make it distinctive. A number of people interviewed by Benton thought poetry 'belongs in any case to the "posh"' (1986: 18). Baldwin (1959), Leonard (1975) and Marsh (1988) also acknowledge the idea of elitism. Leonard's poem 'Poetry' vividly illustrates a feeling of disenfranchisement from the genre. He concludes: 'Poughit. Rih,/That was my education/ – and nothing to do with me' (1975). The need for young people to be able to identify with poets and poetry is just as pertinent today.

Ofsted's 2007 report on poetry teaching indicates that primary school children are given few opportunities to read or write poems which directly connect with their own experiences and the National Curriculum for English at Key Stage 3 stipulates that text choices should be of 'high quality' and 'interesting and engaging, allowing students to explore their present situation or move beyond to experience different times, cultures, viewpoints and situations' (QCA 2007a: 8). However, the retention of *prescribed* reading lists of pre-twentieth-century writers (including poets) from the English literary heritage in this new curriculum (in contrast to the *exemplified* lists of contemporary writers) continues to present challenges for teachers who wish to choose poetry texts which will engage their own students.

Although Leonard views poetry, at least that taught to him in school, as being outside of his culture, in contrast, Muir (1962) and Heaney (1980) both perceive poetry as a vital element within their cultures as 'divination, as a restoration of the culture to itself' (Heaney 1980: 60). In the twenty-first century many GCSE students do encounter a wider, although still restricted, range of poetry. The AQA English GCSE specification includes an extract from Leonard's own 'Unrelated Incidents' which is, ironically, classified by the examination board as being from a different culture (AQA 2005). Whether this poetic diet has any impact on learners' cultural understanding is a question I return to in the next section.

4.6   What is poetry for?

Claims are made for poetry's ability to enable a reader to achieve a state of grace (Hughes 1967, Benton 1986) through communing with poetry. Heaney (1989) credits poetry with some kind of spiritual or restorative power, locating it on the very edge of language, at the point where thought becomes word. These spiritual associations, reflection on experience and the sense of vulnerability which poetry can expose can lead potential readers (including your own students) to reject its advances. In addition, its language and imagery can contribute to the idea that poetry is a difficult, problematic and challenging medium. Given these different and potentially alienating features, how can poetry justify its slot in the marketplace which education has increasingly become? What is poetry for and how can you, as beginning teachers, inspire your students to enjoy poetry in its many different guises? The following sections explore some of these different purposes and suggest ways in which you can explore them in your classroom. Some of the purposes have been drawn from the post-PGCE course questionnaire responses of beginning teachers who participated in the research outlined above. There are also brief references to six case studies of English teachers' poetry histories and teaching repertoires (first reported in Dymoke 2000). In their post-course questionnaire, the now newly qualified teachers were asked to consider why poetry was a part of the English curriculum. Of those completing the questionnaire, 67 per cent answered this question. Their answers highlight purposes of poetry for: language study; developing moral and spiritual understanding; self-expression; multimodal communication; literary heritage; learning about culture; and, in a minority of cases, creativity or pleasure.

4.6.1   Poetry for language study

The beginning teachers' answers embrace a range of views. The majority reflect what I have called the 'Heineken view of poetry' (after Heineken lager's famous advertising slogan), i.e. that *poetry refreshes the language other text types cannot reach*. For these teachers, poetry 'allows', 'enables', 'provides' outlets or opportunities for language study which are not so readily available through other forms. In their view, skills learned through poetry can be 'transferred' or 'applied' to other types of writing. As a result of this transferability, poetry is seen by many as a means to an end, a stopping-off point (or perhaps even a service station) where one can pick up some useful pointers for studying other texts, rather than a final destination. Poetry 'helps', 'encourages', 'broadens', 'expands' or 'improves' awareness and analysis of how written, spoken and visual language works, how words are chosen, the sounds they make and how forms are structured. Consequently, poetry is a 'key' which opens the gates to language, enabling learners to pass through and continue more readily on their largely prosaic journey.

Poetry 'condenses and concentrates language'. It is 'smaller' than other texts as well as being 'unique' and 'inventive'. My earlier research revealed some similar perspectives on the brevity and compactness of poetry to these beginning teachers' views : 'Bruce', a head of department, commented on how poetry could address 'all the qualities of language that we want to address in English but in a small package'. Another teacher admired how poems could achieve 'extraordinary things in a very small space' (Dymoke 2000: 226), which would consequently pave the way for discussion about other types of language. A third teacher, 'Jackie', undoubtedly the most passionate about poetry of those interviewed, saw poetry as a vital, core element within literature and she was reluctant to calculate its potential value in language teaching.

4.6.2   Poetry for moral and spiritual understanding or self-expression?

The moral and spiritual purposes of poetry exercised Holbrook (1961), Hughes (1967) and others but Benton's 1999 survey notes a shift in teachers' attitudes away from consideration of poetry's moral and spiritual values towards an emphasis on its value for developing language skills and discussion about language. The beginning teachers in my sample do not directly refer to spirituality; instead the majority comment on the way poetry gives permission for students, especially less able learners, 'to express themselves', most notably, 'without the conventions of grammar'. Teachers interviewed in both research projects thought that poetry provides insights into a variety of experiences, enabling learners to express or confront emotional experiences or to think through their ideas. In the classroom this might involve asking students to adopt other personae to explore an ethical issue (such as abortion) from different viewpoints, or to explore the public and private presentation of events such as war through poetry, or to give students the freedom to write poetry for cathartic purposes. Students of different ages, interviewed by Ofsted, like the way poetry makes them think more. They also pointed to the potentially different kind of relationship a reader has with poetry rather than prose:

> In a poem you can express emotions. You can't do this in a story . . . You can confide in a poem, it relieves the stress. (Ofsted 2007: 7)

The 'accessibility' of poetry and the 'access' that it provides to self-expression are both connected by some of the teachers I interviewed with perceptions about the concise form, structure and size of poems. These features make writing poetry a less daunting prospect for some learners than embarking on a piece of prose. A head of department (interviewed in the 2000 sample) believed that a high level of achievement for learners of all abilities was possible with poetry: a few lines or an image in a poem can 'sing or shine' and merit praise, and poetry gave learners confidence to be playful with language (Dymoke 2000: 183). The opportunities for playfulness and exploration of an emotion or experience in a short form can also make poetry a particularly successful form to use with those students learning English as an additional language. In discussing patterned forms of poetry, such as Zephaniah's poem 'I want/I don't want', Spiro comments that the poem provides the 'perfect model for the language classroom. On the one hand there is a focus on language. On the other permission to reveal the inner story' (Spiro 2004: 8). You might want to discuss these views about writing poetry with colleagues and students in your school or college.

4.6.3   Poetry as multimodal communication

We have only to think of the ways in which poetry is embedded within the rhythms of everyday life through lyrics, text messages, street talk, protest rallying calls, football songs, playground chants or advertising jingles to acknowledge that poetry is a playful, multimodal medium rather than one destined to be stranded for ever on the printed page. As is shown in Chapter 7, multimodal texts are a key element of English. In *What is Poetry?* Adisa writes that 'Poetry is written on paper, but poetry doesn't live there' (Hoyles and Hoyles 2002: 128). If you leave poetry on the page in your classroom you will be in danger of sounding its death knell: it is an organic, enriching communication tool, which taps into all our senses and is constantly renewing and reinventing itself to afford us new ways to express ourselves. Poetry's multimodal nature is particularly evident when it is performed to live audiences or on the web.

4.6.4   *Poetry Archive* and Poetry Slams

The rapidly expanding *Poetry Archive* (www.poetryarchive.org), along with other web-based resources in North America, New Zealand and elsewhere, has ensured that the digitized voices of a wide range of contemporary poets can be heard in cyberspace. The *Poetry Archive* provides online access to poetry readings and residences together with resources for teachers. Poets' voices can be listened to in the classrooms and homes of people who have perhaps never met or heard a poet before.

Predominant in US high schools and increasingly popular in the UK, Poetry Slams have their origins in jazz club poetry readings held in Chicago in the mid-1980s and draw on influences including elements of hip hop such as rap. Poetry slams are lively knockout competitions in which the poets perform poems (rather than read them off the page) either alone or in teams before an audience, who can also act as judges. The manner and enthusiasm of a slam performance is often just as important as its content or style. Hicks's report on the finals of the London Teenage Poetry Slam (Hicks 2007) demonstrates the passions which competitive poetry events like these can arouse. Slam poetry can be very political: it explores topical concerns including racial, economic and gender injustices as well as more personal issues. Slams can overturn some of the prejudices that Benton (1986), Marsh (1988) and others have revealed among potential readers of poetry. By transcending artificial school subject barriers, together with those of ethnicity and gender, slam events can help young people to gain confidence through a dynamic engagement with the written and spoken word. For more information about slams and how to involve your own students in them go to www.poetryslam.org.uk/slam.html or www.londonteenagepoetryslam.net (both accessed 13 October 2008).

The fusion of dance and poetry as performed, for example, by the Phoenix and Retina dance companies, provides a further illustration that poems need not be 'like caged lions, only some of their qualities, power and beauty . . . viewed from one perspective' (Grainger *et al.* 2005: 141). Many of the beginning teachers I interviewed commented on how poetry teaching needed to embrace multimodality, both in terms of poems selected and teaching approaches used, and be 'not just [about] analysing when stuck behind a desk'. They considered that taught university sessions on performing poetry (using a variety of voices, groupings and drama conventions) and creating kinetic poems (using PowerPoint) had encouraged experimentation with creative ways of 'making poetry come alive'. If poetry is to flourish in any future English curriculum and in your classroom and if you are to flourish as a creative poetry teacher, then you should embrace the multimodal experiences poetry can offer. You might like to:

a) Visit the poetry archive website at www.poetryarchive.org. Listen to some poets you have never heard read aloud or just take a lucky dip and hear what comes up. Go to the teachers' pages and investigate teaching ideas. Explore the students' pages and the excellent links to other poetry sites.

b) Try using the full range of functions on PowerPoint or iMovie to make a kinetic or moving poem (or perhaps a trailer for a long poem). Model your work to your own students. For inspiration go to www.open.ac.uk/crete/movingwords/pages/activities.html (accessed 13 October 2008).

c) Experiment with performing poems in small groups. Encourage your students to think about pitch, tone, volume, silences, use of single, paired or whole-group voices for different choral effects, percussion and movements to bring poems alive. Poems which work particularly well for this activity with KS3 students of all abilities include: 'The Quarry' (Auden), 'Limbo' (Kamau Brathwaite); 'Madcap Rap' (Carter); 'Cat' (Farjeon); 'Men Talk' (Lochhead); 'Trainspotter' (Harmer and Wiley).

d) Use drama activities such as freeze frames to recreate key images or events in a poem, accompanied with voice-over with quotations from the poems; extra scenes, 'off poem' voices or extra lines to explore the context and/or the subtext.

e) Send a poetry in motion postcard to another reader (go to www.poetrysociety.org/postcard.html) or ask students to create and send their own virtual poems.

Involving students in any of these activities will help them to gain a much greater understanding and appreciation of how language and structure create effects and convey meanings. Such interactive approaches are both inclusive and challenging. They should inform any further discussion of the text and ensure that every learner has a stake in this.

4.6.5 Poetry for pleasure

For many critics and writers (including Rosenblatt 1978 and Pullman 2002), pleasure is an essential element of the reading process. Although enjoyment does not necessarily result in learning, all the six case study teachers in my 2000 sample perceived enjoyment as an essential feature and function of poetry in English lessons. However, when questioned at the beginning of their courses in 2005, only 21 per cent of the beginning teachers said that they would like their students to learn that poetry is 'enjoyable' or 'fun'. By the end of the course, a smaller minority (15 per cent) thought that enjoyment of reading and/or writing poetry was a reason for the genre's inclusion in the curriculum. The idea that teachers should teach students to 'appreciate' or 'love' poetry texts (as explored in Goodwyn 2002 and Snapper 2006) seems to have disappeared. My research indicates that some teachers associate poetry solely with school preparation rather than with relaxation (Dymoke 2000). A recent UKLA survey of some 1,200-plus primary and student teachers shows that many of them do not read poetry and appear to have a limited knowledge of poetry texts to draw on in the classroom (Cremin *et al.* 2008).

4.6.6 Poetry for creativity

A head of department, whom I interviewed in 1999, abhorred the pressure he felt under with his GCSE classes to 'produce kids who can write responses rather than kids who can write poems' (Dymoke 2002: 88). The decline in poetry writing observed at the inception of Curriculum 2000 (Benton 2000, Dymoke 2000) has continued as students and teachers become more conversant with acronyms such as PEE (point, evidence, explain) than the creative processes which have shaped poetry texts in the first place. (For a discussion of the dominant PEE see Ellis 2005.) *Playback* responses to the *English 21* debates acknowledged the merits of creative activities in English as being good preparation for imaginative problem-solving in the workplace and elsewhere (QCA 2005b). The greater focus on creativity within the 2007 National Curriculum orders gives some grounds for optimism that there will be more time for creative, non-exam-focused work in future.

All the beginning teachers I questioned at the end of their courses thought poetry could be taught creatively. They drew, almost exclusively, on examples from their taught university courses to substantiate this view and referred to poetry writing, drama and ICT activities they had participated in. A minority considered that their placement schools did not exemplify creative practices but focused on device spotting in poetry lessons. A further 5 per cent saw poetry as an art form: one teacher stated that poetry is in the curriculum 'because it's an art, whereas other parts of English are a craft.' For some, therefore, poetry is admired but separate and less worldly than other elements of the English curriculum. Given their overwhelming endorsement of creativity, it is interesting that a lowly 10 per cent of the sample referred to the opportunities which poetry can offer for creativity (including creative thinking) *as a reason for its inclusion in the curriculum.* For the majority (many of whom were rated as excellent beginning practitioners by their tutors), the utilitarian functions of poetry as a servant of language and assessment are uppermost in their minds.

4.6.7 Poetry for learning about culture

A student interviewed by Gunther Kress and his colleagues, for research for their book *English in Urban Classrooms,* comments on the essential differences between what one learns in English and other school subjects. For Kaleem, science is about the outside world whereas English is about 'the inside, I guess, about society and culture' (Kress *et al.* 2004: 173), but just how important is culture within the study of poetry? Can it provide a way of 'reading the world . . . of writing it' as Freire (1970: 35) has suggested is fundamental to the process of literacy? Poetry 'from different cultures and traditions' forms a major element of GCSE assessment (as structured by the largest market shareholder, the AQA examination board) and varying interpretations of this term are explored in Chapter 1.

At the beginning of their courses, many of the beginning teachers I surveyed had very limited prior experience of studying such texts. Familiarization with texts from 'different cultures and traditions' would be a development need in their PGCE year. By the end of their courses many had taught units or devised materials for Year 10 or 11 'different cultures' lessons. However, only 5 per cent of the beginning teachers considered exploration of culture as *a reason for including poetry in the English curriculum.* This would seem to be a significantly low figure: one which seems disproportionate to the amount of support and time that they had expended on preparing to teach this aspect of the curriculum. The figure leads me to question whether their learning about and teaching of poems from different cultures and traditions has:

a) changed the teachers' perceptions of how poetry can provide a window on cultural experience

or

b) enabled them to develop their students' understandings of culture and tradition.

If neither a) nor b) has been achieved (as the lack of endorsement by 95 per cent could seem to indicate) then this causes me to suspect that this poetry from different cultures and traditions is more likely to be perceived as one element of an English curriculum which must be delivered. Ensuring compliance within the context of a high-stakes testing regime has, inevitably, been the main motivational factor rather than a more idealistic desire to use poetry to explore cultural concerns.

If teaching poetry from different cultures and traditions is something you need support with then you should start by asking why. Is it because you:

- have never previously studied the specific poets before?
- think you have a limited understanding of the contexts out of which/about which they are writing?
- think you are lacking the confidence to deal with the issues explored in the poems?
- are concerned about how the poems will be received by your students in the context of their own classroom?
- are unsure about the linguistic features used in the poems?
- are uncertain about reading the poems aloud with your classes?
- have other concerns?

These concerns are very natural ones but beginning teachers sometimes find it hard to categorize them. By doing so, they could become easier to resolve. Furthermore, it is important to recognize that the concerns are *not* peculiar to the study of poems from different cultures: you could be confronted by the same issues when preparing to teach any new text. However, in many cases, the concerns seem to be accentuated unnecessarily when it comes to teaching poetry from different cultures. One reason for this is that poetry exam questions can tend to ignore the fact that the texts are poems and focus on the cultural issues which appear to be embedded in them instead.

Beginning teachers can be tempted to set aside all they have learned about poetry and assume that a different approach is needed. In my experience of observing poetry lessons, this can lead to situations where students spend a disproportionate amount of lesson time exploring what they understand by the terms 'cultures and traditions' in a homogenized and unhelpful way that has little to do with the texts or the readers themselves. Such activities might involve completion of charts on 'British culture', lengthy discussion of Christmas trees, haggis, fish and chips and, in some more ethnically mixed areas, Diwali, followed by a rapid read-through/annotation of the poems that has no connection with the previous discussion. In order to avoid such disasters you need to ensure that, when you are planning any lesson, you begin by thinking about the students you are teaching and how you will include them:

- What are their cultural experiences and traditions?
- What are the everyday contexts in which they live and learn?
- How similar or different might these be from those explored in the poem?
- What events or issues in the poem might they find most difficult to understand?
- What are the potential difficulties in terms of language? Of imagery?
- What bridges or links will you need to make to aid the students' engagement with the poem?

One of the finest examples of teaching poetry from different cultures and traditions I have observed took account of many of the above questions. I watched a beginning teacher introduce the poem 'Presents from My Aunts in Pakistan' by Moniza Alvi to a low ability Year 10 GCSE English class. She was on placement in a tough, semi-rural school with an all-white, predominantly working-class population and a growing British National Party following. Alvi's poem explores, through the voice of a young British Asian, the challenges and contradictions of a life that fuses different, ever-changing cultural experiences and expectations. The girl's receipt of salwar kameez from aunts in Lahore makes her confront both her origins and her desire to fit in with her school friends.

The teacher began the lesson by focusing on the students' own clothing, asking what they wore at school, at home, when playing sport, on casual and smart occasions, etc. She asked them to explore in small groups why they wore those clothes, how the clothes gave them a sense of identity, how they felt about them and, without using the exact word, what the clothing said about or reflected of their culture(s). Ideas were then pooled on the whiteboard. At this point she showed the class several items of clothing she had borrowed from a friend. These were a sari, several salwar kameez and other items. She passed these items around, allowing the students to touch them, and comment on their colours and textures. I suspect that few of the group had ever touched these types of garments before. She then returned to the questions the group had first explored and asked them to think about these items of clothing in the same ways as they had commented on their own. The students showed great curiosity about the clothing; they commented on the beauty and elegance of the salwar kameez, their colours, their movement, practicality, when they might be worn and what they might signify. The teacher put on the sari and developed her questioning further, pushing them to imagine how they would feel if they were a young British Asian student wearing these clothes in their community. All this was done both economically and sensitively.

Only at this point did she introduce the poem. She read it herself first and then asked the students to read it to each other in small groups. Next, the students were asked to place themselves in the poem, taking the narrator's point of view. They explored the significance of the clothing sent over from Pakistan by two well-meaning aunts and the impact these gifts had on the narrator. By this point the students had a stake in the poem. Their thoughts about clothing and their reactions to the salwar kameez were fresh in their minds. The discussion showed that they could understand the juxtapositions within the poem and were even able to explore the irony of the Pakistani aunts asking for Marks and Spencers cardigans in return.

Undoubtedly there will be times when you will need to do your homework about a new poem, poet or context before you can teach it with confidence. This should not be seen as a chore: English teachers should strive to extend and deepen their knowledge of texts whenever they can and to think about how they can engage their students in them. As they grow in confidence, they also become more experienced at drawing on their prior knowledge of other similar texts or pedagogic approaches to inform their understanding. In teaching poems from different cultures and traditions, there may well be occasions when you will want to draw directly on the experiences of one (or many) member(s) of your class. This will, of course, depend on the context in which you are working but where the opportunity arises, you should take it. Your students might be able to help you with the actual reading of the text (for example Sujata Bhatt's poem 'Search for My Tongue' includes snatches of Gujarati, and Jean 'Binta' Breeze's Wife of Bath speaks Creole in 'In a Brixton Market'). They may be able to explain a reference (such as an item of clothing or food, a sound, an event, features of landscape or climate). You will of course need to be sensitive about how you use the students and ensure they are forewarned, rather than put on the spot. If you do this well, you will give them much greater ownership of their learning.

With any text, you will want to take time prior to the lesson to find out whether the issues it explores are ones that might be difficult for students in your group to discuss openly. For example poems that explore issues of identity, exclusion and isolation such as 'Once Upon A Time' (Okara) and 'Half-Caste' (Agard) could present problems for some students. However, if these poems are approached in a careful manner, they could in fact enable the student(s) concerned to give voice to feelings, perhaps for the first time. As has been shown earlier, poetry can give students opportunities to express their feelings when they would feel overwhelmed by writing in other forms. Such students might include those who are newly arrived in the country, those for whom English is an additional language and those who are developing their fluency. Vicky Obied's recent research on the role of poetry within the developing literacy practices of bilingual children demonstrates just this. In considering bilingual writers' and readers' relationships with texts, she seeks to extend our understanding of bilingual learners from different cultural, social and linguistic backgrounds. She provides a powerful exploration of the language development of two refugee children who, with the assistance of an EAL support teacher, found ways to voice their harrowing experiences in a new language and through the medium of poetry (Obied 2007). One of the poems by 'Soriya' is reprinted below. It conveys the powerlessness she experienced during a night raid of the family home in Afghanistan.

Why Did I Do Nothing?

Scary they were.
Coming at night,
Like giants
Showing only the whites of their eyes.

As the door opened
And they stood, framed by the light
I saw their beards long and dark,
Turbans snaking around their big heads.

Then they shouted.
We could do nothing,

Women sitting fearful,
Men running to hide in the attic.

Now I remember
Why did I do nothing?
I'm angry with myself.

Soriya

Although Obied's research focuses on students from a UK inner city secondary school, her conclusions about poetry's role in supporting learning, and the need for collaborative inter-cultural approaches to develop cognitive understanding, reach far beyond national borders. If you would like further support with teaching poems from different cultures and traditions then you could look at materials designed for the exam specifications. In doing so, be wary of how an understanding of culture is being shaped by assessment demands. Also try to look at other resources such as the web resources recommended below. These will help your students to explore the poems within their contexts and to gain a less exam-packaged view of them. Take opportunities to listen to poets reading their work, either on the web or at a live event.

4.6.8   Some web resources

http://uk.poetryinternationalweb.org
A brilliant site filled with poetry features, poems, podcasts, critical articles, information about events and weblinks from over 30 countries around the globe.

http://www.thepoetryhouse.org
Poetry rooms on poets from Africa, Asia, Australasia, North America and the UK. A useful source of introductory critical material and weblinks.

http://www.open.ac.uk/crete/movingwords/pages/activities.html
A section of this moving words site explores the poem 'Search for my Tongue' through DARTS activities, a video clip of the poem in performance and a Shockwave Flash presentation.

http://www.britishcouncil.org/arts-literature.htm
Includes biographies, critical reviews, author perspectives and booklists for over 500 UK and Commonwealth authors.

http://curriculum.qca.org.uk/key-stages-3-and-4/curriculum-in-action/ casestudieslibrary/case-studies/Cultural_understanding_through_poetry. aspx?return=/search/index.aspx%3FfldSiteSearch%3Dcultural+ understanding+through+poetry
This case study shows how Year 8 students in one school developed their cultural under-standing and had their enthusiasm for poetry fired up by their study of Ghanaian poetry.
(All websites accessed 13 October 2008)

4.7   The game of poetry: poetry and sport

Earlier in this chapter I explored the dynamic and multimodal nature of poetry. Poetry also has both historical and linguistic associations with another dynamic form of expression – sport. In ancient Greece, games had their origins in poetic and musical competition. The lyric poet Pindar honoured the victories of athletes and the first marathon runner Pheidippides is celebrated in Herodotus. The modern Olympics included poetry medals as late as 1948 – a tradition which could be due for a revival. In recent years we have seen a resurgence in sports poetry with websites dedicated to football poems, and poets in residence on the Ashes tour, at Premiership football clubs and even on the Great North Run. The links between poetry and sport could entice otherwise reluctant young learners, fully conversant with the interactivity of PS2 or Nintendo or with the rules of offside and TV sports commentary, into poetry. Although many of these students might be male, it is essential not to preclude female learners or to assume that all learners of one gender learn in the same ways, have the same tastes in texts or the same ways of responding to them.

Although it does celebrate sporting heroes and moments of great prowess or disaster, sporting poetry isn't just about sport: it explores many issues central to people's lives including identity, isolation, joy, ritual, pain, and male and female values. In 2006, I co-edited, with Andy Croft, *Not Just a Game*, an anthology of sport poetry. It includes poems I used with students throughout 16 years as an English teacher. I found that some students seemed to engage with the poems more readily because of the sporting connection and they were able to perform and write poems using related topics or forms. Successful poems ranged from 'Ping-Pong' (Owen) – which works particularly well with Year 7s if read aloud by two teams (each representing one of the table tennis players) – to 'Unfair' (Rosen), which provides an excellent introduction to heated debates about the rights and wrongs of single-sex football teams and other sporting inequalities. Year 10 students explored the making and breaking of relationships through two tennis poems with contrasting moods and layouts: 'A Subaltern's Love Song' (Betjeman) and '40-love' (McGough). All these poems are included in the anthology. In the process of selection, we came up close to sporting language: the vocabularies of different games; expressions used by spectators and commentators; the precise verbs and nouns used for different movements; and the poets' use of spaces and shapes to indicate these. This rich pool of words has certainly influenced my poetry. Your students, who could be very well informed about the nature of the shimmy, the nutmeg or the googly, already have a rich fund of vocabulary they can draw on in their own writing.

You might want to consider how poetry is like sport/a game with your students. Some suggested points of comparison can be found in Table 4.3.

As you read more poems together, you could add ideas to this list. Challenging students to conceptualize poetry as a game can be a useful way of extending more able learners'

Table 4.3 How is poetry like sport?

Sport involves:	Poetry involves:
choosing moves, using spaces, applying knowledge	word play, dexterity and flexibility with language
movement and keeping eyes on your opponent, the ball, the space	rhythm, fluidity, pace and spaces, words and silences
set plays, overall shape and rules of game	forms (sonnets, haikus, odes, ballads, concrete, free verse), rhymes, knowing rules and breaking them
limited kit needed to play sport, to swim, to run, to kick a ball in the park	a pencil and paper will suffice for writing a poem; a poem is all you need to read a poem.
practising and trying out different moves to improve skills	drafting and trying out different word combinations: 'like Beckham practising his free kicks for hours before doing them for real' (Jackie Kay in Dymoke 2003: 66)
spectators and participants worldwide: anyone can participate in this democratic activity	everyone: everyone can write, read, perform and listen to poetry and many do at some point in their lives whether at partnership ceremonies, funerals or on other special occasions
being in touch with atmospheric conditions and responding to the opportunities or challenges they offer (whether it be a blisteringly hot road, a calm sea or a muddy pitch)	responding to stimulus, to spoken, written or visual language, to events and circumstances and seizing on these to write poetry
creativity and energy	creativity and energy
risk-taking and learning something new about yourself	writing poetry involves taking risks and making new discoveries: 'It's like diving into a place you don't know.' (pupil cited in Ofsted report 2007: 9)

thinking about poetry. Might certain poets play certain positions? What about amateur and professional sport? Fitness regimes and sporting superstitions? Are there direct comparisons between these aspects of sport and poetry and, if not, what other links can they find?

As is touched on in Table 4.3, much poetry is concerned with wordplay. Playing with words can be a useful bridge to more developed writing. Rhyming games and poetic consequences can help students to get their creative juices flowing. Games can lead to weird juxtapositions of words which will send students off in unexpected directions. Once they become confident with simple wordplay, they might want to move on to writing epigrams or even parodies.

The Furniture Game is a popular poetry game. First described by Sandy Brownjohn (1982) and subsequently reworked by many others, it is used in writing workshops with all ages. Writers are asked to imagine a famous person (or someone known to them) in terms of a number of objects such as a piece of furniture, a drink, a flower, a piece of music, an item of clothing and so on. This can be introduced in quite a structured way with one line of description per item. However, once writers become more confident they can leave this framework behind and let their imaginations fly. Here is an example by Sofie Khachik, written when she was a student teacher. The identity of the famous person is revealed at the end of the chapter.[1]

Retrospective

She is early morning in the quiet time
When night ends teetering on the precipice of day.
A cat crouching at the traffic lights
After a wilful night rollicking by the bins,
Exchanges an eye with the heroine of our tale.

She is an orchid lifting her face to light
With a slightly funny face tipping a graceful stem.
Without warning, she sails down moon river,
Suitcase packed; off to see the world,
In a yellow taxi cab or an African rickshaw.

Walking down Madison Avenue, she embodies
Elegant columns of black and sheaths of couture;
A wisp in a Givenchy dress, tiptoeing to a party
Ricocheting from group to group,
Destined to be the water, rather than the glass.

When the day is done, she is a nightingale
Singing a final refrain, waking only for a weather report,
Before resting like a Rennie Mackintosh chair
In a gallery spotlight: stark and curved.
A work of art.

Sofie Khachik

For another example (which moves far away from the original format), look at Simon Armitage's poem 'Not the Furniture Game' in his 1992 collection *Kid* (Faber and Faber, pp. 69–70).

The web is a good source of poetry games, many of which could be used by pairs on a laptop or by whole groups on an interactive whiteboard. For example, go to www.windowsproject.demon.co.uk/wpinfd.htm for a downloadable PDF of 30-plus poetry games (accessed 13 October 2008).

Another site exemplifying the multimodal nature of poetry is http://ludocity.org/wiki/Poets_versus_Policemen (accessed 27 October 2008). This is a role-playing poetry game played out in an open space over several hours and involving fugitive poets and policemen keeping a look out for poetic behaviour.

Whatever games or activities you are using to kick-start poetry writing, it is essential that you try them out beforehand as the quality of web and print versions of poetry games can be very variable. Steer clear of those which seem inflexible: writing within a very limited framework can result in very pedestrian poetry. Sian Hughes (1998) warns that poetry games and wordplay activities will not always lead to a complete draft of a poem but they can help to tone young writers' poetry muscles for when that time comes. In addition, you should avoid the temptation to stand on the touchline in poetry lessons or to be the referee. Make sure *you* participate and model the writing and reading of poetry: students need to see that you too 'struggle with words' (Nicholls 1990: B27) and savour them.

Finding texts and classroom strategies which stimulate boys' reading could be a particular challenge for you (as has been explored in Chapter 2). In terms of poetry, boys can be attracted to its wordplay, the intellectual challenge which some poetry provides or its exploration of ideas in a very compressed form. Pike (2000) argues that students need to be given opportunities to investigate the nature of poetry itself and the processes they engage in as readers. His research indicates that poetry appears to offer fewer rewards to its readers than plays or novels because, as Steve, one of his respondents, says: 'it's not like a book where you find out what happens next' (Pile 2000: 45). This perception could support an argument for using predictive or pre-reading work within poetry lessons to develop readers' ownership of poems and their responses to them. Many of the DARTs activities outlined in Chapter 1 can be used to develop students' reflections on poetry. One of my most successful poetry lessons with a Year 10 class featured a cloze exercise to explore 'Wind' (Hughes). I think I gave the class a greater investment in the poem by ensuring there was plenty of opportunity for pairs of students to argue over their word choices with other pairs and to develop their own versions of 'Wind' before encountering the complete original. Particularly significant for me was that this activity appeared to mark a turning point in the way many (but not all) of the boys in the group engaged with poetry. They seemed to relish puzzling over the word choices and were perhaps able to envisage more readily how writers struggle with words as they created particular effects with the words they had chosen themselves.

4.8 Teaching poetry from different periods

Poetry written before (and even during) the twentieth century can present particular challenges for students in terms of understanding the language, form and/or the contexts in which it was written. You may have identified this as a personal concern too. Although you might be reassured to learn that you are not alone in identifying this need (Dymoke 2007), you will want to boost your confidence. How can you do this? Firstly by reading and listening to as wide a range of poetry from different periods as possible and immersing yourself in the language and concerns of the writers. Make sure you establish your own responses to the poems before seeking out other views. If you have limited experience of pre-twentieth-century poetry then the anthologies listed in Appendix 1 would provide a useful introduction.

If you are teaching in England you will want to refer to the National Curriculum; the 'Range and Content' sections of the KS3 and KS4 for English are at http://curriculum.qca.org.uk/key-stages-3-and-4/subjects/english/keystage3/index.aspx (accessed 27 October 2008). The lists of writers includes poets whose work is considered 'rich and substantial enough to repay sustained reading and offer scope for pupils to explore and analyse their language, structure, themes and ideas' (QCA 2007a: 12). You will also need to consult current lists of examination texts (see below). Identify the poets you are unfamiliar with and remind yourself of those you have previously studied who may have been writing in the same period. Talk to your tutor about your personal priorities and think about how you can extend your knowledge and understanding beyond what might be immediately required in your teaching placements. By taking this approach you can become more confident about compiling selections of poems for comparative or thematic work.

It will also be essential to familiarize yourself with the period in which a poem was written and the different ways in which it has been received by audiences. You should set aside time to read critical and contextual material from a variety of sources and to think about the questions that different readers would want to ask about a poem. For an example, look at the following poem by Alexander Pope and the questions which follow it. This approach has been inspired by Adrian Beard's *Texts and Contexts* (2001):

Epigram Engraved on the Collar of a Dog which I Gave to His Royal Highness

I am his Highness' dog at Kew;
Pray tell me, sir, whose dog are you?

Alexander Pope

- First write down all the questions that you have about this poem.
- Now try to group these questions into:
    a) those you would want answers to/understanding of *before* you would feel comfortable using the poem with a group
    b) those that you would want to explore *together* with your students
- Now look again at what you have asked yourself.
    - Can you see different areas emerging in your (a) questions? Could you put them into sub-groups? Are some focused on language? Are some concerned with factual historical or biographical details? Which of the answers to your (a) questions would you want to actually give to your students *before* reading the poem? Which *after* reading? Which answers/understandings would you want them to discover for themselves through their own research and reflection either before or after reading the poem?
    - What do you think are the most significant (b) questions to explore with students? How can you phrase these into open-ended questions which will promote discussion and development of personal response? (For example there is a world of difference between the closed question 'Who is the dog talking in the poem?' and the more open question 'Who might be talking in the poem and why do you think this?')

Try to use this questioning framework with new poems. It will help you to think through potential issues and structure your planning. Remember, you cannot be expected to know everything that every critic has said about a text but you should have a good grasp of when and how a text was written and some of the different ways it could be read. Furthermore, you need to be open to hearing/developing other ways of reading it with your students.

4.8.1 Social, cultural and historical contexts

You will be asking students to develop their understanding of poetry written in different social, cultural and historical and contextual circumstances from their own. Use of paintings and other visual artefacts, such as household objects from the period, or archive material like diaries and letters, can help to make historical periods seem more real. If you want to use a collection of items or something unusual then contact your local museum which might have a loan scheme for borrowing artefacts. In *Two Poems by John Keats* (1998), Gabrielle Cliff Hodges explores how close visual reading of paintings can support students' readings of different versions of stories in the narrative poems 'Isabella' and 'The Eve of St Agnes'. These activities could lead students to write alternative versions in poetic form.

Drama-based activities to set the scene of the poem or to bring students into the world of a text through exploration of their own/the characters' feelings at key moments are also invaluable. Snapshots, captioned tableaux and thought-tracking activities work well with ballads like 'The Sisters' (Tennyson) or 'The Rime of the Ancient Mariner' (Coleridge). Role on the wall (pooling comments on a large-scale character outline) can be an effective method of tracking a group's developing impressions of a character like the Duke in 'My Last Duchess' (Browning).

Another approach, suggested in *Studying Blake's Songs* (Bleiman and Webster 2005), is to consider modern parallels for a poet. For example, who might be a twenty-first-century Blake, Byron or Coleridge? Who are the flamboyant and/or outrageous voices in today's artistic community? Who are the radical figures who break with convention and introduce new forms? If the poets were alive today, what might people say about them?

4.8.2 Language

A major barrier to understanding could be the language of the poem. Students should hear a good reading of it to help with this. A small number of recordings of pre-twentieth-century poets are available through the Poetry Archive website and the British Library. *Poetry Please* on BBC Radio 4 regularly includes good-quality readings of poems taught in schools. To investigate which poems have featured recently, or to listen again, visit www.bbc.co.uk/ radio4/arts/poetryplease.shtml (accessed 13 October 2008).

To focus specifically on a poet's diction and investigate potential linguistic patterns, repetitions, sounds and themes you could try collapsing a poem into a bank of individual alphabetized words. This technique, first devised by Millum and Warren (2001), provides you with a very different way of reading a poem. The bank could also be used as a source for the students' own poetry which could, in turn, lead to some interesting comparative work.

4.9   Teaching poetry for examinations

If you are teaching poetry for an examination you should aim to use as many active approaches as you can (including those suggested above) and provide students with opportunities to listen to and perform as many different readings as possible. This will ensure that:

a) the students' encounters with poetry are memorable
b) they will have opportunities to develop their personal responses, rather than being spoon-fed an answer.

Most examination boards provide an anthology at GCSE which includes poetry from different periods and cultures. You should be able to borrow a copy from a library or from the English department where you are based. If you studied for GCSE English or English Literature yourself any time after 1998 then some of the poems will already be familiar to you. The body of work in these anthologies can appear overwhelming. Therefore, you will need to be well organized (so you can cover all the poems necessary in the time allotted) and work smartly to ensure that your approaches will prepare the students fully. Make sure you look at examples of poetry questions at an early stage in your planning and discuss these with an experienced colleague. These can be downloaded together with mark schemes from most of the exam board websites (see Chapter 2). You will find that some of the questions (particularly those set by AQA) require students to make rather tortuous comparisons between poems.

There are strict rules about annotation of examination texts at all levels. Literature examinations are either 'open book' (i.e. a clean text, usually without any notes, can be used in an exam room) *or* 'closed book' (no text can be brought in). Each module or paper might be different. Both formats have their advantages and make different demands of exam candidates. You may have a preference for one type but think about the challenges these formats present for your students so that you can build preparation into your planning. If the students are permitted to use a clean anthology, how are you going to ensure that they can find their way around it quickly in an examination? If they are in a 'closed book' situation, how can you prepare them so they know the poems well enough to make links and use quotations to support their ideas? There are no set answers but if students are going to draw confidently on their personal experiences of the poems then you will need to plan for short periods of reflection, idea-sharing and careful note-making (not dictation).

Students will need to draw on their prior learning of technical terminology when discussing how language is chosen and shaped on the page and the effect it has on the reader. They will also need to compare groups of poems, exploring the contrasting treatments of themes, issues and events within them. When planning your scheme of work, try to avoid cramming too many poems into one lesson. I know this is easier said than done, but beginning teachers often make this mistake, with the result that they skim the surface of several poems. This confuses students and leaves them with little to say about any of the poems. To help them to structure their ideas about different poems and make links between them you could use grids or charts or you might ask them to devise a Venn diagram or a mind-map. By using a visual organizer, along with colour coding, symbols and labelling, the students can explore connections between poems in memorable ways which can be displayed and revisited. Providing opportunities to review previously logged interpretations of poems at the end of a unit of work or during revision is a vital part of the work on any examination text. You could use the flipchart facility on an interactive whiteboard or a poster space in your classroom wall to record developing impressions over time and revisit them prior to the examination. Asking students to write short journal entries (see Chapter 2) is a similar, more private approach.

4.10   Conclusion

Whatever approaches you use with poetry, this chapter has highlighted the need for a varied approach to stimulate different types of learners and give them ownership of their responses. Although use of carefully worded comprehension questions might be appropriate in some situations, these should be used very sparingly. Otherwise 'the dead hand of the exam' (Dymoke 2002) will rest heavily on your students and could lead them to reject poetry for ever once they have jumped their last exam hurdle.

Note

1. Audrey Hepburn.

5 Non-Fiction Texts

5.1 Introduction

This chapter begins by considering definitions of the broad term 'non-fiction'. The suggested range of textual forms that appears in the National Curriculum is investigated, including literary non-fiction, travel writing, reportage, print media and more ephemeral informational texts which serve very explicit or practical purposes. It continues with recommendations for broadening the scope of students' reading, together with a look at issues of gender and genre. Strategies for analytical, comparative and creative work are also embedded throughout.

The classification 'Non-Fiction' is an increasingly slippery term which can be interpreted in many different ways. In some senses, it appears to be a negative label, encompassing all that is not fiction and implying, through use of the prefix 'non', that there is a hierarchy of texts with Fiction at the pinnacle. If you look at the section signage in bookshops you will see that 'Non-Fiction' has become a catch-all for everything that is not the fast-paced thriller, the fantasy saga or Oprah's latest favourite novel. It embraces biography, criticism and travel writing and, in most cases, poetry and drama – two genres which surely lend themselves to fictional presentations of events.

Within another milieu, higher education, non-fiction also appears to be being rebranded. The seemingly unstoppable rise of Masters courses in Creative Writing has sparked the introduction of 'Creative Non-Fiction', which embraces life writing and travel writing. This label suggests that there are perhaps additional scales within the textual hierarchy and that not all non-fiction is creative (or some is more creative than others). Where does one draw the line? Is an autobiography more creative than a piece of advertising copy? Is an account of travelling across the Sahara of greater value than an encyclopaedia or guidebook entry on the same location? Such questions raise questions about the nature and purpose of these texts. Does a text which inspires or causes us to reflect ultimately have greater value than one which persuades or informs its readership? Do seemingly different texts in fact have features in common? These are questions you might want to explore with your own students at the beginning of a non-fiction unit. You could begin by asking how they might categorize or rank the texts listed below:

Personal letter	eBay website page	Poem
Blog entry	Politician's memoirs	Novel
Travel guide	Gig review	Graphic novel
Literary biography	Encyclopaedia	Instruction manual
Glossy magazine advert	Recipe book	Match report
Guinness Book of Records	Obituary	Holiday brochure
Film trailer	Comic	*Doctor Who* Annual
Shakespeare play	YouTube clip	*Radio Times*
Film poster	Highway Code	Autobiography
Chinese takeaway leaflet	Special offer coupon	Broadsheet editorial

You could offer them categories such as:

a) importance/status
b) creative use of language
c) usefulness

Alternatively they could use a card sort activity to group the texts in different ways, such as the audiences they are written for or the contexts in which they would be produced. They could classify the cards according to the different ways they could be read. For example, which texts would they scan for a quick gist of key points? Which would they read in depth? Make judgements about? Sift for relevant information? Enter into, copy, paste or make changes? Which would they summarize?

Any such activity would probably reveal that we read texts in different ways and that it is difficult to make hard and fast rules about how texts are constructed and the purposes they serve. It could well point up what Andrews calls the 'hybrid' nature of such texts and their resistance to classification (2001b: 131).

5.2   Non-fiction and the National Curriculum

Since the late 1990s, there has been a shift in emphasis within National Curriculum English towards learning about the conventions of non-fiction text types. This was welcomed by those said to favour an 'adult needs' model of English (DES 1989) which equips learners to cope with texts they will be required to read and/or write in the 'real' world of work. For others, non-fiction and its use for teaching literacy has presented a significant challenge to the status of literary texts, engagement with which has been at the core of English teaching since its inception as a distinct subject. Some believe literacy and language are best taught through literature because of its affective power (Pike 2004) or perceive the focus on literacy as presaging a 'bleak spectre of utilitarianism' (Marshall 1998: 109) that will loom over an English curriculum solely concerned with enhancing economic performance. Barton has a somewhat more optimistic view: non-literary texts can serve as a kind of stepping stone en route to engagement with more status-laden literary forms and provide 'a more neutral base for developing our pupils' sensitivity to the way language is used' (Barton 2001: 143). Barton also delights in the idea of different combinations of texts (both literary and non-literary) 'rubbing shoulders' with one another in the classroom, with the juxtapositions leading to new insights for their readership.

As has been shown previously, Wray and Lewis's Exeter Extending Literacy (EXEL) project has focused on ways of helping primary teachers to extend their pupils' literacy. In developing the Extending Interactions with Texts (EXIT) model, the researchers concentrated on reading and writing of non-fiction, areas which, they argue, had been previously neglected by both researchers and practitioners (Wray and Lewis 1995, 1996). Wray and Lewis wanted to move away from the emphasis on extracting information that had been the usual focus in classroom-based non-fiction work. Their model (outlined in Chapter 1) aims to capture the recursive processes of reading a text (albeit in a linear form). It focuses on the interactive processes of reading such texts and the essential role of the reader in constructing meaning. Moss argues that the strategies proposed in the EXIT model and texts produced by educational publishers, especially, now work together to promote and perpetuate a particular way of reading concerned with finding and assimilating new information so that 'discourse, object and practice converge' (Moss 2007: 100).

Having established this model, Lewis, Wray and Mitchell (1995) explored the use of expository writing frames or QUADs (questions, answers, details, source) (Cudd and Roberts 1989) and other structures such as grids and charts, which supported knowledge construction and interaction with non-fiction texts in the primary classroom and enabled learners to move away from copying out sections of text from a source, which had previously been a feature of much topic-based work at this level. These approaches to textual analysis are now common practice in many secondary classrooms across a range of subject areas. To support students' own non-fiction writing, Wray and Lewis (1996) proposed the use of writing frames. These would provide a framework or scaffold that would be introduced by class discussion and modelling by the teacher. The researchers have always stressed that writing frames should be used flexibly within whole-class work on non-fiction for particular children, *not as whole-class worksheets*. They state that, once students have gained in confidence, they will extend their knowledge of the genre and its language features and broaden their linguistic repertoire (see Wray and Lewis 1996). When used in this way, writing frames can be an extremely effective tool for supporting less confident writers. However, in my experience, these strategies are now commonly used for fiction and poetry writing and too often as undifferentiated worksheets issued to all learners in a group. Their best uses remain those allied to the original purpose of supporting reading and writing non-fiction.

The focus on boys' attainment and literacy which came to the fore in the 1990s led to the widely voiced conclusion that there was insufficient non-fiction in school English to stimulate boys' interests, with the result that they felt excluded from the curriculum (Millard 1997). Non-fiction does form a significant element of many boys' reading diets but they do not read more non-fiction than narrative (Whitehead *et al.* 1977, Hall and Coles 1999). The stereotypical idea that female readers prefer to escape into the feminine emotional world of narrative fiction, away from a male functional/factual world, ignores the reality that the most dominant type of non-fiction is prose argument in the form of news and magazine stories which engage readers in a particular point of view (Moss 2007). The visual element of non-fiction is also considered to be an attraction to boys: Moss and Attar (1999) explore how boys navigate their way through non-fiction texts by using visual images. In later work, Moss shows how, during quiet reading time, primary-aged boys eluded 'their standing in the reading hierarchy' (Moss 2007: 87) through choosing non-fiction texts and concentrating on the visual images within them. In contrast, the girls she observed were prepared to keep reading fiction allotted according to their level of reading proficiency and to select books appropriate for their place in this hierarchy.

5.3   Range of non-fiction reading

We next consider the range of textual forms suggested in the National Curriculum before continuing to explore the purposes of non-fiction and how these have shaped the nature of assessment in English. In the National Curriculum, the range of non-fiction reading at KS3 and KS4 should include:

> h) forms such as journalism, travel writing, essays, reportage, literary non-fiction, [print media] and multimodal texts [including film and television].[1]
> i) purposes such as to instruct, inform, explain, describe, analyse, review, discuss and persuade. (QCA 2007a: 12)

Non-fiction texts such as those listed above present many different demands on the reader. Each uses language in very particular ways and, like all other text types, has what Kress calls 'a high degree of internal structure' (1982: 98). For the most part this internal structure is hidden from the reader or speaker's view: the conventions of the text are so familiar to the user that the text's structure is taken for granted and appears to be natural. Genre theorists argue that this implicit knowledge, of textual structure and 'linguistic features beyond the sentence' (Kress 1982: 97), needs to be taught. These views have permeated the teaching of Literacy/English since the advent of the Literacy Strategy. In the last ten years the teaching of non-fiction conventions has become a major feature of the taught English curriculum.

5.3.1 Literary non-fiction

In choosing texts to use in the classroom, it is important to bear in mind that, as with fiction, non-fiction texts 'must be rich and substantial enough to repay sustained reading and offer scope for pupils to explore and analyse their language, structure, themes and ideas' (QCA 2007a: 11). At KS4 the guidance reflects students' maturation: it stresses the importance of selecting texts through which students can 'relate to their own experiences, and also develop their understanding of less familiar viewpoints and situations' (QCA 2007b: 12).

The National Curriculum no longer exemplifies authors of literary non-fiction suitable for study. This leaves plenty of scope for selecting texts which are of interest to and appropriate for your students. If this is a new field for you, then you may want to familiarize yourself with the wide range of texts which fall into this category by dipping into the non-fiction collections listed in Appendix 1. Alternatively, if you would prefer to investigate the work of a specific author in a more sustained way, the following texts would be suitable for use from KS3 onwards:

Angelou, M. (1984) *I Know Why the Caged Bird Sings*. London: Virago.
Bennett, A. (2005) *Untold Stories*. London: Faber & Faber (essays and diaries from this collection).
Brittain, V. (1978) *Testament of Youth*. London: Faber & Faber.
Bryson, B. (2004) *A Short History of Nearly Everything*. London: Black Swan.
Deane, S. (1997) *Reading in the Dark*. London: Vintage.
Durrell, G. (1973) *My Family and Other Animals*. Harmondsworth: Penguin.
Frank, A. (2007 reissue) *The Diary of a Young Girl*. London: Penguin.
Hornby, N. (1992) *Fever Pitch*. London: Penguin.
Palin, M. (1992) *Pole to Pole*. BBC Books (also available on DVD).
Sassoon, S. (1975) *Memoirs of a Fox Hunting Man*. London: Faber & Faber.
Simpson, J. (1998) *Touching the Void*. London: Vintage.
Slater, N. (2003) *Toast: The Story of a Boy's Hunger*. London: Fourth Estate.
Westall, R. (2006) *The Making of Me: A Writer's Childhood*. London: Catnip Books.
Wordsworth, D. (2002) *The Grasmere and Alfoxden Journals*. Oxford: Oxford University Press.

In engaging with texts, young readers need to gain a sense of the whole text's construction. This advice can present challenges for any class teacher. Quality non-fiction texts, like all good literature, can be about far more than first appears. Matthews and Newton argue that literary non-fiction (diaries, travel writing and autobiographies especially) presents greater problems for learners than other factual texts. In their view, they 'almost appear as fiction' (Matthews and Newton 2005: 14) and yet have been created by writers working under greater constraints than poets, novelists or dramatists because their starting points are themselves and their own situations. The result of this potential confusion is that students bring to their writing about these texts 'the same armoury of textual analysis tools usually deployed when examining fiction, not always with entirely successful results' (ibid. 2005: 15). For an account of how these difficulties can be overcome at GCSE level, refer to Matthews and Newton's account of the teaching of Michael Palin's *Pole to Pole* in *The Secondary English Magazine* (December 2005 issue).

It will be vital for you to ensure that you choose texts very carefully and offer your students choices wherever possible. Apparent student interest in football should not mean that *Fever Pitch* is an automatic choice for a whole group. English teachers have told me that some students find this book very hard going – especially if they are not Arsenal supporters!

Touching the Void

Touching the Void has become a popular text in schools in recent years for use with students aged 14 to 19. It is a gripping survival story about two mountaineers climbing the Siula Grande in the Andes. A life-changing moment occurs when one man falls. He is left dangling over a seeming abyss and the other decides to cut the rope to save himself, certain that he must be sending his companion to his death. Written by Joe Simpson, the mountaineer who fell yet survived and dragged himself back to base camp, the story is ostensibly told from the perspectives of the two men. This choice of viewpoint raises questions about the construction of reality within a non-fiction text which are interesting for very able students to grapple with. (The film adaptation adds a further dimension to this debate as both men appear in it to reflect on their experiences but the climb and accident are reconstructed by actors.) Most readers (or viewers) of this text should experience the full gamut of emotions. It raises questions about the nature of friendship, survival, trust and faith as well as capturing the tensions of the life-changing moment very effectively. The book comes with a map of the mountain range, which is a useful resource for plotting key events and other note-making activities. Visual, aural and written material about Simpson and subsequent climbs he has undertaken (including his final thwarted trip to the Eiger) can be found on his website at www.noordinaryjoe.co.uk (accessed 13 October 2008).

The image Simpson projects of himself and his subsequent portrayal by the media both provide further food for thought. If you are considering using this text in the classroom with lower ability students you may well want to look at Mike Wilson's adaptation of the novel, *Ice Mountain*. Written in the third person and in much abbreviated form, it still makes the spirit of the book accessible to a much wider audience. Adaptation of a non-fiction text of their choice for a different audience could also be a suitable writing challenge for very able students.

5.3.2   Literary diaries and letters

Diaries such as Alan Bennett's diary of the first production of *The History Boys* (in *Untold Stories*) or Brian Friel's (1979) *Sporadic Diary* about the writing of *Translations* both provide readers with behind-the-scenes insights into the journey from script to stage which can inform and extend their appreciation of the original texts. Insights into the contextual/personal influences on writers' choices of subject and form can provide new ways into textual study for examinations (see for example Reid (ed.) 2007 *The Letters of Ted Hughes*). They are also fascinating in their own right. In addition, critical work on life writing, such as *Diaries and Journals of Literary Women from Fanny Burney to Virginia Woolf* (Simons 1990) offers further ways of understanding the constructed selves which diaries offer their readership.

5.3.3   Blogs

In taking stock of advances in technology at the end of 2006, one multimedia editor commented that 'the revolution will not be televised, it will be YouTubed. And podcast. And blogged. And immortalized as a Wikipedia entry' (Logan 2006: 11). He summarizes not only the multiplicity of new ways in which texts can be created and transmitted but also highlights that these are mediums through which ordinary members of the public, untrained and from outside of traditional global media empires, can at last have access to the tools of production in order to make and distribute their own perspectives worldwide. Blogs (short for weblogs) are a related but increasingly distant cousin of the diary. They are perhaps more democratic and interactive than the traditional written form. The first blogs were very much like basic diaries: they included simple comments on websites visited and ratings for these (Richardson 2006). Now they are a kind of constantly evolving text form which offer authors of all ages, and from all walks of life, opportunities to publish and share reflections, comments, recommendations, concerns, jokes, photos, video clips, weblinks, and to ask and answer questions instantly with a potentially vast worldwide audience. The blog postings could be daily, monthly or even hourly. There are no rules but these are, by their very nature, collaborative texts: 'they ask readers to think and to respond. They demand interaction' (Richardson 2006: 18). A key part of their appeal is that they can be easily and constantly updated and published from anywhere with an open internet connection. The blog is a rapidly expanding form of communication which can appeal to a wide readership or a very special interest group. The sites of the most successful bloggers like Arianna Huffington (huffingtonpost.com) and Petite Anglaise (petiteanglaise.com), can attract thousands of hits a day, while other blogs by writers like Neil Gaiman (journal.neilgaiman.com) and

David Belbin (www.davidbelbin.com) are read by a more specialist audience. It is ironic to see how some of these highly successful bloggers have begun to publish their blogs and their blogging experiences in old-fashioned book form, a form which arguably retains a legitimacy and lasting influence that newer mediums cannot yet emulate. However, just as email has now been surpassed by Facebook as a means of informal communication, the blog could be perceived as the staid diary of tomorrow once an even more technologically advanced form of text arrives on the scene. For more about blogs, and their close cousins, wikis, see Chapter 7.

5.3.4 Essays

Ironically, although students, and teachers, will be all too familiar with the 'essays' they write and mark, the literary essay is probably the least widely read non-fiction form for twenty-first-century readers. At their best, essays are extremely thought-provoking and present their arguments in a concise and coherent way – ideal models in fact for your students' own writing. If this is a new area for you, you could start by reading:

> Berger, J (1990) *Ways of Seeing*. London: Penguin. A highly influential text on how we read images from advertisements to oil paintings.
> Jamie, K. (2005) *Findings*. London: Sort of Books. A sparely written and moving collection of essays about aspects of the natural world and life in Scotland.
> Orwell, G. (2003 paperback) *Shooting an Elephant and Other Essays*. London: Penguin Classics. A classic with essays on a wide range of topics.
> Swift, J. (1996 edition) *A Modest Proposal*. London: Dover Thrift. Swift makes a most convincing case for eating children to solve the problems of the Irish famine – a polemic to stretch new Year 12 students.

5.3.5 Travel writing

Travel writing is not all about journeys to exotic locations. Some of the best examples below are located close to home and look at the world around us through a different lens. Some examples of texts include:

> Bryson, B. (1996) *Notes from a Small Island*. London: Black Swan.
> Chatwin, B. (1988) *Songlines*. London: Picador.
> Deakin, R. (2000) *Waterlog: A Swimmer's Journey through Britain*. London: Vintage.

5.4 Print media, reportage and journalism

These categories cover similar ground and it will be important for you to use each term correctly with your students.

Print media is a broad term which encompasses any type of printed work that reaches an audience (for example a free newspaper, a supermarket leaflet, a magazine, a flyer, a brochure). Working with print media in the classroom can be enjoyable and accessible to students across a wide ability range: audience and purpose can be much more immediately apparent than in other textual forms. For Barton these are 'texts without proper immigration papers, shifty and vaguely ill-at-ease in the class. Yet these texts can speak with an astonishing directness to pupils' (2001: 150). This illicit quality can be used to advantage in the classroom. In my experience, students can view analysis and creation of non-fiction as a break from more literary work. They are able to draw more readily on their own experiences, tastes and their interactions with such texts as consumers. They are surprised by how much they already know about how such texts are constructed, their 'grammar of design' (Kress and van Leeuwen 1996/2006), and how texts of similar types compare. Because of its purposes, much print media is ephemeral – an issue you will want to address and one you should consider when selecting your sources: make sure that they are sufficiently up to date to engage your students. However, you might find it interesting to compare texts from different times, for example leaflets on healthy eating or tourist attractions from a range of historical periods. This activity could raise key questions about language and cultural change and increasingly sophisticated uses of design features. Your local museum may be able to help you out with artefacts or you could visit the British library website (www. bl.uk). For an example go to http://www.bl.uk/learning/images/texts/tour/large1137.html (accessed 13 October 2008). The plain advert from a 1912 Lyme Regis guidebook featured on this webpage should provoke plenty of discussion about a different time where cloths were purchased for 'Five o'clock tables', non-stock items could be 'procured by return' and advertisers did not need to bother with an address or telephone number (if they had one).

Reportage is the direct reporting of events *actually witnessed* by the journalist who is on the spot, taking part or caught up in events. It can be presented in a variety of media. Reportage from history includes Pliny describing the destruction of Pompeii and Samuel Pepys reporting on the Great Fire of London. Current affairs reportage includes reporting directly from war zones, conflicts, natural disasters, famines or major events like the fall of the Berlin Wall or the moment Nelson Mandela left his prison cell for the last time. BBC television's John Simpson and Luke Harding of the *Guardian* are known for their reportage. *The Faber Book of Reportage* (Carey 1987) or *Cupcakes and Kalashnikovs: 100 Years of the Best Journalism by Women* (Mills 2005) would provide useful starting points for exploration of this subgenre.

Journalism is writing about/interpretation of events which the journalist has not witnessed at first hand. The writer might have composed the piece by collating and summarizing information from a range of different sources, such as interviews, published reports, statistics and eyewitness accounts. The text could be broadcast on radio or television, on a website or in a newspaper or magazine. Comparative work that explores how different journalists have covered the same story for different television or newspaper audiences is a common classroom activity which may already be familiar to you from your own education.

If you are planning such an activity, try to choose a story which is:

- accessible for your students
- reported from different angles in the publications you choose
- laid out or presented in striking ways with interesting headlines, graphics, photographs or footage.

Breaking and dramatic news stories are usually a better choice than slow-burning, drawn-out ones. Although it is not vital that your students have some prior knowledge of the stories they are comparing, a more immediate item of breaking news is more likely to provoke greater interest than an older/dead story. Do not assume they will know very much about the political allegiances and favoured topics of the news media. Although it may be cheaper to investigate just the front page/opening item in a news programme, an opportunity to look at the whole newspaper/view a whole (short) bulletin could lead to a more in-depth analysis of language, audience and purpose. Alternatively you could explore how the story develops over a number of days and at what point it disappears from the headlines.

When making comparisons between different newspaper reports, you will want to ensure your students are familiar with key terms such as those in Figure 5.1.

- Berliner: mid-sized newspaper format, includes the *Guardian*.
- Broadsheet: largest size of newspaper in the UK, usually with long vertical columns, includes the *Daily Telegraph*, *Financial Times* and the *Sunday Times*.
- Byline: literally who the report is written by (not all journalists achieve this status).
- Caption: short heading which informs reader about a photo or other visual.
- Column: vertical division of text on a page. Alternatively, a regular small section of a newspaper written by the same writer or on a particular topic.
- Compact: smallest size of newspaper (same size as tabloid but term 'compact' is preferred by some papers like *The Times*).
- Crosshead: single words or phrases which serve as headings for individual paragraphs.
- Editor: person in overall charge of the content of the newspaper or programme.
- Headline: main title for a news report (in large type).
- Layout: how the text and visuals are laid out on the page.
- Masthead: top section of the front page; includes the name of the newspaper, adverts or promotions for features inside.
- Red tops: tabloid newspapers such as the *Sun*, the *Star* and the *Daily Mirror*, which have red mastheads.
- Reporter: person who writes the news stories.
- Sub-editor: stories are submitted to a sub-editor, who edits and prepares them for publication.
- Subhead: smaller heading, usually found under main headline.
- Tabloid: smallest newspaper format; includes red tops, like the *Sun*, as well as the *Daily Mail* and many weekly or regional newspapers. Red top tabloids are often perceived as downmarket and associated with sensational reporting.

Figure 5.1 Newspaper design, layout and production terminology

If you want your students to develop their own skills in writing reports for broadcast or print media then I would strongly recommend that you try to organize a simulation activity. This requires them to work in news teams, taking on different roles in order to produce a newspaper front page or TV/radio bulletin in 'real time'. Software such as *Stop Press* or *Newsmaker* includes simulation activities (with news items gradually breaking, changing and even disappearing over the course of a morning) or exploration of news items in depth from different angles. Alternatively you might want to enter students for the *TES* School Newspaper or BBC school report competitions or take a group to the National Media Museum in Bradford where they can work against the clock to record their own TV bulletin. Such activities require careful planning. You will probably need to negotiate a change to the timetable and you could even involve other subject areas such as Art, Humanities or Citizenship to make it a much bigger project. (The emphasis on creativity, cross-curricular work and enterprise in the 2007 National Curriculum could be useful levers in your negotiations.) Whatever you arrange, your students will learn about far more than just how to write a news story: English beyond the classroom should become much more real for them.

All the types of non-fiction explored here should be relatively easy to access and use as resources in your teaching. However, these texts may have been written or broadcast primarily for a literate adult audience. When you are selecting materials, look closely at their readability and accessibility for your students. Consider using alternatives aimed at a younger audience or think about providing a glossary of key terms for less confident readers.

5.5 Multimodal texts

Multimodal texts use a combination of two or more modes of communication (aural, visual and written) to create their meanings. Examples include the combinations of: words and images in a magazine article; words, images, video clips and sound on a website; images, speech and sound in a documentary film. Many non-fiction texts operate in more than one mode and your students should be given opportunities to explore how these modes work together and/or in opposition to create a finished text. You will find references to multimodal texts in this chapter but for more specific details refer to Chapter 7. You might want to start thinking about multimodal texts by returning to the list of non-fiction texts at the beginning of this chapter. Which of those would you describe as multimodal? Is one mode more dominant than the others in their construction?

5.6 Purposes

When they are reading for meaning, students will need to:

reflect on the origin and purpose of texts and assess their usefulness, recognising bias, opinion, implicit meaning and abuse of evidence. (QCA 2007b: 7)

Teachers are advised that this reading will involve:

> looking at how texts reflect the purposes for which they were written and the impact they were
> intended to have on the reader. Texts could come from commercial organisations, employers, gov-
> ernment sources, political and charity campaigns and websites. (QCA 2007b: 7)

The purposes of non-literary and non-fiction texts listed in the National Curriculum are:
'instruct, inform, explain, describe, analyse, review, discuss and persuade' (QCA 2007a: 12
and 2007b: 14). These selected purposes arguably have very utilitarian functions. Clearly
students should learn how to mediate texts which have an impact on their everyday lives
and their place in their world. However, it appears that there is no longer any place for
non-fiction which serves imaginative, exploratory or entertainment purposes. Twenty-first-
century National Curriculum English seems to be a serious business with no time for the
dreaming, laughter or enjoyment which could be triggered by reading an engaging blog or
piece of travel writing or watching an amusing commercial. Or is it? Such purposes may be
more difficult to assess but this should not be a reason to preclude them. It will be essential
that you look beyond the purposes stipulated in the curriculum orders and adopt a flexible
approach in your teaching.

5.6.1   Approaches to exploring purposes

In considering each of the purposes of texts, it is vital to make links across the three attainment targets and to think about how reading non-fiction texts will inform students' speaking
and writing. Students are required to develop their speaking and listening skills for a range
of purposes: 'describing, narrating, explaining, informing, persuading, entertaining, hypo-
thesising and exploring' and expressing ideas, feelings and opinions' (QCA 2007b: 3.1).

The written forms that students are required to gain experience of include many which
can be broadly classified as non-fiction:

> . . . autobiographies . . . diaries, minutes, accounts, information leaflets, plans, summaries, bro-
> chures, advertisements, editorials, articles and letters conveying opinions, campaign literature,
> polemics, reviews, commentaries, articles, essays and reports. (QCA 2007b: 3.3)

Whichever forms and purposes you focus on, you will need to ensure you have a sound
grasp of the lexis and grammar (including visual grammar) of the texts you are teaching so
that you can explore the deliberate construction of these texts and their intended impact on
an audience confidently with your students both through modelling and through involving
students in discussion/annotation. Images projected by an OHP, digital projector or an interactive whiteboard can be read quite easily by a whole group. Alternatively you could stick
texts on large sheets of sugar paper or load them on to laptop screens ready for annotation
by small groups. In choosing your approach and your text(s), try to ensure not only that the
language is appropriate to include and challenge all learners but that the font sizes, uses of

colour and image are clear enough to be read by students with visual impairments. For further advice on these issues (which should inform your selection and production of *all* your classroom resources) refer to www.officefordisability.gov.uk/resources/background0602. asp (accessed 13 October 2008).

5.6.2   Purposes and creative approaches

This section takes a closer look at non-fiction purposes and suggests some creative ways into exploring them in the classroom.

Instruct

Instructions such as how to construct a set of shelves, rewire a plug, take a free kick, install a piece of software or set up an answering machine message can be multimodal texts which include verbal, written and/or visual (static or moving image) elements. The purpose of instructional or procedural texts, as they are often called, is to instruct someone how they should do something very specific which has a definite end-product or outcome. Successful instructions will outline what the aim or outcome is and, in some cases, why. They will tell the reader quite clearly how to achieve this outcome, what equipment/materials are needed and the stages of the process in the chronological order that they should happen. Spoken, written and visual instructions all follow slightly different conventions. The written conventions will be recognizable to most readers:

- the text is laid out in a specific order
- instructions are written in the present tense
- the imperative is used
- sentences are usually short and refer to completion of one action at a time
- the tone expects/assumes the reader will carry out the instructions
- vocabulary is usually straightforward with use of extensive verbs
- a final sentence may anticipate or celebrate what has been achieved.

Although adherence to conventions may be similar within instructional texts of the same type, the context in which a set of instructions is being given will have an effect on the language used. For example, a set of instructions telling you how to remove a car tyre would be couched in very different language from those written for a Formula 1 technician changing tyres in the pits. Verbs may assume prior knowledge of techniques and references to specific jargon or acronyms may proliferate according to the specialist nature of the audience.

Analysis of the language of recipes is one of the most common forms of instructional writing explored in classrooms. A very structured and teacher-led approach to analysing the language of recipes is exemplified in the *Grammar for Writing* materials (DfEE 2000). This approach implies that recipes have a very rigid format. Although written recipes do tend to follow conventions, in that they include information about ingredients needed and the methods or stages of preparation, the style of recipe can vary enormously. Cookery writers like Nigel Slater, Jane Grigson or Elizabeth David will engage with the historical, literary or personal associations of a dish or key ingredient, usually as a preamble to the recipe. Their writing is imbued with memory and the sensuous experiences of picking and buying ingredients, preparing, tasting and eating them. Celebrity chefs like Jamie Oliver and Nigella Lawson have exuberant styles and use language which is distinctly different from the recipes you might find on the back of a packet of pasta or in a manual for an item of kitchen equipment. Some written recipes use diagrams or photographs, while others rely solely on written instructions. Television recipes are presented in such a way as to enable the viewer to experience the skills involved in making a particular dish and even to taste it vicariously. On radio, the careful use of sound is very important in conveying the different stages in the cooking process. Both mediums might refer their audiences to further information and a copy of the full recipe on the programme's website. Opportunities to listen again are often also available via websites or podcasts. Such variations in the instructional style of recipes can make for interesting comparative work which emphasizes the richness of the form and enables students to explore the other purposes of a recipe (beyond that of instruction).

Creative ways in:

a) Ask students to work in pairs to draft (and perhaps record) a podcast script for a simple set of instructions (such as: how to wire a plug; how to peel and core an apple; how to apply mascara; how to separate and whisk an egg white; how to tie a bow-tie; how to use predictive text to send a text message). Make sure you have the relevant props with you. Each pair in the room should then pass on their script to another pair who should try to complete the task by following the instructions *to the letter*. The pairs should then review the draft and annotate it with any additional phrases or changes they think are needed to clarify the process before handing it back to the original pair, who should then try out the instructions for themselves.

b) Provide a list of potential ingredients from which students could create a sandwich, milkshake or snack. Ask them to imagine they are on *Masterchef* or *Ready Steady Cook*. They have to create a tasty end-product from some of the listed ingredients and write a recipe for it in 15 minutes. If you were able to make this a cross-curricular task they could actually try out the recipes in a food technology lesson.

c) Write a recipe for an emotion such as jealousy, happiness, anger or embarrassment.

d) Take a set of instructions and use the words in it to write a text in a different form such as a found poem or a piece of description.

Inform

Texts which inform are often concise and yet densely packed with information. In terms of textual conventions, these texts make use of:

- headings, subheadings and boxed sections which break up the prose into smaller sections and provide structure
- discourse markers such as *firstly, consequently, in addition*, which provide a logical structure
- diagrams, charts, drawings or photographs to exemplify aspects of the text or provide further information

- complex or technical vocabulary
- a formal and concise style
- references back and forwards to points made elsewhere in the text.

Creative ways in:

a) Many of the texts your own students will be using in other lessons will fall into this category. This in itself could make for some interesting comparative work in that you could, as a class, draw up a list of key criteria for judging a successful information text: which of their texts do they think presents its information most clearly? Which is the most appealing? Which is the most difficult to read?

b) Alternatively you could choose one topic such as the 2008 earthquake in the UK and compile a collection of different information sources about this topic (for example from books, Wikipedia, specialist websites like the National Geographical Survey, newspapers, YouTube). This could then lead to sorting activities: which of these information texts is the most comprehensive? Which is the most reliable? Which is the most interesting? Which inform you solely of the facts and which include opinion? Students could go on to write their own informative piece for a school textbook on earthquakes yet to be published. They could consider how they will use the information sources you have analysed together with other sources they may have themselves.

c) What are the different ways in which you could inform the local community about something that has happened (for example an unexpected and temporary school closure due to a burst boiler)? Who are the different audiences who will need this information? What exactly will they need to know? What are the most appropriate channels/methods of communication you could use to ensure that accurate information reaches them quickly? Which methods would be less reliable? Why?

Explain

A text which explains could take various forms. Explanations have many similar features to information texts. They serve to give reasons for why or how something works or has occurred. For example: why hurricanes happen; how a hydroelectric dam works; why Oliver Cromwell came to power; how too much sugar can ruin your teeth; why you missed the bus or failed to complete your assignment. Such texts might include manuals, posters, leaflets, letters, presentations, conversations, personal emails or text messages. In each case you will need to explore the audience of the text and the purpose of writing (or speaking).

Some contend that explanation texts can be divided into three subgenres: temporal, causal and factorial. Although the structure of each subgenre is similar, Lewis and Wray (1995) suggest that the connectives used in each case can vary. Causal explanations will use, for example, *therefore, thus, as a result*. Temporal explanations will use connectives such as *subsequently, eventually, finally*. In contrast, factorial explanations that involve the reader in making judgements about reasons and deliberating about the main reason, will include phrases like *the main reason, another reason* and so on.

Creative ways in:

a) *Reading and Writing Non-Fiction* (Ayres and Dayus 2000) has a series of useful activities on explanation texts which includes a page on transforming an explanation from *Horrible*

Science – Disgusting Digestion into Standard English to explore different audiences for explanation texts. Your students could also decide how they would adapt a piece of plain explanatory text for a younger audience.

b) Best explanations – which student can give the wildest, wackiest, most detailed or most improbable explanation for arriving late to a lesson?

Describe

Students may be familiar with the language of description from their reading of fiction. However, description is also a vital element of different types of factual texts, including those which attempt to persuade someone to visit a holiday resort, or which describe the appearance of a missing person, the match-winning free kick or an item for sale on eBay. A description captures the atmosphere and illustrates a particular scene. The writer may draw on all the senses in their writing and make use of imagery to help evoke a mood. Alternatively a description can be a very succinct list of features with little elaboration.

Creative ways in:

a) A matching activity for short examples of different types of descriptive writing and potential audiences.

b) Ask your students to describe an item of their clothing in different ways as if it were: for sale in a clothing catalogue; being written about by a journalist at a Paris fashion show; an item on a lost property list; something worn by an Oscar winner for an interview; a piece of traditional costume as described in a holiday guide book; the clothing of the main character in a novel.

Analyse

Texts which serve analytical purposes look critically at a subject and explore aspects of it as though under a microscope. They take a particular stance on the subject under scrutiny, drawing selectively on evidence to support a point of view. Depending on the intended audience and subject, the analysis may be written in highly technical language.

Creative ways in:

a) Much of the writing students will be expected to complete about other texts (especially literature) will be analytical. It may be a good idea to ask them to take stock of their own analytical style, to identify which of the conventions are present and which they might need to develop to improve their grade.

b) Ask students to highlight the key linguistic features in different colours on a photocopied piece of analytical writing. Complete a statistical analysis of the frequency with which each feature occurs. Students could present their findings as an oral presentation or a written report.

Review

Texts which review, look back over, revisit or listen again to something and make a judgement about it. This 'something' might be a live performance, a film, CD, a poetry anthology, a restaurant meal or an art exhibition. Programmes like Mark Kermode's *Film 24* on BBCNews24, *Front Row* on Radio 4, as well as *Heat* magazine and weekend newspapers all include examples of reviews. Review texts tend to:

- Begin by summarizing the story/content/context of the item to be reviewed. This might include reference to the artist's previous work or achievements.
- Offer a personal response to the item under review, indicating the impact it has had on the reviewer.
- Draw on the reviewer's previous experience of other/similar texts in the genre.
- Exemplify the reviewer's reaction to the text with reference to some key moments/passages/lyrics/clips which are then explored in more detail.
- (Usually) leave the audience in no doubt about what the reviewer thought of the text – unless the reviewer is being diplomatic about a friend's work.
- End with some brief details about publisher, tour dates, release details, etc.

Most well-written reviews will leave something to the audience's imagination, such as what happens in the end of a film/book but, infuriatingly, some do not!

Creative ways in:

a) Reviewers can have very idiosyncratic styles. Students could compare different reviews of the same film or album. The *Guardian* newspaper's review round-up page in *G2* might be a good source as a starting point for this discussion. Students could work in small groups to construct their own reviews page in a similar style with short comments on a range of programmes, films, computer games and books they have read.

b) Students could imagine they are restaurant critics for a national newspaper. How would they review their packed lunches or meals served in the school canteen?

Discuss

Discursive texts present arguments about issues or events (Chapter 6 explores one kind of discursive spoken text – the debate). Discursive texts all tend to explore differing viewpoints before arriving at a conclusion based on the evidence they have explored. Written types include editorials, academic papers, and historical or philosophical texts. Discussion usually:

- is written in the present tense
- begins with a statement or overview of the main arguments to be explored
- draws on arguments for
- draws on arguments against
- includes arguments for and against either grouped separately or argument/counter argument for each point presented together
- draws on supporting evidence for each argument
- has a logical structure with points linked together by causal connectives
- arrives at a recommendation within its conclusion.

Creative ways in:

a) Ask the students to carry out a vox pop around school or within a year group on a topical issue. They should then collate the arguments for and against and present them as a paper for discussion by the school council or the tutor team.

b) Compare two newspaper editorials on the same subject. Draw a diagram or chart which shows the differences and similarities in the way the issue is discussed in each publication.

c) Conduct a formal debate on a topical issue (see guidance in Chapter 6).

Persuade

Texts whose purpose is to persuade include advertising of different kinds, political speeches, election campaign literature, travel websites and brochures, property details, etc. These texts aim to sell you a future in which you might be, for example, happier, safer, freer, thinner or more successful. They are texts which are only interested in telling you one side of the story – the positive side about their product, party or special interest group. For the most part, they are closely targeted at very specific audiences: nothing about their design, structure or choice of language will have been left to chance.

Such texts usually:

- begin with an opening statement or image which asserts a viewpoint or asks the reader/viewer a question which intrigues and hooks them
- expand on this opening through a series of points which elaborate on, repeat and reinforce the message or the USP (Unique Selling Point)
- reiterate the opening statement very clearly in conclusion
- use statistics, references to reports, or comments from other users to endorse their message
- address themselves very deliberately to their intended audience through, for example, their use of language, humour, music, images, cultural references, layout, etc.

Creative ways in:

a) In my experience, students can be fascinated by exploring the language of adverts, especially if they are given a choice of product to investigate and are able to draw on their prior knowledge. Students could be asked to present a collage of adverts for a generic product (such as perfume, cars, chocolate or mobile phones) which is marketed for different audiences with an accompanying analytical piece of writing exploring the persuasive techniques.

b) In marketing teams, the students should prepare all the elements of a pitch for an advertising campaign for a new product. This could be a two-week project with the final pitch being delivered to an external panel. (If you would prefer this to be small scale then refer to suggestions in Chapter 6.)

5.6.3   Triplets

Within the previous (1999) version of the National Curriculum a similar range of purposes was listed to these outlined here. However, these were organized in triplets:

- Writing to imagine, explore, entertain
- Writing to inform, explain, describe
- Writing to persuade, argue, advise
- Writing to analyse, review, comment

You need to be aware of these triplets as they will still be referred to in schools until 2011: the creators of GCSE English exam specifications used the triplets directly in the design of their assessments (both for writing and, with slight variation, for speaking and listening). For specific information about the style of questioning refer to the examination board websites listed in Chapter 2. The triplets have dominated assessment in English for too long: they have become the bane of many teachers' lives. Although, as Andrews notes, the groupings did mark a positive move of 'persuasive, argumentative texts from underneath the umbrella of the "factual" informative category' (Andrews 2001b: 130), the triplets highlight the unstable nature of textual categorization. They present a contorted and compartmentalized view of what it means to read, write and speak English. (For example, surely an advertiser can *entertain* and *persuade* readers to *imagine* a future, through *description,* in which a particular product will transform their lives, and yet these purposes of text were listed in discrete triplets.) These triplets appear to have been dispensed with, although much will depend on the redesign of GCSE specifications (for first examination in 2011) before we can be completely sure of their passing.

5.7 Conclusion

In preparing to teach non-fiction you will need to ensure you can talk confidently about its varied lexis and grammatical structures. It will also be a good idea for you to read widely across the literary non-fiction genres and to develop squirrel-like instincts for storing, recording or bookmarking useful non-fiction texts that you will come across in your everyday life. Of all the genres explored in this book, non-fiction is perhaps the most varied and immediate and the one with the most potential for stimulating discussion about language use by all students in your classes.

Notes

1. Bracketed insertion denotes requirements at KS4 only.
2. KS3 progamme of study also includes 'shaping'.

Spoken Texts and Scripts $\boxed{6}$

Chapter Outline

6.1   Introduction

This chapter explores ways into teaching texts that have been loosely grouped together as 'spoken texts and scripts'. This wide-ranging focus includes consideration of: our everyday speech as text; presentation skills and use of presentational tools; formal speeches; script composition; bringing drama texts off the page; the place of Shakespeare and other playwrights in the curriculum and approaches to teaching them. Once more I touch on issues of subject knowledge and point to sources of support for your further development in this rich and rewarding area for classroom study.

6.2   Everyday speech as text

The English curriculum has long been dominated by the study of written, canonical or high-status texts composed by others, with the result that the oral and everyday or ephemeral texts we make ourselves (i.e. the dialogues we create in everyday conversation, the jokes we tell, the directions we give, the lists we make) are frequently neglected in the classroom. This was not always the case. Knowledge about Language (KAL) became a popular and yet controversial aspect of English study in the early days of the National Curriculum, in no small part due to the development of the LINC training materials (see Chapter 1). Influenced by functional theories of language, particularly those of Halliday, who places meaning at the centre of theories of language (see Halliday and Hasan 1989), LINC emphasized a view of the 'richness and variety of language . . . a description of texts in social contexts over the description of isolated decontextualised bits of language' (Carter 1990: 5). This view was also reflected in textbooks that appeared at the time (for example Bain 1993, Bain and Bain 1996). Many of these could be readily used in a classroom today.

The arrival of a new curriculum model has once again placed more emphasis on spoken language at both primary and secondary level. The National Curriculum for English clearly states the importance of spoken language study in all four of its 'key concepts' in order to develop students' competence, creativity, and cultural and critical understandings. In terms of themselves as speakers, students need to be able to:

- use a range of ways to structure and organize their speech to support their purposes and guide the listener
- vary vocabulary, structures and grammar to convey meaning, including speaking Standard English fluently
- engage an audience, using a range of techniques to explore, enrich and explain their ideas. (QCA 2007a: 2.1b, c and d)

and to

- understand aspects of language structure and variation, including the international significance of Standard English and the impact of technology on the way we speak and write. (QCA 2007b: 3.4)

The development of students' knowledge about how language functions to create meaning is a key element within all the above curriculum requirements. Your students will be in a better position to explore how meaning is created if your approach to planning and teaching begins with contexts and situations that they have experienced. For example, if we look at 2.1b (the first point above), you could start the students off by asking them to think about their construction of a very short piece of spoken informational text – a joke. In his work on the art of common talk, Carter has acknowledged that even young children have 'the capacity for telling and receiving jokes which depend for their effect on a recognition of the creative play with patterns of meaning' (Carter 2003: 18). He continues by commenting on the creativity of everyday talk with its 'wordplay, puns and formulaic jokes' (ibid.: 18). Such a rich and accessible field is ideal for student investigations. You could begin by asking them to record some of their favourite (inoffensive) jokes as source material and explore in small groups the following questions about the creative processes involved:

- How do they tell jokes?
- When and where do they tell them?
- Why do they tell jokes?
- What are the key features of a joke's structure – can they see certain patterns in the language?
- What about intonation, pitch, timing or choice of vocabulary and phrasing? Do these vary according to the kind of joke being told? Do they vary according to the different contexts in which the jokes are told?
- Could the same joke be told very differently by two people or two people of different genders, cultures or ages?
- How does the joke-teller keep an audience engaged?
- How does the joke-teller know if his or her purposes are achieved?
- What occurs linguistically *after* a joke has been told?

If you wanted to develop this discussion further you could explore issues of body language and listen to sound/DVD clips of different joke-telling styles. You could also investigate the differences between spoken and written jokes (and what is lost/gained when a joke is spoken or when a joke is told via email or text message).

An alternative to joke-telling would be to focus on instructional talk, a form first explored in Chapter 5. For example:

- How do your students give spoken instructions to one of their peers about something technical like how to locate a particular sound file on an MP3 player or how to find their way to the next level of a computer game? What are the key terms that they use?
- How many of these terms would be familiar to the audience concerned?
- How much of the instruction is spoken and how much is demonstration?
- How would they amend their spoken instructions for someone who had never used the equipment before?
- What do they notice about the ways in which the instructor and the person under instruction interact in each case?

One of the reasons experienced teachers were challenged by developments like KAL, and subsequent initiatives such as the KS3 *Framework for Teaching English* and the AS/A2 English Language and Literature specifications introduced in 2000, is that these made them feel insecure about their knowledge of how language functions and its associated terminology. Many of those who are new to the profession also find language to be a major knowledge gap (Cajkler and Hislam 2004). This may well be an area which you will need support with. If you are fortunate enough to be on a PGCE English course which attracts linguists as well as those with literature or media degrees, then make sure you tap into their expertise (and share some of your own in a different area in return). There are also a number of helpful textbooks and websites you should consult. The best of these are listed at the end of the section on everyday speech. It is important not to panic, however: remember that no single teacher knows everything! We all continue to learn throughout our careers and to draw on advice from others. I hope you will discover that language study is a fascinating area and one which you will want to immerse yourself in.

6.3   Grammar for talk

In terms of the language of spoken texts, if you and your students want to learn more about the features of your own spoken language then you will find that two QCA publications – *New Perspectives on spoken English in the classroom* (2003) and *Grammar for Talk* (2004) – will provide valuable starting points for your investigations. See Figure 6.1 for an example of key features.

- 'Heads' are found at the beginning of clauses. They help listeners to orient themselves to a topic:
  The ugly bungalow on the corner, is that where she lives?
  A friend of mine, Tom, his cousin loaned us the tent we took to Glastonbury.

- 'Tails' are found at the end of clauses, normally echoing an antecedent noun. They help to reinforce what we are saying:
  She's a brilliant badminton player Rachel is.
  It can leave you feeling very weak, shingles, can't it?

- In an 'ellipsis', subjects and sometimes verbs are omitted because we assume our listeners know what we mean:
  (I've got) Lots to tell you about our trip to Moscow.
  (Do you want to go for a) Pint?
  (It) Sounds like a plan. (to do what you've suggested)

- Discourse markers are used to mark boundaries between one topic and the next in a conversation:
  anyway, right, OK, so, what's more, etc.

- Adverbials and adverbs are used after tags and at the end of clauses (due to the unrehearsed nature of speech, and time constraints) to orient the listener and soften what has been said:
  You are with me, aren't you, almost?
  It should be a lot easier playing them now Pietersen's captain, shouldn't it, in a way?

- 'Vague language' softens or diminish expressions, making them sound less assertive or bossy:
  thing, stuff, sort of, whatever, or something.

- Deictic features (such as *this, these, that, those, here* and *there*) help to locate an utterance spatially. Temporal deictic words and personal pronouns are also common:
  Could we just move this over there into that alcove?
  Then I'd like to pop in to that little shop over there.

- Use of modal expressions so that utterances don't sound too assertive:
  possibly, probably, I suppose, I don't know, perhaps, etc.

- Chains of clauses in a stream of spoken language which are linked by coordinating (such as *and*) or simple subordinating conjunctions (such as '*cos* or *so*):
  I was just about to pack up and, well, I saw this last branch that needed cutting and I picked up the secateurs and then a red ant got in my gardening glove and it bit me and whooah – I went crashing forward and the blood went everywhere.

- Subordinate clauses stand alone and serve to highlight a topic or signal to a listener that they could take a turn in the dialogue:
  And now I've got to wait for the next train, which is bad news.

(adapted from Carter, R., 'The grammar of talk: spoken English, grammar and the classroom' in QCA 2003)

Figure 6.1 Basic forms of spoken grammar

Which of the features of spoken grammar listed in Figure 6.1 are new to you? Which can you identify from your own speech? You could use snippets of classroom, school corridor or even staffroom conversation as a basis for analysis with your group. In each case it will be important to consider the social contexts in which the conversations take place and how these have had an influence over delivery, structure and content.

Once you have reflected on the technical features of your spoken language you could also take a more holistic approach and consider how your (and your students') use of the English language has developed. Some of the questions you might want to explore are listed here but you will want to add your own ideas too.

- Do you speak English with your family?
- Do you use words from other languages within your personal vocabulary? If so, how do you mix them with English words?
- Are there words and phrases which you use that are peculiar to your particular region, dialect or family?
- How would you describe your own spoken English? How much does it adhere to Standard English? How does it differ from your use of the written word?
- Have you always spoken in this way or have you been influenced by relocating to a different region or country?
- Do you switch between different language codes when you talk in various contexts? What were the first words of English you remember speaking?
- Do you think and/or dream in English all the time?
- Has your use of English changed as you have grown older?

Some recommended stimuli to provoke these discussions are:

a) The website www.bbc.co.uk/voices/. This enables you to record and listen to voice recordings from different parts of the UK, to explore local word maps, issues of multilingualism and language change. Also for other regional case studies go to www.bl.uk/learning/langlit/sounds/case-studies/. If you are intending to use either of these sites in the classroom make sure you check out they will function with your school's server as some internet gatekeepers can be sensitive to their content (both sites accessed 14 October 2008).

b) Two fascinating short texts which explore contrasting aspects of spoken English. In 'A Language Autobiography', Shari Sabeti considers issues of identity and isolation through her use of English, which separates her from her Persian roots (Sabeti 2002). In contrast, Ian McEwan's 'Mother Tongue' centres movingly on the gradual loss of his mother's spoken English through Alzheimer's and the effects of her language on him at different stages in his own life (McEwan 2001). Both texts would be very suitable for classroom discussion, especially with Post-16 groups. They may inspire you to write your own language autobiography.

6.4   Recommended language support texts for teachers

Ballard, K. (2007) *The Frameworks of English: Introducing Language Structures* (2nd Edition). London: Palgrave Macmillan.

Crystal, D. (1995) *Cambridge Encyclopaedia of English*. Cambridge: Cambridge University Press.

Crystal, D. (2004) *Making Sense of Grammar*. London: Longman.

Edwards, V. (1996) *The Other Languages: a guide to multilingual classrooms*, Reading: RAILC.

Gravelle, M. (ed.) (2000) *Planning for Bilingual Learners*. Stoke-on-Trent: Trentham Books.

McWilliam, N. (1998) *What's in a word? Vocabulary development in multilingual classrooms*. Stoke-on-Trent: Trentham Books.

Maybin, J. and Swann, J. (2006) *The Art of English: Everyday Creativity*. London: Palgrave Macmillan.

O'Connor, J. (2003) *The Pocket Guide to English Language*. Cambridge: Cambridge University Press.

Ross, A. (2006) *Language Knowledge for Secondary Teachers*. London: David Fulton.

Websites

www.cybergrammar.co.uk – Debra Myhill's site is very helpful for consolidating subject knowledge about language.

www.universalteacher.org.uk – Andrew Moore's site is especially useful for A level Language related support and teaching ideas.

www.phon.ucl.ac.uk/home/dick/tta/KS3.htm – Dick Hudson's Key Stage 3 Grammar site will help you to secure grammatical key terms.

(all accessed 14 October 2008)

6.5 Presentation skills and use of presentational tools

One of the key skills of spoken English that your pupils will need to develop is an ability to present their ideas to others in a range of different situations, both individually and as a member of a group. Oral presentation can be a very daunting prospect for some less confident members of your classes whereas others, who perhaps seem overconfident speakers, will need to be encouraged to *listen* to advice (and to their peers) so they can hone their skills to their best advantage. You will need to think carefully both about the ground rules you establish for speaking and listening activities and about how you organize groupings for presentations. In teaching effective presentation skills, you should also model these yourself, both in your everyday use of spoken language and in your explicit focus on different types of spoken texts.

The DVD *Teaching Speaking and Listening* (DfES 2007) has a variety of useful lesson video clips, transcripts, background papers and a glossary to support your planning and teaching of speaking and listening. It contains an example of modelling by Robin Launder, who introduces the use of persuasive language for his Year 10 class through modelling and links this to a discussion of the key features of spoken persuasive texts. The students then develop their own short dramatic presentations to sell a variety of everyday objects (such as hats and plastic cups) in lively, persuasive ways. The DVD also exemplifies approaches to different types of talk: dialogic, exploratory and Socratic.

- *Dialogic talk* involves speakers and listeners in exploring and building both their own and other people's ideas to develop coherent thoughts about a question, topic, text, etc. under discussion (Alexander 2003).
- *Exploratory talk* involves paired, critical and constructive discussion usually on a given question or piece of information. The sharing of information, the reasoning engaged in and attempts to arrive at an agreement are all key elements of this exploratory process (Mercer 1995).
- *Socratic talk* involves guided observation of a discussion. Usually a small group of speakers are each observed by a number of other people. The speakers' contributions to the discussion are subsequently evaluated by those who have observed them.

In your classroom work, you will want to experiment with each of these different approaches with all kinds of texts. Try to vary the methods you use to suit the topic concerned and to ensure that students continue to be challenged and engaged.

6.5.1   Using PowerPoint

If you are asking students to present ideas to the rest of the class then you may want them to use dramatic techniques such as role-play or short scripted scenes that have been developed through improvization. For a formal presentation (for example, of research findings, interpretations of a poem or a pitch for an advertising campaign) it may be more appropriate to ask the students to create and then present a PowerPoint presentation. If you do give students the choice to present their ideas using this medium you need to be very sure that this is the most suitable format for them to use: a carefully drawn single OHT, a poster or some handwritten bullet points on a whiteboard might suffice. Be wary of introducing them to what Bigum defines as 'digital busy work' (2003: 3), that is, using new technologies to carry out 'lower-order tasks' (Lankshear and Knobel 2007: 101). In exploring Bigum's definition, Lankshear and Knobel use the example of 'PowerPoint slides where each slide is filled with text that the student reads to their classmates directly from the screen' (2007: 101). Such presentations may well have been constructed with little guidance or understanding of what makes an effective presentation. Indeed, as Lankshear and Knobel state, some web archive support materials appear to encourage students to cram each blank slide full of information, with little thought given to careful selection or potential copyright issues. The resulting creations are constructed by students who have concentrated much more on the technological processes involved in using software or internet applications than on the interpretation and presentation of their own ideas. If you do want your students to use PowerPoint then you need to be clear about students' prior knowledge of the software.

By the time they reach Year 8, most students will be very familiar with the features of PowerPoint (and might prefer to present their ideas in other formats). They may have already endured some unsuccessful presentations by their teachers, too! In planning your speaking and listening activity, aim to include discussion of what makes a good (and legal) presentation. You may want to model a short, successful presentation yourself or design some contrasting sample slides to discuss as a group. Think about limiting the number of slides the students can include and allow separate blocks of time for them to plan the slides, draft their script and rehearse how they will use the slides in their presentation – in my experience the drafting and rehearsal stages are neglected far too often. When planning lessons and assessing students' achievements in this area, try not to overlook the value of the exploratory talk they will have engaged in during the drafting stages. Through his observation of collaborative activities at the computer screen, Neil Mercer (1995) notes that teacher recap on previous activities and explicit rehearsal of discussion ground rules can cause the amount of exploratory talk to escalate. In my own research with student teachers and pupils on the potential of wireless keyboards for enhancing teaching and learning, some of the most stimulating formative discussions that I observed took place in a classroom where the student teacher's expectations for collaborative talk had been established and were reiterated before the start of each lesson (Dymoke 2005).

You might of course have limited experience of using presentation software yourself. Although most recent graduates will have used PowerPoint in their seminar presentations, those of you who are changing careers or have had little contact with ICT beyond internet surfing will want to develop your skills in this area during your training. If you fall into this category then do not panic. Make sure that you talk to your tutor and other beginning teachers on your course *at an early stage* about your ICT training needs. You will undoubtedly find that someone will help you to get started. In this way you can build your confidence and (if you are training in England) prepare yourself for the ICT skills test.

6.6   Speeches and debates

We have already explored some aspects of everyday spoken English in this chapter but one other aspect you might want to look at in your classroom is *The Speech*. In investigating speeches, students can explore construction, purpose, delivery and audience reactions. They can go on to experiment with writing their own speeches to persuade or entertain others. Famous twentieth-century speeches delivered for political/commercial, celebratory or elegiac purposes by orators like Nelson Mandela, Martin Luther King, Mahatma Gandhi, Margaret Thatcher, Winston Churchill and Earl Spencer are widely available in transcript form and through recordings posted on YouTube. A website primarily aimed at American teachers (www.webenglishteacher.com/speech.html, accessed 14 October 2008) also includes some interesting material such as annotated speeches and background material.

You might want to introduce your students to formal debating conventions and even to enter a team for a debating competition (such as those run by the English Speaking Union or your local university). An awareness of formal discussion skills and the origins/conventions of parliamentary debate are key elements of the Citizenship curriculum in KS2 and KS3. If you are able to team up with other colleagues in your school, you could organize an inter-tutor group competition. In my experience students can rise to the challenges of this formal approach very well, taking the debate much more seriously than they would a normal classroom discussion and listening well. Be warned that the debates can become very heated!

If you are focusing primarily on investigating persuasive techniques, I can almost guarantee that someone in the department you are working in will have taught such a unit before, so talk to them about their resources. Persuasion appears to be one of the most frequently taught aspects of English in Key Stage 3 so be wary of overkill. One approach which can engage students effectively is to ask them to persuade someone else to buy something unsaleable, bizarre or that they would never need. However, do tread carefully with this approach as some very strange items are sold on eBay. One Year 8 class I observed last summer decided how they would sell mud from Glastonbury (a version of this activity is shown at http://news. bbc.co.uk/cbbcnews/hi/newsid_4130000/newsid_4139600/4139610.stm, accessed 27 October 2008). This approach proved to be an effective stimulus for their own (even stranger) ideas.

6.7   Teaching drama texts

Drama is an essential genre for your students to experience. Teaching a play for the first time can be challenging for beginning teachers. There's the need to allocate parts. The potential for public humiliation if no one volunteers to read. The need to navigate your class through a text which has a very particular layout on the page. The prospect of a close and scary encounter between a less than confident reader and characters speaking pithy language. The immediacy of the text and the pace required to read it in an engaging way. The shortness (in most cases) of the scenes and the challenge of how to explore what arises from them. These factors are undoubtedly apparent in many prose texts, but they can become magnified in drama. Few plays offer space for the teacher or student to hide. The long stretches of prose with which you might, just might, hold an audience's attention (or at least keep them quiet) are absent here. Having said all this, try to cast your fears aside. I can honestly say, both from my own English teaching experience and from frequent observations of student teachers, that, as Hamlet says, 'the play's the thing', wherein you'll catch the conscience, or at least the imagination, of your pupils. In the last few months I have been constantly reminded of how much pupils enjoy play texts. I have observed a group of low ability and usually disruptive Year 10 students engrossed in Willy Russell's *Blood Brothers*, arguing over whether Mickey or Eddie should go out with Linda. I've listened to a girl, excluded from every other subject, desperate to read the main role of Linda and articulating an understanding of the character's feelings in a way which stunned the usual class teacher. I heard Year 9 students raving about a production of Anne Cassidy's *Looking for JJ* that they had just seen on tour, able Year 10s fired up by the injustice of the witch hunts in Arthur Miller's *The Crucible*, Year 11s arguing over Eva's real identity in J.B. Priestley's *An Inspector Calls* and Year 13s immersed in the passion and destruction of John Ford's *'Tis Pity She's a Whore* – a play which makes *The Sopranos* seem like a family comedy.

If you make the right choice of text and are able to plan a stimulating sequence of lessons around it, then you could well find that teaching a play could be one of your students' most rewarding and eye-opening experiences of literature. In choosing which texts to teach you will, of course, in part need to be guided by what's in the stock cupboard, listed in the exam specification and what your colleagues might advise as appropriate for your students. The most successful texts will undoubtedly be the most well-thumbed ones (and the texts which always get booked up quickly by your colleagues, so plan ahead). Below is a list of some of the most commonly taught play texts in schools – excluding Shakespeare, who will be discussed later in this chapter. This is not a comprehensive list but features a number of the most common titles, some of which have now been taught in schools for many years. Many of them are frequently set as examination texts. Which of the plays do you recognize from your own previous studies? Which might you want to familiarize yourself with?

6.7.1   KS3 Drama texts

Anne Fine: *The Granny Project*
Nigel Gray: *Black Harvest* – play version of Anne Pilling's novel
Jan Needle: *A Game of Soldiers* – play and novel
Joe Standerline: *Stone Cold* – play version of the novel by Robert Swindells
Paul Whitfield: *Precious* and *A Game of Two Halves*
The KS3 Drama Book (English & Media Centre) includes *Helmet* by Douglas Maxwell and scripts/
    videos of a number of other short plays

6.7.2   KS4 Drama texts

Willis Hall: *The Long and the Short and the Tall*
Arthur Miller: *The Crucible; A View from the Bridge; Death of A Salesman; All My Sons* (Miller is also
    widely taught at Post-16 level)
J.B. Priestley: *An Inspector Calls*
Willy Russell: *Blood Brothers, Educating Rita*
R.C. Sheriff: *Journey's End*
Oscar Wilde: *The Importance of Being Earnest*

6.7.3   Post-16 Drama texts

Aphra Behn: *The Rover*
Alan Bennett: *The History Boys*
Carol Churchill: *Light Shining in Buckinghamshire, Top Girls*
John Ford: *'Tis Pity She's a Whore*
Brian Friel: *Making History, Translations*
Athol Fugard: *Master Harold and the Boys*
David Hare: *Murmuring Judges*

Ben Johnson: *Volpone*
Christopher Marlowe: *Dr Faustus*
Thomas Middleton: *Women Beware Women*
Tom Stoppard: *Arcadia, Rosencrantz and Guildenstern are Dead*
John Webster: *The Duchess of Malfi, The White Devil*
Timberlake Wertenbaker: *Our Country's Good*
Oscar Wilde: *Lady Windermere's Fan*
Tennessee Williams: *A Streetcar Named Desire, Cat on a Hot Tin Roof, The Glass Menagerie*
William Wycherley: *The Country Wife*

When first exploring a play script with a class, especially at KS3, you will want to ensure that they are familiar with the particular conventions of layout and other dramatic key terms. These conventions and their definitions can be found in Table 6.1.

Table 6.1 Play script conventions

Term	Definition
Script	The written text of a play, film, television, radio broadcast (including adverts). Anything that has been created to be read out loud and performed.
Audience	The people who watch or listen to the play.
Act	The major division of a play – like a book chapter. A play could have 1 to 5 acts or more. Within each act there are usually a number of scenes of continuous action.
Scene	Each act is broken down into a series of short scenes. A scene often focuses on one key event. Every new scene could take place in a different setting.
Line	The script may have line numbers (especially if it is a Shakespeare play or a media script). These can help readers and actors to find their place in a text and can be useful for production and design teams.
Stage Directions	Instructions written in the text which tell an actor where or how to move, how to behave or speak a line. Can also include instructions for sound, lighting or other visual effects. Often printed in a different font to the spoken words and/or in brackets.
Narrator	A person outside the action who gives the audience information about events, characters, etc. In a radio, film or television script the narrator's voice might take the form of a voice-over.
Chorus	One person or a group of people outside of the action who comment on events in the play or provide background information.
Setting	Place, time of day or date when/where a scene occurs.
Soliloquy	A character's speech which is usually given when the actor is alone on stage. It reveals their thoughts to the audience only.
Aside	A comment made by one character to another (or by one character to the audience) which no one else is supposed to be able to hear.
Dramatic Irony	The audience might know more about what is happening in the play than some of the characters. Because the audience are in the know, they might find some of the things characters do or say to be ironic.
Dramatis Personae	The list of characters in the play.

These terms could all be introduced at the beginning. Alternatively, you might find it more effective to introduce them gradually and to build up a set of class definitions linked to the specific play you are reading. If students are writing about a script and its construction, you will want them to use many of these terms confidently. If they are devising their own scripts, they will want to use some of the features in their own writing.

Many drama specialists would suggest that a more successful route into reading plays (which can often be complex and demanding texts) can be through working with them as 'briefs for performance' (Kempe and Ashwell 2000: 214) which can be interpreted in different ways. In thinking about how you will use play scripts in your English lessons you will soon come to realize that if the students' engagement with the text is to be a meaningful one, it cannot be a solitary experience. If you ask them endless questions about what happens at the end of each scene (which they must write about in silence), you will kill any sense of drama stone dead. On the other hand, you may well be confronted by the physical constraints of the classroom space you are teaching in and the other facilities available to you. Time and rooming constraints will not allow you to spend every lesson acting out the play in the school's only large drama space, and anyway such activity might not involve or challenge all of your students equally. In offering what they describe as a 'viable alternative' (ibid.: 215) to these polarized desk-bound and stage-bound methods of working with texts, Kempe and Ashwell suggest that the model of teaching dramatic texts used needs to offer:

- ways of getting the students to engage with the text from the first encounter
- ways of getting them to see the text as a whole as quickly as possible
- ways of encouraging them to consider their personal responses to the text
- methods which will help them see the characters and narrative as dramatic creations, rather than as real people and situations
- ways of regarding the text as an incomplete experience, the meaning of which they – as readers, actors, directors and audience will have a hand in creating. (Kempe and Ashwell 2000: 215)

They continue by outlining a plethora of learner-centred activities for developing students' understandings about the construction of play scripts, how they can be performed and interpreted. It would not be practicable or appropriate to reproduce these here. However, their simple and highly effective idea for introducing script writing should whet your appetite for more. I have used a version of this very successfully with Year 8 students and include it below.

6.7.4   Four-line plays

In *Progression in Secondary Drama*, Kempe and Ashwell (2000) describe the introduction of four-line plays to focus the students' attention on the relationship between gestures, movements, spatial relationships, timing, pauses, intonation, pitch, etc., in dialogue and how these elements mesh together to create meanings.

1. The students are given a four-line play which they should try to act out in pairs in at least six different ways. For example:

   A: Long time no see!

   B: No.

   A: What do you think?

   B: I'm not sure.

   They must not add anything else to the script but should talk about what happens to the words when they add pauses, gestures, speak them with different emphasis and so on.

2. The pair should then decide on a context for the script. For example, it could be that A is an optimistic parent talking to a rather guarded teacher B at a consultation evening and waiting for the verdict on his child's progress. Alternatively A could be in the refreshments queue at half-time in a football match where her team have performed dreadfully. She bumps into B, a former friend who is in two minds about speaking to her and uncertain about what he's seen on the pitch so far.

3. The students rehearse their performance of the lines, again not adding anything but ensuring that they make the context they have chosen for the exchange as clear as possible.

4. The lines are then performed to the rest of the group, with the teacher guiding reflection by the whole class on how effectively the pair have conveyed the situation. Once all (or a selection) of the pairs' performances have been seen the teacher could then open up a discussion about the different ways the lines have been interpreted.

5. The next stage is for students to write their own four-line plays in pairs and to pass them on to another pair without giving any hint of what situation was in their minds when they wrote it. The pairs rehearse the new lines in their own way, perform and discuss them as before.

Kempe and Ashwell suggest that a potential extension of this activity is for the original writers of the plays to rehearse the four lines themselves. They should notate them with directions on how they performed them and then pass these versions to another pair, who should see if they can replicate the writers' intentions in their own performance. The activity as a whole raises so many issues about interpretation, the processes involved in performing scripts, the difficulties of notating a script and even authorship and ownership of texts.

When working with play scripts, teachers can sometimes be tempted to read them in a static way, almost as though they were prose. If your students are to appreciate the real power and intentions of a dramatist's language then you will need to give them opportunities to bring the text off the page, as has been exemplified in the four-line scripts activity above. One way you can do this is to act out some of the scenes in small groups. You could have several groups acting out the same scene and lead in to a comparison of different interpretations. You could also organize small groups to take different scenes so that your class runs through the action of a whole Act with contributions from different class members. Another approach, which could potentially lead to greater in-depth discussion, is for a group of volunteers to be directed by the rest of the class about how they should deliver their lines, move around the space and interact with one another. Such a strategy will enable you to open up discussion about the characters and, hopefully, explore a range of interpretations about their behaviours and motivations. Many plays can be read through quickly in class so you could read the script all through in several lessons and then revisit key sections of the play in much greater depth using some of the strategies listed below. If you decide on the quick read-through approach, make sure you choose your readers carefully and move through the first reading briskly.

The strategies suggested here are not exclusively for use with plays: many of them will work extremely well with poetry, prose fiction and non-fiction texts too. They are used extensively by creative teachers in many subject areas for non-text-based work to explore social issues or perspectives on historical events. Ask yourself:

a) How could you use the strategies in Table 6.2 with a script (or another text/topic) that you know well?

b) What might the potential benefits of each listed activity be for increasing your students' levels of participation?

c) How could you use the activities for developing students' understanding of the text or empathy for the characters?

For other examples of drama strategies, refer to Neelands and Goode (2000) and to the NATE (2000) publication *Cracking Drama*.

6.8   The place of Drama in the English curriculum

Drama has an important place both within the National Curriculum orders for English and across all curriculum subjects. The study of play texts, assessed predominantly through written responses, is a feature of KS3 assessments, GCSE and Post-16 examinations. Drama forms a key element of Speaking and Listening programmes of study for both KS3 and KS4 English for all students as is exemplified below.

6.8.1   Specific references to drama within the Speaking and Listening strand

Key processes
Pupils should be able to:

j) use different dramatic approaches to explore ideas, texts and issues
k) use different dramatic techniques to convey action, character, atmosphere and tension
l) explore the ways that words, actions, sound and staging combine to create dramatic moments.

Explanatory notes
Different dramatic approaches: These include tableaux, hot-seating, teacher in role, 'thought tracking' and forum theatre.

Table 6.2 Drama strategies (adapted from Neelands and Goode 2000)

Activity	Definition
Context-building activities	*Scene-setting conventions or those which add extra information to the context of the unfolding drama*
Using Objects	A number of objects are selected which provide clues about a character and introduce that character or their setting to the students. The objects should trigger questions by the group, helping them to develop their interpretive skills and to enter the world of the drama. Real or imagined objects can also be given to a character by the students.
Role on the Wall	A key role or representation of an issue such as homelessness is presented as an outline, diagram or picture on the wall. Information about the role is written on, added with post-its, changed and augmented as the drama progresses. A collective interpretation of the complexities of the 'role' emerges.
Collective Character	A character is improvised by a group of pupils and any one of them can speak as the character. (Alternatively one person can take on the role and the others whisper comments and suggest lines of dialogue.)
Narrative activities	*Conventions emphasizing the story or what happens next in the drama*
Hot-seating	A character, played by a student or teacher, is interviewed in role by the rest of the class in order to explore the person's motivations, reactions to events and to gain insights into relationships. The person is usually seated facing the rest of the group.
Time Line	This is a physical representation of the relationships between events. Students work on a number of small group scenes which occur before and after a key dramatic encounter. The groups are then asked to consider how each scene relates to the key encounter (in terms of impact on it, timescale or relationship with characters) and to physically position themselves (or a group representative) in relation to an image or group sculpture of the key encounter.
Teacher in Role	The teacher adopts a role within the context of the drama in order to control the action, create tension, engage or challenge others in the group and develop the narrative.
Poetic activities	*Conventions focusing on/creating the 'symbolic potential' of the drama*
Forum Theatre	Action by a small group or an individual in front of the whole group, who observe and own the action. They can intervene in it, provide commentary and advice, suggest replays or re-workings of the action, question those in a scene or even replace them.
Captioning	Students devise captions, headlines, labels, titles or select short quotations which anchor the moment they have created visually. The short text provides an interpretation of the moment or a summary or perhaps raises further questions about it.
Reflective activities	*Conventions which underline the inner thoughts of the drama or enable review of the drama from inside its dramatic context*
Freeze Frame, Marking the Moment or Tableaux	Small groups or individuals freeze the action or mark it at a key moment where a new understanding has occurred for them. This could be achieved visually (through creating a still image) or through other means such as speech, poetry or mime. Others observe and pass comment on the way this key moment has been captured.
Thought-tracking	The action is stopped so that those in role can express their inner thoughts and feelings and distinguish these from what they have made explicit outwardly.
Group Sculpture	Volunteers from the group are modelled into a shape, sculpture, monument or exhibit by others in the class to represent an aspect of the topic/text being explored. The images created can often be abstract and enable students to develop collective interpretations.
Conscience Alley	The group divides into two parallel lines facing each other. A person in role walks between the lines and individuals on each side say what is on the person's conscience as they pass. The two lines could represent different aspects or views of the dilemma the character is facing.

Different dramatic techniques: These could include: varying volume, tone and pace, use of pause, gesture, movement and staging, choral speaking, monologue and dramatic irony. These apply to both scripted and improvized performances.

Range of activities should include:

> c) individual and group improvisation and performance
> d) devising, scripting and performing plays.

Curriculum opportunities:

> g) watch live performances in the theatre wherever possible to appreciate how action, character, atmosphere, tension and themes are conveyed
> h) participate actively in drama workshops and discuss with actors, playwrights, directors and other drama professionals the impact and meaning of different ways of performing and staging drama, wherever possible. (From QCA 2007a: *Programme of study for key stage 3 and attainment targets*)

6.8.2   Drama in English examinations

At KS4 and at Post-16 level, each examination board takes a slightly different approach to assessing students' understanding of play scripts. Writing about plays is often assessed via coursework. This approach can enable students to engage with the plays in more creative ways than through a written examination. For example, they might explore varying interpretations of the plays through analysis of film and live theatre productions they have watched. The plays listed earlier in this chapter include many texts that frequently feature on set text lists. For precise details about the way plays are assessed by each examination board you should check the exam specifications on the various exam board websites (listed in Chapter 2) and talk to experienced teachers in your placement schools. Whether you are teaching a play for coursework or final examination, if a production arrives nearby then you should try to arrange a theatre visit for your students. Make sure you seek advice about how to carry out the risk assessments required for such visits and the exact form of words the school will require you to use in any letters home requesting parental consent and payment donations. Although this might seem to involve a lot of organization, the shared experience of seeing a play should make it worthwhile. Early each term the *Guardian* newspaper publishes lists of all the set plays in production around the country. Keep an eye out for reviews too and collect them to use with your students.

6.9   Shakespeare

William Shakespeare has his own special place in the English curriculum (in England and Wales at least) in that he is the only author whom students are required to study throughout their compulsory and post-compulsory secondary school education. They are examined on his work at GCSE and AS/A2. At KS3 (in England) a new form of teacher assessment, to replace SATs, was due to be announced, following consultation, after this book went to press.

How has he come to have such an illustrious position? Is it merited in your view? Why should students be tested on their understanding of his work? These are questions which, as a beginning teacher, you will need to think about (and have views on). Shakespeare moved centre stage, in curriculum terms, following the publication in 1984 of *English 5–16: Curriculum Matters 1* (DES). This document was a precursor of the 1989 Cox Report that led to the first National Curriculum. Leach (1992) states that Cox had four reasons for wanting to include Shakespeare in the National Curriculum:

1) the wisdom encompassed in 'great literature' such as that of Shakespeare
2) the notion that 'great works' are central to our culture and literary heritage, therefore every child must be introduced to them
3) the influential nature of Shakespeare's language (and his extraordinary use of it)
4) the insights into human character offered by Shakespeare.

She also highlights two other reasons:

5) Shakespeare's place in or influence on the development of the English language
6) Deprivation of such language study could deprive students of the chance to develop their competence in using Standard English.

One of the leading advocates of the teaching of Shakespeare in schools in the twentieth and early twenty-first century was Rex Gibson. Founder of the highly influential Shakespeare in Schools project, Gibson abhorred the desk-bound nature of so much Shakespeare teaching which he saw as being weighed down by centuries of scholarship. He was committed to giving students the opportunities to explore the richness of Shakespeare's language through practical classroom activities. His inspirational training programmes for teachers influenced many teachers' approaches to Shakespeare (including mine): we were encouraged to move back the desks and bring the language of Shakespeare's scripts to life. Gibson's *Teaching Shakespeare* (1998) remains one of the essential texts for all beginning teachers. One of its central tenets is that 'successful Shakespeare teaching is learner-centred. It acknowledges that every student seeks to create his or her own meaning, rather than passively soak up information' (Gibson 1998: 9). This is a comment which should be made about the study of any author's work. Gibson also saw successful classroom Shakespeare as being a collaborative, social activity which should invite students and teachers to participate in an 'imaginative conspiracy' in their classrooms (ibid.: 13) – similar to that experienced between actors and an audience in a theatre. He recognized that teachers may well come to Shakespeare with memories of badly taught, dry lectures in which the plays were weighed down by academic notes. He urged them to be enthusiastic about the plays, responsive to new insights that their own students could offer in the classroom and to avoid the temptation of 'bardolatry' (ibid.: 154) which could put their students off.

Gibson's active approaches are many and various. They require careful classroom organization as they embrace whole-class, large-group 'companies', small-group, pair and individual work. If you plan well and use them in a balanced way your students will develop their own responses to Shakespeare's language much more readily. You might also find that the activities could influence your approach to other texts. The activities include some excellent strategies for understanding the thoughts or 'sense units' (ibid.: 166) of a dramatic speech, gaining a feeling for the rhythms of the speeches and savouring the rich variety of the language. These include:

- 'Walking the line' – each student walks around the room (in whatever direction they choose) speaking a line at a time and making a sudden ninety-degree turn at the end of each line.
- 'Walking the punctuation' – similar to above but turning sharp right or left with every punctuation mark or every full stop.
- 'Walking your sense unit' – students walk as above but they make their own decisions about when to turn according to where/when they sense a change in the direction of thought.
- 'Performing an everyday action' – students speak small units of speech as they perform everyday tasks such as making a cup of tea, putting on make-up, counting up money or, in pairs, such as carrying a heavy load or throwing a ball to each other. This can cause the speaker to say the words afresh, breaking them up slightly differently and causing new insights to emerge.
- 'Conversation' – partners speak alternate sense units or punctuated sections of a soliloquy, thus emphasizing the internal conversation which seems to take place in the script.
- 'Echoes' – in small groups one student slowly speaks the lines and the others echo every word connected with war, jealousy, suspicion or whatever the underlying theme might be. This helps them to develop a sense of how Shakespeare creates atmosphere through his use of language.
- 'Insult Generator' – this can provide an introduction to character work, to the richness of Shakespeare's language or simply be a way of enabling everyone in the group to speak some Shakespeare without fear and have some fun. The teacher prepares a sheet with three columns of Shakespearean words. Students construct their own insults by selecting a word from each column. They either walk round the room insulting each other or devise an insulting conversation with a partner. They could add 'thou' to the beginning of their insult but otherwise must only use the words on the sheet, i.e.

scurvy	hare-brained	pantaloon	viperous
pigeon-livered	puke-stocking		

- Since Gibson first wrote about this activity many different versions are now available in textbooks and on the internet (for an example go to www.pangloss.com/seidel/shake_rule.html, accessed 14 October 2008).

Whether you are teaching a Shakespeare play or any other drama script, the students' enjoyment and understanding will be markedly increased if they are able to see a live production. A trip to Stratford-upon-Avon is worth considering and a day spent there can include a Birthplace visit, Ann Hathaway's cottage and a play. If you want to develop

students' understanding of the context in which his plays were performed then I think watching a performance at Shakespeare's Globe Theatre at Bankside in London is an even better option. The season runs from May to October and productions are staged in all weathers. Groundlings tickets are very cheap and the theatre offers a number of extras for education groups.

Both the Royal Shakespeare Company (RSC) and the Globe websites are invaluable sources of archive material such as production stills, video clips, design and backstage information to support your teaching. Go to:

> www.rsc.org.uk
> www.shakespeares-globe.org/globeeducation/

(both accessed 14 October 2008)

6.9.1   Shakespeare and examinations

Students' understanding of Shakespeare is tested in different ways in English schools at the end of KS3, KS4 and at Post-16 level. Until October 2008, teachers chose from two plays at KS3 and students were required to answer questions focusing on set sections (not necessarily whole scenes). The first appearance of Shakespeare in these test papers (and the introduction of the tests themselves) was vigorously contested in 1993 when they were originally introduced and boycotted by many schools. However, preparation for these tests sadly dominated many Year 9 students' experience of English, even though many of them appeared to study *only* the two scenes they would be tested on, in isolation from the rest of the play. This reductive approach gave students no sense of the play as a text written for performance and bypassed many of the practical approaches advocated by Gibson (1998), Leach (1992) and others. With the scrapping of the statutory English tests at KS3, this strangulation of Shakespeare is, thankfully, at an end and teachers should in future have far greater flexibility to choose plays and plan teaching strategies and learning outcomes which are appropriate for their own students. For further announcements about the form of the classroom teacher assessments which will replace SATs, keep an eye on announcements on the National Assessment Agency website at www.naa.org.uk and at www.qca.org.uk.

At KS4 (for GCSE) currently the coursework options offered by some examination boards appear to provide greater opportunities for engagement with different interpretations and productions as well as consideration of the social and historical contexts in which the plays were written. Shakespeare coursework is assessed for students' skills in reading. Although most students write their coursework, some boards give students the option to demonstrate their understanding of Shakespeare through an oral rather than a written piece. This option is not taken by many schools but it can be an excellent route for some students, especially those who are more confident orally than on paper. For further information about this you should check the examination boards' websites (see details in Chapter 2).

At Post-16 level Shakespeare remains one of the core authors to be studied for English A level. Each examination board includes the plays in different papers with different assessment weightings. Coursework options again offer opportunities for comparative work and exploration of different productions of plays by Shakespeare and other dramatists (see for example Edexcel's compulsory AS English Literature coursework unit *Explorations In Drama* for examination from 2009 onwards). Shakespeare is one of the authors on the Prescribed World Literature List for the International Baccalaureate (IB) Language A1. For their detailed study, students must choose one or two Shakespeare plays together with texts from other genres depending on their level of entry.

6.10   Conclusion

This chapter has shown how spoken texts, produced in many and various forms, are an exceptionally rich and immediate source to use in the classroom. They can also be the most inclusive and readily accessible forms to make, investigate, perform and listen to with your students. It has been argued that, if Shakespeare were alive today, he would be writing soap operas for television or film scripts or even graphic novels. The next chapter explores the opportunities that you will have for teaching and learning about such multimodal texts in your twenty-first-century classroom.

Multimodal and Moving Image Texts 7

7.1   Introduction

This chapter begins by exploring definitions of multimodal texts and moving image texts. These are terms for types of texts which have rapidly taken a central role in young people's everyday lives beyond the classroom and are slowly being acknowledged within school curricula, where more conventional print-based forms continue to hold sway. This chapter considers influential research into the reading and composition of these texts, together with approaches to teaching production and analysis and strategies for assessment. It includes sections on graphic novels, blogs and wikis, fan fiction and other social literacy practices and insights into the composition processes of a documentary film-maker.

There is a lot of overlap between the terms 'moving image' and 'multimodal'. As you would expect, moving image texts use moving images and include cartoons, silent films, blockbuster movies, television adverts and footage shot on mobile phones. Many of the images in these films are accompanied by sound effects, music and/or written text, which means the texts are also multimodal. Multimodal texts operate in two or more modes to create their meanings. Combinations of modes include:

- words and images (for example in a picture book or comic)
- images, words and sound (for example in a computer game)
- words/hypertexts, sound, digital photos and/or video clips (for example on a webpage).

Although the term multimodal is perhaps more readily associated with digitally constructed texts, many seemingly more conventional text types fit into this category. For example, think about the different modes in which a play script or a poem operate. These texts might have been written down but, when spoken aloud or performed to an audience, they also operate in other modes. In performance, a play script communicates to its audience through spoken utterances, sound effects and music, movement and visual effects. Watching a play at The Globe will confirm the multimodal nature of this experience. Poetry is the oldest multimodal text, developing from the oral tradition into written form. The written poem comes alive when performed, reaching out to a much wider audience (as anyone who has attended a Poetry Live! event or listened to the Poetry Archive on the web will affirm). I would argue that the act of reading the poem silently and experiencing Rosenblatt's 'event' (1978) of the poem in your head is the sign of a multimodal text at work.

7.2   Picture books, comics and graphic novels

Picture books, comics and graphic novels are also multimodal texts. The relationship between the visual and the verbal embodied in these texts has been given scant attention in mainstream curricula and yet they draw on visual conventions which should be learned by all readers if they are to develop their understanding of how meanings can be conveyed and participate fully in dynamic processes of communication. Linney (1995) notes that members of disadvantaged communities frequently have low levels of visual literacy and a limited awareness of these conventions which include: figure and fore/background distinctions; line and shape; space and pictorial depth; time and movement; shading; scaling; showing what is usually invisible; thought and speech bubbles; the meanings of pictorial symbols; and 'visual amputation' (where only parts of objects are shown within the frame) (Linney 1995: 49). Graham (1990), Lewis (2001), Styles and Arizipe (2002) and Johnston and Mangat (2003) have explored the importance of picture books in literacy learning, their constructions and how ethnic groups are represented within them. Styles and Arizipe (2002) show how young (primary-aged) readers can interact with images in ways which were not predicted by less observant adults.

Nevertheless, assessed opportunities for exploration of the visual and verbal within secondary school curricula tend to concentrate on their juxtaposition in the layout of print media texts such as advertisements or magazine covers. Why is this? The avoidance of hugely popular, complex and demanding texts such as graphic novels reveals a great deal about official notions of what constitutes literature. Nevertheless, the time is now ripe to recognize issues regarding visual grammar more fully within text selection, classroom learning and, even, assessment practices, and to make a case for classroom study of comics, graphic novels and picture books.

Comics and graphic novels present their stories in more accessible (but frequently no less subtle) ways than prose texts and are potentially more attractive to reluctant young male readers. Although comics feature in Media Studies teaching (including GCSE assessment), the use of *bandes dessinées* (the term preferred by many artists, from the French for 'drawn strips') in English classrooms is less common. Carol Fox (2007) describes how students can develop an understanding of narrative structure and such aspects as duration, proximity, narrative voice and repetition through reading comics and graphic novels. Belbin and Brick (2007) provide an amusing and useful introduction to the visual conventions of the form in 'If Shakespeare were alive today', in which a resurrected Leonardo da Vinci explains them to the Bard. An extract from this strip is shown in Figure 7.1.

For Fox, the compression of thought structures within texts like *Maus* (Spiegelman 2003) and use of repeated frames suggest strong links with other text types – especially poetry – and present an opportunity for readers to explore potential crossovers between seemingly discrete genres.

Comics and graphic novels also have an important, but under-acknowledged, role in developing young people's critical engagement with social, political and personal issues. This can be seen in the work of graphic novelists such as Raymond Briggs, Joe Sacco and Marjane Satrapi amongst others, who explore living in times of conflict and oppression. In terms of comics, John Stuart Clark has collaborated with other artists and writers to produce a series of six UNICEF comics designed to raise awareness about aspects of the

Figure 7.1 An extract from 'If Shakespeare were alive today' (Belbin and Brick 2007). Reprinted by kind permission of the authors

United Nations Convention on the Rights of the Child (Clark 1998–2003). They include stories about asylum seekers, bullying, sexual abuse, a child's right to education and the treatment of young people in detention. Circulated free, these comics have reached over 500,000 young readers.

Appendix 1 includes a list of picture books and graphic novels, texts which would work well in a secondary English classroom and are worth reading whatever your age.

7.3 Research into reading and composing digital multimodal texts

The interactive nature of reading is arguably heightened when engaging with a multimodal text because, in many cases, the text will require you to take action beyond merely turning the page and thinking about your response to what has been read. It makes more explicit/ complex demands on you to intervene in the text, to enter into its composition and become one of its authors. The distinctions between the acts of reading and writing and the roles of different participants can become blurred with digital multimodal texts especially: 'we become digital versions of ourselves' (Thomas 2007: 161). This notion of blurring extends to: the places and times where these texts are constructed; the nature of the texts themselves, which not only defy conventional genre categorization but also blur distinctions between topics and tones; the ownership of the texts; and the identity of the author(s).

If we return to the derivation of text from the Latin verb *texere*: to weave, then the weavers/ writers of that text and the users/readers of it are the same people, their acts of writing and reading occurring simultaneously and in a multiplicity of locations. The multimodal text is not a cloth made by one weaver using a particular thread and previously defined pattern to create a finished form. Buckingham writes of the 'convergence of previous distinct cultural forms and practices' (2003: 173) which occurs in the production of digital texts, a convergence which is led by a profit motive. For others the text is a collaborative exercise, spliced together or 'remixed' (Lankshear and Knobel 2007: 8) with many different threads continually rethreaded by other weavers/users to alter the look, feel, sound and shape of the fabric. Its surfaces can be appliquéd, embroidered, dyed or patchworked with other texts to make new hybrid texts which are embedded with many different associations, priorities, emphases, perspectives and connotations. It can be threaded with routes that lead away from one fabric and into another. The new text-fabric is a twenty-first-century material, a shape-shifter responsive to changes in the mood and context of its many readers/writers. These users may be less concerned with an end product or official recognition through publication but more interested in the process of making and experiencing the text as it develops or in the presentation of themselves as collaborators in this process. These experiences could include posting a comment or a hyperlink on a blog, creating a new storyline in an online gaming programme, or redrafting another wiki contributor's draft of a poem. If the maker has the appropriate computer hardware, software and high-speed internet access then these texts can be made for little cost. It is, however, essential to acknowledge that equality of access to the means of production remains an issue in many communities even in the digital age.

Within the collaborative making of multimodal texts there is a sense of 'relatedness' (Lankshear and Knobel 2007: 13): people create and participate in texts in what Gee calls 'affinity spaces' (Gee 2004: 83). He argues that these are very different from the spaces where learning occurs in schools: these are cyberspaces where like-minded individuals, sharing a common passion or interest, can actively make and remake meanings about subjects which are dear to them. Relationships develop primarily through interests rather than through contextual factors such as race, gender or class. The collaborative groupings created within these spaces challenge perceptions about when and where text-making can occur: it can happen at any moment and originate from anywhere in the world with an open internet connection. The immediacy of access to all kinds of texts (through websites, online library catalogues, online games, blogs, etc.) and to potential collaborators challenges the traditional dominance of offline print media produced within clearly defined publication timelines and frameworks. It also challenges the traditional identities of students and teachers by introducing opportunities for learning allegiances with collaborators of different ages/ levels of experience outside the parameters of, for example, the traditional school timetable and the classroom space. For teachers who are beginning to work with multimodal texts (and the multi-literacies which such texts rely on for their creation), Cynthia Lewis reminds us that there are some key issues to consider about the practices afforded by such new technologies and the contexts in which these practices are situated (Lewis 2007). It will not suffice for a teacher to have participated in curricular training in use of (for example) Blogspot, Dreamweaver or Blackboard: they must also engage with the 'new mindsets, practices and identities' (Lewis 2007: 230) that arise from new technologies and types of communication. She identifies these as being concerned with:

- agency – arriving at an awareness of how a domain works and how one might work within that domain
- performativity – the identities of those who construct the texts and how they invent, present, reflect on and publish their individual and collaborative selves at different stages in the process
- circulation – how the texts are circulated across space and time, the speed with which they are circulated, who is included and excluded from this process and how it is controlled. (Lewis 2007)

Participation in a multimodal text is perhaps the only true way to learn about how they work and to realize their potential for developing literacy in the broadest sense. Not all texts will ever be suitable for classroom use (nor should they be) but, as beginning English teachers, you should take the time to reflect on the types of digital texts which some of you and infinitely more of your students will already be familiar with and the literacy practices which they will have engaged in. In this way your teaching will be informed by these practices and be open to the possibilities they could offer you. You should also not make assumptions about the level of student competence in using the technology. They may be less fearful of it than adults but they can still be frustrated by its failings or lack the information that will help them to make progress (Buckingham 2003). Gee points to the danger of leaving new literacies out of school curricula, with the result that only those with access to digital technology and resources outside of their classrooms will be sufficiently versed in the use of these textual practices to be able to participate effectively in society as future citizens (Gee 2004). The need to acknowledge such practices was clearly demonstrated to Ross Harrison, a beginning English and Media teacher, in the following classroom experiences:

> Early in my second school placement I was engaged in a discussion on knights and chivalry with a top set Year 7 in preparation for studying 'The Lady of Shalott'. While brainstorming 'heroic deeds', one particularly enthusiastic pupil remarked that a knight could be sent on dangerous missions like assassinations. A little perplexed, I quizzed him further on what exactly he meant. 'They would be given a marker,' he said. 'They would have to spy on their target, get information on them then kill them.' I was just about to suggest to him that his idea wasn't exactly what I was looking for, when he quickly followed up with, 'Like *Assassin's Creed*.' It was clear now. *Assassin's Creed* is a videogame for the Xbox 360 and PlayStation 3 consoles, which puts the player in the role of a medieval 'assassin' saving the Holy Land from corruption. . . . What interested me about the pupil's comments was his understanding of the causality, of the internal (that is, in-game) narrative constructed by the three simple actions involved – get marker, gather intelligence, conduct assassination. I say simple, and in execution it is, but underneath lies something thrillingly complex. It displays narrative choice, and an agency quite intrinsic to the medium . . .

In a second example he explores the impact of students' exposure to narrative texts outside school on their response to classroom-based writing tasks and his own growing awareness that reading for pleasure is not limited to reading print texts. He describes a Year 8 student's reworking of *Boy* (Dahl 1986) into 'The further adventures of Boy':

> . . . it was an extremely imaginative story involving Dahl coming across warring, yet 'modernised' (i.e. Westernised) tribes in the jungle. I asked where he had gotten his inspiration from. At this point he enthusiastically told me about *Warhammer* and *Civilisation*, two strategy-cum-RPGs that allow the player to influence political and social factions, and build allegiances or enemies depending on their actions in the game. In *Civilisation*, he told me, he could influence the development of tribal societies by offering them Western assets such as money and arms in return for their co-operation. I was both impressed and a little astounded that this pupil, not traditionally academically able, had not only spoken fluently about quite advanced concepts for his age, but had also managed to apply and rework them into a short story involving Roald Dahl in 1930s Africa. It seems his experience with constructing in-game narratives had given him confidence in his own creative ability, allowing him to construct his own narrative. (From Harrison 2008, reproduced by permission of the author)

The National Curriculum has finally acknowledged the need for learning about multi-modal texts which, it must be reiterated, are not just digital texts. However, the 2007 programmes of study do not exemplify very fully the types of texts which might come under the multimodal umbrella. The next section looks in more detail at different multimodal texts, and explores issues of reading and writing these texts in and beyond the classroom.

7.4   Websites

In the early days of the internet websites were perceived as informational texts but with the arrival of Web 2 and increased interactivity, millions of people around the world now use websites for very different purposes, whether these be for: information (such as research for leisure activities or to look up 'facts' for homework); shopping; entertainment (gambling, watching a film, looking at holiday photos, writing an episode of fan fiction); social communication or critical discussion (with avatars, like-minded individuals or long-lost schoolfriends, to make their protests heard, to sign petitions or simply to exist in a different identity in a virtual world). The list of reasons and purposes for reading are endless and overlapping. Embedded hyperlinks within pages enable us to skip and flick through vast multimodal libraries, open many windows at once, plan routes through our own reading and 'bookmark' key sites for return visits. On our return, these texts may have changed, moved location or even disappeared entirely, such is their ephemeral and transmutable nature. Online reading is in the ascendancy, particularly among 'digital natives' (Prensky 2001: 1) such as teenagers. According to a month-long 2008 National Year of Reading survey, song-lyric websites, computer game cheats online and their own blog or fan fiction are ranked in the top five text types that teenagers enjoy reading (see www.yearofreading.org.uk for further details (accessed 14 October 2008)).

7.4.1   Reading on screen

When talking about web activity, we still use the lexis of reading and talk of pages and bookmarks. However, in accessing any website, you are immediately confronted with a number of different options about how to read the screen, options which are different from those faced when reading a graphic novel or a film. Digital natives among us probably surf and use sites without a second thought, but ask yourself: do you start reading at the top left-hand-side in line with western reading conventions and steadily move to the bottom of the page? Or does your eye immediately rove to the furthest right column? Do you ignore all the different sections and immediately steer your mouse to the menu options? Do you click on a hyperlink in the middle of the screen and ignore everything else on the page?

Gunther Kress's theoretical framework for multimodality (2003) and research undertaken by Bearne *et al.* (2007) for UKLA both raise issues about our web-based reading journeys which would not only be interesting to explore with your students but should have a bearing on your classroom approaches. Kress warns that we need to be attentive to the different modes operating within a text and to realize that, although the processes of reading on screen are not the same as the sustained concentrated attentive reading of, for example, a novel, they are no less complex or demanding. When reading a novel, you are led by the author and the overall text design along a clearly coded path (Kress 2003). In following this path, your role as a reader is to decode, interpret, reflect on and transform what is laid before you into images, feelings and so on. Unless you deliberately choose to skip a paragraph or read the end of the book first, you read the words in each clause, sentence, page and chapter in an order previously determined by the writer.[1] In reading on screen, you enter into a different dynamic: you move away from a coded pathway and are freed to make your own decisions, to apply 'principles of relevance to a page which is (relatively) open in its organisation and consequently offers a range of possible paths, perhaps infinitely many more' (Kress 2003: 162). Bearne *et al.* set out to explore whether the skills required for reading paper-based texts were different from those on screen. Observed reading processes included:

- using a range of strategies to make sense of multi-modal on-screen texts
- browsing and actively searching by topic or key word/idea, selecting and retrieving information
- attending to (and interpreting) different elements of an on-screen text including sound, movement, image and word
- following/guiding on-screen texts, commenting on structure, organisation and presentational features as well as the text-maker's point of view and the effect of the text on the reader
- becoming a discriminating reader, adjusting reading approaches to fit demands of the text and task, sustaining and revisiting reading
- relating texts to social and cultural experience (Bearne *et al.* 2007: 5).

This range of strategies points to the development of a set of sophisticated reading skills. The research team asked whether the persistence shown by many of the observed readers did not in fact demonstrate a type of sustained reading which differed from that demanded by an extended, print-based text. They also questioned the extent to which the observed reading was 'extended and challenged in classrooms' (Bearne *et al.* 2007: 29) in school contexts where critical reading of web-based and other multimodal texts is still in its infancy. Their concerns pertain to:

a) the lack of models of on-screen multimodal texts in classrooms where teachers have different levels of experience of reading/analysing such texts
b) the multimodal sources used which do not equate to their students' own reading experiences or preferences.

In the early years of media teaching in the UK there was a popular misconception (among politicians especially) that TV soap operas were low-level leisure-time viewing, highly unsuitable for classroom study, and that their inclusion somehow degraded the subject of English. In the digital age, popular websites seem to have become the focus of this misconception. Participation in these websites and other out-of-school literacy activities may be deemed by some to be a distraction from learning but, thanks to the work of Street (1995), Lankshear and Knobel (2003), Gee (2004) and others regarding sociocultural theories of literacy, the texts and literacy practices encompassed within these milieux are now recognized as a legitimate field for study. Morgan (1998) and Buckingham (2003) remind us that social theories of literacy challenge the textual emphases predominant in literature learning because the social, economic and historical contexts of production, distribution and viewing demand consideration alongside more conventional literary foci on critical analysis and composition. This does not mean that all such practices can or should lend themselves to classroom study. Nevertheless, your work as English teachers should be informed by both the social and the academic literacy practices of your students: to marginalize them is to undermine what Bourdieu calls their 'cultural capital' (1986). Jennifer Stone (2007) has identified the range of different genres young people participate in when using popular websites. These include narrative, descriptive, satire, discography, review, interview and song lyrics. She evaluates the intertextuality and multimodality of the websites together with the literacy skills required of student participants (in terms of how they cope with lengthy sentence structures and complex vocabulary). Stone contrasts these webtexts with less demanding examples of biographical writing that American students are asked to read in school.

This may well be a suitable point for you to pause and consider your own on-screen reading practices and the construction and content of the websites you visit. How will you model these and engage your students in critique? You could first think about mapping your own screen reading or logging and annotating (with the aid of your browser's 'history' list) the path(s) that you take in the first ten minutes after entering a website. What reading processes do you engage in? Which sites or parts of sites do you read in a sustained way? Which do you learn from? Which do you get sidetracked by? Which hyperlinks do you follow or ignore? Why?

Now think about analysing your reading critically. You might find the questions in Figure 7.2 helpful. They can be adapted for discussion with students about their preferred websites or for comparative work on websites on similar topics.

The above questions could be used with any multimodal text. Your own subject knowledge and previous experiences of different modes as both consumer and producer will inevitably influence your approach to teaching all kinds of texts. Burn and Durran suggest that 'in the making of complex multimodal texts formal attention to the different modes is uneven, depending on curricular legitimation, academic training and the degree to which different modes are formally fixed in grammatical systems' (2007: 58). In their view, consideration of the use of dramatic speech and action within such texts is notably absent from traditional media pedagogies. Their fine book, *Media Literacy in Schools* (2007), makes a strong case for inclusion of these modes. It offers a model of media education firmly rooted in learning about the media through practical experience and critical reflection on media processes. In exploring critical frameworks for analysing multimodal texts you should think about how your students can be guided to read critically and how their own multimodal texts could be assessed. Wyatt-Smith and Kimber (2005) have explored the assessable 'multiliterate

Textual organization

What do you notice about the way the text is laid out on the page(s)? How is it organized? What sorts of headings, sections, captions, boxes and menus are used? Are the hyperlinks obvious?

Design features

What about the colours and fonts used? Are they well chosen to create a particular look to the page? Are they readable? Is there a coherent design at work?

Navigation and interaction

Does the text entice you to interact with it? Are you guided in your reading? Are you drawn from one section of the page to another? Can you read it in any order? How easy is it to navigate from one page to another or from this site to other sites (and back again)? How easy is it to search for a specific topic within the site?

Lexis

What can you say about the lexis? Is it intended for the general reader or the expert in a particular subject? Does it acknowledge an audience of a particular age or level of experience or both in its choices of words and grammar? Is the text accurate, well written and clearly expressed? Is it littered with spelling and grammatical errors? Is it written in complex, lengthy sentences? Is the vocabulary simple or sophisticated?

Visual images

What can you observe about the choices of images – the still pictures, animations, video, logos and symbols? What impression do they create? Are they high-quality images? How are they arranged on the page? How have they been chosen? What do they appear to symbolize or represent? What have you noticed about the juxtapositions of images? How do images, written text and sound work together?

Sound

What about the sounds on the page? What can you hear as you navigate around it, click your mouse or carry out other actions? What sort of ambience is there in the on-screen environment? What impact do the sounds have on your response to the page? Can you control the sound? Are you given choices about it?

Your response

What can you say about your own reading of the page(s)? What is the overall impact of reading? Have you bought or sold something, gained a greater understanding of an issue or simply enjoyed looking at the site? Do you feel you have learned something from reading? Have you been made to laugh, to feel curious, angry or confused?

Have you been invited to post comments or to vote ? How easy was this? How aware are you of other users' participation in the site? What do you know about these contributors?

Will you revisit the site, bookmark it or recommend it to others? Why? How does it compare with other sites on similar topics?

How reliable do you feel the text is that you are reading? What are the indicators of this reliability? Will you double-check elsewhere?

Figure 7.2 Investigating your screen reading

features of performance' in multimodal texts produced by students. They question how teachers can move beyond an assessment model which traditionally privileges monomodal texts (print-based and sometimes oral) 'to capture the student as learner: a learner who selects, evaluates and reconstitutes multimodal resources for meaning making' (2005: 25). They suggest an assessment model consisting of four criteria: e-proficiency; content; cohesion and design (see Figure 7.3).

Performance Terrain in Shaping Online, Multimodal Texts		
Criterion 1: E-Proficiency (in this view, proficiency goes beyond control of technical operations, extending to discriminating use)		
Criterion 2: Cohesion (Unifying the structure, representation, organization of ideas, links)	**Criterion 3: Content** (Working with existing knowledge to create new knowledge)	**Criterion 4: Design** (Creating an aesthetic, artful design)
In designing the text, the student has:	*In using existing knowledge, the student has:*	*In designing the text, the student has:*
Structured the text utilizing appropriate headings and subheadings for linking ideas and guiding the reader	Provided the intended audience with sufficient and relevant information	Selected relevant images that work in conjunction with written, auditory language to convey meaning
Provided strategic organization that invites reader interactivity with internal explanatory links as well as links to other related sites/texts	Structured or chunked information appropriately, both within and across a node (paragraph, slide, page)	Chosen visual and spatial features that achieve harmony (background colour/font selection), balance of design and aesthetic appeal
Provided appropriate structures, e.g. functioning links, menu, consistent linking style to facilitate interactivity	Manipulated written, visual and auditory language to achieve defined purpose/s	Combined written, visual and auditory language to convey meaning
Clear navigation/linking within and between nodes/screens/sites	Transformed/reshaped existing information, combining different sources to formulate 'new' knowledge – that is, going beyond cutting-and-pasting	Observed the grammars and logics of verbal (traditional grammar), visual (positioning, symbolic representation) and electronic text (specific logics related to particular software choice)

Figure 7.3 Assessment criteria for multimodal text production (Wyatt-Smith, C. and Kimber, K. (2005) 'Valuing and evaluating student-generated online multimodal texts: rethinking what counts', *English in Education*, 39 (2), 22–43. (Reproduced by permission of the authors and NATE.))

7.4.2 Hyperlinks

One of the key features of any website is the hyperlinks embedded within it which give the reader/user access to many different and immediate pathways between linked texts. This affordance of the web environment offers opportunities for exploring intertextual links between visual, sound and print modes. These can open up alternative interpretations of a subject through new juxtapositions of texts. Beach and O'Brien (2005) suggest ways of exploiting this affordance to enable students to gain a clearer understanding of intertextuality. For example, one group of tenth grade (UK Year 11) students were asked to construct links from quotations in *Fahrenheit 451* to contemporary song lyrics and film clips portraying the prevalence of control, power and censorship in society. Another group investigated intercontextuality by reconstructing advertising images. In spite of these innovative approaches, Beach and O'Brien, in a similar vein to Bearne *et al.* (2007), express concerns that critical enquiry is not always a prominent feature of students' reading and creation of intertextual links. In analysing a project on multimodal poetry texts and literary devices carried out by seventh-graders (Year 8) and pre-service teachers, the authors identify three types of links representing three different levels of critical thinking:

- an 'iconic function' was used to illustrate another text
- an 'indexical function' was used to extend a text to show shared meaning
- a 'symbolic function' was used to question the meaning of a text. (Beach and O'Brien 2005: 50)

Their categories indicate another potential method of assessing some of the skills used in multimodal text production and make a useful contribution to discussion of multimodal texts at a time when their assessment is not widespread in mainstream English curricula.

This section has so far dealt with websites in general. We will now turn our attention to some specific types of websites and the affordances that they offer for reading and creating texts.

7.4.3 Blogs

Blogs were introduced with other non-fiction texts in Chapter 5. This section considers the affordances that these multimodal texts offer their users and implications for classroom use. Your students may never have read a literary diary but they are more likely to have had some experience of reading and/or writing blogs. The blogosphere, consisting of over 70 million blogs (Technorati 2007) is not alien text territory for them and the potential for using blogs in the classroom is considerable. Blogs have spawned many subgenres including personal, political, fashion and literary blogs. These all focus on individual views – views expressed usually in written form by created online identities who perform their texts to known and unknown audiences in cyberspace and hope to receive feedback. The act of writing for an audience is very strong for some of these writer-performers. For my ongoing research into published writers' composition processes, popular blogger, Troubled Diva, told me: 'My writing is very largely performance-based and I am used to having instant feedback for everything I write. In fact I am so steeped in blogging and journalistic culture that I can barely see the point of writing *without* an audience.' He goes on to explore how he 'play[s] to the gallery' of his audience, an audience which helps to 'shape' content rather than collaborating in his blog writing. Although blogs have arguably crossed over into the mainstream and have become a popular social literacy practice, there is still a sense that 'insider' knowledge is needed before you can truly belong to a blogging community. I say this as someone who has, so far, resisted writing a blog but posts comments on other blogs and is fascinated by the constructed personas of bloggers and their reasons for blogging.

Eide and Eide (2005) argue that blogs promote different types of thinking:

- critical and analytical (bloggers are actively reading and engaging in texts rather than passively viewing them)
- creative, intuitive, and associational thinking (blogs have to be constantly updated and the best thrive on 'outlandish' updates or spontaneous associations leading to new links)
- analogical thinking (professional communicators, lawyers, thinkers and academics who are members of the blogosphere enable students to witness argument in action).

They can also:

- be a powerful medium for increasing access and exposure to quality information
- combine the best of solitary reflection and social interaction.

Research into blogging is a fast-growing aspect of 'new literacies' research. Davies and Merchant (2007) suggest that the new affordances offered by blog technology enable researchers to explore and reflect on themselves as both subjects and objects in a medium which challenges conventional thinking about what it means to be a writer. They highlight the collaborative nature of the medium and the 'allegiances' (2007: 184) struck up between bloggers who share knowledge and reference/hyperlink each other's blogs. A blogger's textual practices also spill over into use of other online forms such as Flickr or MSN and develop a sense of 'shared endeavour' (ibid.: 176) both on and, in some cases, off line as a result of the afforded interactivity.

Within the classroom context, Ray (2006, as cited in Wood 2008) describes four main uses of blogs:

1. *Blogs to communicate*: an electronic bulletin board as a fast method of communication with other interested parties, such as students, colleagues and parents.
2. *Blogs as instructional resources*: homework support provided through publication of tips, explanations, models or use of hyperlink libraries to help structure student research.
3. *Blogs as collaborative tools*: group student blogs to facilitate collaboration on investigations, group novel or script writing, etc. The blog enables participants to reflect on their creative/investigative processes.
4. *Blogs as showcases for student projects*: a means of publishing student work on the internet, which can be easily accessed by members of the school community.

Blogs are not without potential problems, however. Equality of access remains a key issue and student safety is paramount: bloggers create virtual identities for themselves and students could fall prey to online bullies or predators. In addition you should weigh up the ease of setting up a blog against the increasing amounts of time it could take you to write, update, and monitor as it develops.

If you do want to set up a blog for an English project, www.blogger.com is probably the easiest site to use: set-up is free and it has an intuitive interface (Parker 2008). If you want to interact with other English teaching bloggers and share resources and reflections on classroom practice, you could sign up to the fast-growing www.englishspace.org. You could also visit Ewan McIntosh's www.edu.blogs.com for regular reflections on social software, its use in schools, research and other subjects (all websites accessed 14 October 2008).

7.4.4   Wikis

First developed in 1995, wikis are a type of blog. Their name is derived from *wiki-wiki*, a Hawaiian word meaning 'quick'. They facilitate collaborative writing online in ways which surpass what can be achieved in a blog. Individuals within a wiki community can directly intervene in texts written by others to edit, develop or even delete their work. The prime example of a wiki is *Wikipedia* – an online encyclopedia containing, at the time of writing, over 2.2 million articles written and rewritten by strangers all round the world. The scale and scope of this wiki is 'fact-encirclingly huge . . . idiosyncratic, careful, messy, funny, shocking and full of shimmering controversies' (Baker 2008: 5). Baker conveys the enjoyable and potentially addictive nature of participating in Wikipedia. He also explains the terminology used by participants at different levels within this online community. It would be interesting to explore Wikipedia with students to consider issues of truth and reliability and investigate:

- how they could contribute themselves and edit other people's work
- how their contributions are received
- how long a new entry exists online
- how and why decisions are made to delete people's work.

Most wikis consist of templates of a contents page and other outline pages which anyone can then develop in their own style. They enable a community to work together online, either to produce a publishable product or to share and comment on work in progress. Some moodles or VLEs (examples of virtual learning environments) like Blackboard now include wikis, chatrooms and blogs along with additional features to promote reflection and synchronous and asynchronous communication like email groups and discussion boards. However, these elements are only accessible to the registered users of that specific online community. Although a VLE-based wiki can be safer because of its enrolment restrictions, if you want to set up a wiki which could be accessed by students working in different schools or on other continents then it might be preferable to set up your own. This can be done very quickly. For an example go to www.pbwiki.com (accessed 14 October 2008) and follow the steps in the 'educators' section: you can be under way in five minutes. When creating any online environment you do need to be very aware of cyber safety issues. Make sure all involved (and parents/carers) are also aware of these. Ensure that:

a) your wiki is set up so that only those students you want to contribute can do so (other people will be able to browse the wiki)
b) students are very careful about how much personal information they publish online
c) passwords for wiki managers and contributors are changed regularly.

7.4.5   Using a wiki – a case study

A Canadian colleague, Janette Hughes, and I set up a wiki to research the affordances it could offer for developing beginning teachers' skills and confidence in teaching poetry. Established in September 2007, the poetry wiki has enabled a mixed convenience sample group of 56 pre-service English and Language Arts teachers from the UK and Canada to share: reflections about the nature of poetry; first experiences of teaching poetry; teaching resources; and drafts and edits of each others' poetry online. Some found this supportive medium gave them confidence to write and share their own poetry for the first time. One student wrote:

> I must confess that this is the first poem I have ever written and I think I severely over-used 'and' and 'the' which I tried to remove. Thanks, A, for the advice to break the lines down, etc. I have done that and I think it describes the sequence and commands of the traffic lights better. B, I also love your suggestion of 'pushed', 'pulled' and 'stretched' actually being manipulated by the text. I will try and contribute more to this page and to you, my fellow Haikus. I am in awe of 'We Danced Through the Ashes' [another poem posted on the site] and I think you have a real talent.

Others began to experiment with the multimodality offered by this medium: they pasted images which inspired their writing and hyperlinks to other poetry pages. After writing a haiku sequence, one student created a very powerful film of sounds and images inspired by his own work. Some, less successful, work with webcams was also tried. The relative ease with which you can paste in additional material was not fully exploited by the participants in this research. However, the wiki gave both researchers and beginning teachers much food for thought about how learning in their own cyberclassrooms can be developed further.

The nature of this 'insider research' (Lankshear and Knobel 2003, Davies and Merchant 2007) is not without its problems. In commenting on students' drafts, I was very conscious of my other roles and experiences as a tutor, assessor, poet and researcher. I tried to set these aside but, inevitably, they informed my responses and the way other participants reacted to them. Some students were understandably wary of the blank pages opening up in front of them and, in the early stages, preferred to post comments in the boxes below. When reading the screen, these boxes are less apparent. Some tentatively introduced their own work as a 'little poem' or their 'very very rough draft'. We asked everyone to make at least one posting in response to a series of definitions of poetry (like those in Chapter 4) so that they could at least see how the wiki environment worked. After that, the teachers were cajoled and reminded of the wiki's existence rather than subjected to heavy policing.

Some students responded to the wiki enthusiastically. A small number became frequent contributors to different groups, both to seek readers for their own poems and to share recommendations. They also began to reflect on themselves as writers and to comment on other people's work. Comments were generally polite, although often specifically focused on technical aspects of the drafts that they liked. Very few made direct interventions in others' draft work. Some seldom contributed, choosing to remain silent visitors. In evaluating the affordances of the wiki, it appears to have offered this group opportunities to:

- write and edit online at any time of night or day
- use a method which potentially takes away some of the fear of sharing drafts
- gain a wider range of perspectives on their writing
- share their views and experiences of poetry teaching with others
- learn about other teaching approaches they could use
- develop technological skills in multimodal communication through use of written, visual and sound modes.

These affordances could have an impact on the beginning teachers' developing classroom practice and attitudes to poetry. They have been arrived at without the difficulty of organizing additional face-to-face meetings during a very busy training year. The wiki has, however, placed extra demands on the two moderators' time (to monitor and respond to postings) and given the participants additional (albeit mainly optional) tasks to complete. Involvement in the wiki did not replace teaching sessions on poetry but supplemented these. Teacher participation was dependent on the availability of regular access to (preferably high-speed) internet connections. The Canadian teacher candidates were a small group and based at a 'laptop university' where this was not an issue. The UK-based students had greater variability of access at home, in their placement schools and in their HEI base – a factor which inevitably affected the number and regularity of contributions. Resourcing and teaching load will be key issues in planning future use of the wiki. (For more detail on the specific outcomes of this research, refer to Dymoke and Hughes 2008.)

7.4.6   Online gaming and fan fiction

Game playing is a multi-literate activity with the best games placing considerable cognitive demands on players (Buckingham 2003). Researchers including Black (2007), Steinkuehler (2005, 2007) and Thomas (2007) have focused their sociocultural literacy research on the online gaming activities of young adults. They are interested in the worlds that gamers inhabit and create when they socialize informally online in a 'new third place' (Steinkuehler 2005: 17) that exists beyond work and home and stress the need for educators and researchers to be much more aware of the 'capacity of such spaces to profoundly shape the cognition and culture of net-generation kids' (ibid.: 29), the same kids who may be failing to engage with the school curriculum.

Massively Multiplayer Online Gaming (MMOG) is online videogaming in which the players create their own digital characters (otherwise known as avatars) to play the games and interact with other avatars. The environments created by the software are alternative complex worlds akin to those of 'Middle-earth' in *The Hobbit* (Tolkien 1937) and *Dungeons and Dragons* (Gygax and Arneson 1974). *Dungeons and Dragons* was the forerunner of so many online Role Playing Games (RPGs) today in which groups form allegiances, slay monsters, fight other clans for control of land, trade goods and so on. *World of Warcraft* is the most popular game on the market. Others include *Lineage 1* and *Lineage 2* – the subject of much of Steinkuehler's research. MMOG is said to have 9.5 million participants worldwide who spend on average 20 hours a week in virtual worlds. Their participation mainly consists of conversation or different levels of written chat, which can take place simultaneously and focus on players' individual or shared actions in a game. In addition, they take part in multiple literacy practices both beyond and alongside the games. These include contribution to fan websites, blogs and discussion boards, creation of digital videos, manuals and writing fan fiction.

Fan fiction, the writing of fiction about/around an avatar or other characters in an online game or other text, can engage its creators in complex, sometimes collaborative, literacy practices such as text transformation and manipulation. Rebecca Black suggests fan fiction sites are learning environments whose emphasis is 'moving toward procedural knowledge that involves the acquisition of skills and strategies for learning how to learn and to continue learning' (2007: 133). She identifies how certain authors elicit social review and confirmation of their membership of a fan-fiction group from their online peers through public presentation of their work, reflection on the trials of writing it and display of their 'expert knowledge' (ibid.: 133). These online practices both blur and break the boundaries of narrative, literacy and concepts of identity (Thomas 2007). In a case study of two adolescent females (Tiana and Jandalf), Angela Thomas asks the young women to describe their creation of a piece of fan fiction. Their description (in Figure 7.4) emphasizes not only the complex drafting undertaken but how their work crosses genres and modes to create hybrid texts.

If you were to hear such constructive dialogue in an English classroom you would be extremely pleased. As educators we urgently need to consider how we can learn from and acknowledge these multimodal literacy practices when working with our students.

7.4.7 Other social software sites

Many of the comments about MMOG could also apply to *Second Life*®. Rather than being a competitive game, *Second Life*® is a virtual, 3D world in which, once enrolled, you can reside

> *The process we work through to create our fan fiction is to first role play the narrative out using Yahoo Instant Messenger. We go on Yahoo, sometimes spend about 5 minutes talking about where the plot is going, and then just write. If there's any confusion the narrators step in, or we use OOC (out of character) chatter to help out. But we rarely think about what we're doing, we just write like heck and get as much done as we can in a short time. When we get big plot bunnies [i.e. narrative plotline ideas], sometimes we email each other about them though. Usually though we just improvise . . . yeah . . . that's about it. We write so much better when we don't think about what's going on.*
>
> *The fan fiction is then written out by me. I save all the RPG [Role-Playing Game] chats and rewrite them from their script format into fan fiction that is more like standard narrative form.*
>
> (From: Thomas, A. (2007) 'Blurring and Breaking through the Boundaries of Narrative, Literacy and Identity in Adolescent Fan Fiction', in M. Knobel and C. Lankshear (eds) (2007), *A New Literacies Sampler*, pp.139–40, reproduced by permission of Peter Lang.)

Figure 7.4 Tiana's description of her literacy practices with Jandalf

and which you can help to create by adopting an identity of your choice and interacting with other residents. Increasingly schools, universities and commercial organizations are developing a presence in this world. You may find opportunities to work with your students in the specially secure 'Teen Second life' site that operates within it. In 2007, a hundred students from the National Association for Gifted and Talented Youth (NAGTY) in the UK participated in a pilot scheme in a virtual place called 'Schome', a blend of home and school. Instigated by the Open University, this pilot was designed to encourage students and staff to think about the development and improvement of education systems in real and virtual worlds. The final report concludes that engagement with Schome and the rest of the website led to enhancement of SParkers' (or students') '*knowledge age skills* (e.g. communication, teamwork, leadership, creativity)' but 'a substantial initial learning curve' needed to be overcome before the site's educational potential could be fully realized (Twining 2007: 3).

Flickr.com is a social software site which provides online space for sharing photographs and written text and (for paid subscribers only) short videos and soundtracks. Contributors decide who can look at their work and post comments. On a simple level, Flickr can be used for sharing holiday photos with distant friends but it also provides exciting opportunities for collaborative text-making. The facility to tag photographs means that the images can become part of a vast searchable database. Contributors with similar interests can easily create their own multimodal texts such as photo-stories to share with their online group(s) (for more on such communities see Davies and Merchant 2007). Flickr's geotagging feature enables users to link visual and written texts to very precise locations around the world – a useful facility whether you are planning a climbing holiday in Spain like my partner's father or exploring how a poet captures the sense of a particular place in her work. Tagging is an

example of a 'folksonomy' (Knobel and Lankshear 2007: 19), an evolving system of classification devised by photographers who decide how they want to label their work instead of
complying with pre-ordained categories established by others. Flickr has helped to 'nurture
the spread of citizen journalism' (Keegan 2008: 4) in that users can upload photos of breaking local and international news (whether this be a minor English earthquake or a Tibetan
monks' uprising) to share with a worldwide audience. Regular users of the site remark on
its value as a visual diary or visual learning log (see for example Teacher Dude who blogs
his reflections on his developing photography skills at http://teacherdudebbq.blogspot.
com/2007/06/on-learning.html (accessed 14 October 2008)).

The plethora of other social software sites now available such as Facebook, Bebo, MySpace
and YouTube have led to an explosion of creative activity online and, in most cases, to a
democratization of these processes. However, big business has not taken long to catch on
to the commercial potential of new media. If students are to engage critically in aspects of
multimodal production they should also be able to reflect on the implications of ownership.

7.5 Offline texts

7.5.1 Video computer games

Multimodal video computer games (like *Halo Wars*, *Crash*, *Grand Theft Auto* and others)
played on a PlayStation 2 or Xbox were made and played before more recent MMOG
developments. Gee perceives such commercial games as 'deep technologies' (Gee 2007:
95) which challenge traditional approaches to schooling in that learning is seen as a pleasurable activity that can be developed through 'situated practice' (Gee 2004: 108). In playing video games, he suggests that the competence > performance model privileged in
school learning is reversed: players have to perform first: to adopt a particular mindset,
'thinking, acting, valuing and deciding like a professional of a certain sort' (Gee 2007:
111) *before* they can become competent. In the UK, Burn and Durran (2007) have focused
on the study of games as a cultural form. They have engaged secondary school students
in the process of making games and in developing a critical understanding of the narrative construction, character conventions, rules and economies which underpin the games.
Their students have used *MissonMaker*, a software authoring tool, to design the 'ludic
elements' (Burn and Durran 2007: 124) of their games and to engage in complex multimodal practices and multi-literacies.

7.5.2 Kar2ouche

Kar2ouche animation software is used widely in UK schools. It takes storyboarding into a
multimodal dimension. Originally developed by Immersive Education and researchers at
Oxford University, this powerful tool enables students to create different layers of a digital

multimodal text and develop their own interpretation of a speech, short extract or whole scene from a number of Shakespeare plays, operas and other texts. They can draw on and manipulate banks of ready-made images of characters, props and settings. They can lay down tracks of sound and music effects and recordings of dramatic speech, or add their own. Speech and thought bubbles, captions and commentaries can be added and the texts can be personalized. Kar2ouche is enjoyable software to use with students of all ages. It can be time-consuming and is best used in a very focused way, at least to start with (for example insist on a tight timescale and ask students to produce a sequence of six frames on a key speech). It is important to build in time for discussion and critical comparison of sequences created. Use an interactive whiteboard or digital projector to ensure that everyone in a group can view and take time to look at each frame critically. Ask students to explain the creative choices they have made. Students who have used Apple's iMovie or Microsoft's Movie Maker programs will have no difficulties with this software. Alternatively, Kar2ouche and other even simpler interactive CD-ROMs like *Poetry in Motion* (a pre-1914 resource) can provide a stepping stone to more sophisticated digital editing packages.

7.6   Moving image texts

Moving image texts are one type of multimodal text. The literacy associated with moving images is one element of media literacy which is itself a subset of multi-literacies (Burn and Durran 2007). To develop their understanding of how moving images work to create meaning, students need to learn about different shots a film-maker can use (from the extreme close-up to the long shot), the way these shots can be manipulated and the affordances that they offer to the narrative process. Students need to learn how these shots can be woven together by jump-cutting, cross-cutting, fading, dissolving and so on and to extend their knowledge of how moving images and different types of sound (both diegitic and nondiegetic) work to create the overall effects. Students bring to your classroom prior knowledge of how images make meaning. They may not be able to say what iambic pentameter contributes to the impact of a Shakespeare sonnet but they will instinctively know that a low shot moving up the body into the face of a film actor conveys a sense of menace. This knowledge means that, as a teacher, you could be faced with a very different classroom dynamic when using film from that experienced in a more traditional print-based lesson. The students may not yet have a complete vocabulary to articulate how the grammar of the moving image works. As a result both 'dialogic and dynamic approaches' (Buckingham 2003: 153) are required, which draw on prior knowledge and experience and engage students in reflection and learning of new knowledge. Within English lessons, the British Film Institute perceives that students' 'moving image-based knowledge of genres, narrative structures and character function can contribute to their self-confidence as readers and writers' (BFI 2000: 4). This should not, however, be seen as just a stepping-stone to engagement with canonical literature (Marsh and Millard 2000). Although filmed versions of Shakespeare plays can be a vital resource to support literary study, film is a medium in its own right and should be considered as such. In effect, moving image literacy can arm students with the critical vocabulary they need and support their developing understanding of how to use the medium to make meanings.

Making meaning with moving images, whether for screening on television or in a cinema, is very much a collaborative process and a business. Taghi Amirani is a documentary film-maker whose highly acclaimed, sharply observed films have been broadcast on BBC and Channel 4 in the UK and on public television in the USA. He is another participant in my ongoing research on textual composition. He sees his collaborators as 'camera, sound editor, commissioner, researcher, driver, runner, accountant . . . and of course the on-screen contributors of the film'. Each documentary he makes, whether it's about allotments, bioluminescence or the closure of an Iranian newspaper, goes through a similar series of evolutionary stages on the journey from proposal to rough cut to first screening. Many of these occur before anyone has picked up a camera: '[I] find a subject [I] am curious about, fired up by, research, get access to the story/people, maybe shoot some sample footage, write a proposal, pitch the idea, get funding, make the film.'

The BFI and Film Education have been instrumental in developing moving image education in the UK. Information about their educational work can be found at:

www.screenonline.org.uk/education/index.html
www.filmeducation.org
(both accessed 14 October 2008)

Both organizations provide excellent resources to develop students' skills in the analysis and creation of moving images of different kinds. The BFI is committed to building teachers' confidence and pedagogy. Its model of progression in cineliteracy is based on three conceptual areas:

- The language of moving images – focusing on the ways in which moving image texts are internally *constructed*
- Producers and audiences – exploring the ways in which moving image texts are *made and delivered* to audiences
- Messages and values – concerned with the *interpretations* of the world offered by moving image texts and the effects these may have. (BFI 2000: 50)

This model underpins the practical guidance offered to Secondary teachers in *Moving Images in the Classroom* (BFI 2000). Obtainable at www.bfi.org.uk/education/teaching/miic (accessed 14 October 2008), this useful downloadable guide to teaching and learning with moving image focuses on eight techniques:

- Freeze Frame
- Sound and Image

- Spot the Shots
- Top and Tail
- Attracting Audiences
- Generic Translation
- Cross-media Comparisons
- Simulation

The publication includes advice on the integration of moving image work across a range of curriculum subjects. It could inspire you to plan cross-curricular projects – a key aspect of the National Curriculum.

Film Education also focuses on developing a critical understanding of how individual films are marketed. Many of their subject specific and cross-curricular resources are free; others can be purchased in DVD compilation packs. Every October, Film Education runs a School Film week with free screenings and practical activities. Both organizations have regular mailings for teachers.

A further invaluable source of information to support your teaching of moving images is the Internet Movie database – www.imdb.com (accessed 14 October 2008). This is many movie addicts' first port of call for information about specific films and television programmes. The site includes trailers, film and television stills, film biographies and movie news.

7.7   Conclusion

This chapter has explored some of the under-recognized and new directions that texts are taking and the collaborative processes which facilitate their production. More than ever before, you will need to be aware of your students' literacy skills, personal tastes and prior learning beyond the classroom. You will need to ensure that these are acknowledged and embraced so that you and your students move beyond the comfort zone of the whole-class reader and the prescribed anthology poem to make new meanings together. It is a risky, creative and exciting time to be a teacher of texts.

Note

1. There are, of course, notable exceptions to this rule: B.S. Johnson's 1969 novel *The Unfortunates* was published in loose-leaf format and readers could organize the chapters for themselves.

Appendix 1

Recommended Texts

Children's and Young Adult Contemporary Fiction for KS3 and KS4

This list serves as an introduction. Publishers are included but many of the fiction titles are available in various school and paperback editions. Find out what students are reading in your placement schools and try to read as widely as possible.

David Almond: *Skellig*; *Kit's Wilderness*; *Clay* (all Hodder)
Rachel Anderson: *The War Orphan*; *Paper Faces* (both Oxford)
Bernard Ashley: *Little Soldier* (Collins); *A Kind of Wild Justice* (OUP)
David Belbin: *Love Lessons* (Scholastic); *Denial* (Hodder); *Dead Teachers Don't Talk* (Five Leaves)
Malorie Blackman: *Noughts and Crosses*; *Checkmate*; *Hacker* (Corgi)
Tim Bowler: *River Boy*; *Storm Catchers* (both OUP)
Frank Cottrell Boyce: *Millions*; *Cosmic* (both Macmillan)
John Boyne: *The Boy in the Striped Pyjamas* (David Fickling)
Kevin Brooks: *Martyn Pig* (The Chicken House)
Melvin Burgess: *Junk*; *Sara's Face* (both Puffin Teenage)
Betsy Byars: *The Midnight Fox* (Puffin); *The Eighteenth Emergency* (Red Fox)
Anne Cassidy: *Looking for JJ* (Scholastic)
Aidan Chambers: *Postcards from No Man's Land* (Red Fox)
Gennifer Choldenko: *Al Capone Does My Shirts* (Bloomsbury)
Michael Coleman: *Tag* (Orchard)
Robert Cormier: *I am the Cheese*; *Heroes*; *After the First Death* (all Puffin)
Gillian Cross: *The Demon Headmaster*; *Tightrope* (both Puffin)
Roald Dahl: *The Wonderful Story of Henry Sugar*; *The Witches* (both Puffin)
Farrukh Dhondy: *Come to Mecca* (Collins)
Chris d'Lacey: *The Fire Within* (Scholastic)
Berlie Doherty: *The Snake-stone* (Collins); *Dear Nobody* and *Deep Secret* (both Puffin)
Harry Edge: *Spray* (Hodder)
Anne Fine: *Flour Babies*; *The Tulip Touch* (both Puffin)
Nicholas Fisk: *Grinny*; *Sweets from a Stranger* (both Puffin)

Jamila Gavin: *Coram Boy* (Mammoth)

Morris Gleitzman: *Two Weeks with the Queen* (Puffin); *Blabbermouth* (Macmillan); *Once* (Puffin)

Mark Haddon: *The Curious Incident of the Dog in the Night-time* (David Fickling)

Laurie Halse Anderson: *Speak* (Hodder)

Russell Hoban: *The Mouse and his Child* (Faber)

Anthony Horowitz: *Stormbreaker* (Walker Books)

Tanya Landman: *The Goldsmith's Daughter* (Walker Books)

Michelle Magorian: *Goodnight Mister Tom* (Longman)

Jan Mark: *Heathrow Nights* (Hodder)

Michael Morpurgo: *Kensuke's Kingdom* (Mammoth); *Private Peaceful* (Harper Collins)

Beverly Naidoo: *Journey to Jo'Burg* (Collins); *The Other Side of Truth* (Puffin)

William Nicholson: *The Wind Singer* (Egmont)

Robert O'Brien: *Z for Zachariah* (Puffin)

Mal Peet: *Keeper: Tamar*; *Penalty* (Walker Books)

Philip Pullman: *Northern Lights*; *Ruby in the Smoke* (both Scholastic)

Bali Rai: *(Un)arranged Marriage* (Corgi); *Dream On* (Barrington Stoke); *Rani and Sukh* (Bloomsbury)

Celia Rees: *Witch Child*; *Sorceress, Pirates* (all Bloomsbury); *Truth or Dare* (Macmillan)

Meg Rossoff: *How I Live Now* (Puffin)

J.K. Rowling: *Harry Potter and the Philosopher's Stone* (Bloomsbury)

Louis Sachar: *Holes*; *Small Steps* (both Bloomsbury)

Alex Shearer: *Tins* (Heinemann)

Marlene Fanta Shyer: *Welcome Home Jellybean* (Heinemann)

Meera Syal: *Anita and Me* (Flamingo)

Robert Swindells: *Stone Cold* (Puffin); *Daz 4 Zoe* (Puffin)

Mildred D Taylor: *Roll of Thunder, Hear My Cry* (Puffin)

John van de Ruit: *Spud* (Puffin)

James Watson: *Talking in Whispers* (Collins)

Robert Westall: *The Machine Gunners*; *Blitzcat* (both Macmillan)

Jacqueline Wilson: *Bad Girls*; *Vicky Angel* (both Corgi)

Dianne Wynne Jones: *Charmed Life* (Collins)

Benjamin Zephaniah: *Refugee Boy*; *Face* (both Bloomsbury)

Paul Zindel: *The Pigman* (Lions)

D. Hahn and L. Flynn (eds) (2006) *The Ultimate Teen Book Guide* (A & C Black) – includes interesting links between books and ideas for your own/your students' further reading.

Picture Books and Graphic Novels suitable for KS3 and KS4

Raymond Briggs: many titles including *When the Wind Blows* (Penguin); *The Tin-Pot Foreign General and the Old Iron Woman* (Hamish Hamilton); *Ethel and Ernest: a true story* (Jonathan Cape)

Anthony Browne: many titles including *King Kong* (Picture Corgi); *Into the Forest* (Walker Books); *PiggyBook (*Walker Books)

Armin Greder: *The Island* (Allen & Unwin)

Gilbert and Jaime Hernandez: *Love and Rockets* (Fantagraphics Books, Seattle)

Roberto Innocenti and Ian McEwan: *Rose Blanche* (Red Fox)
Frank Miller: *Batman: The Dark Knight Returns* (Titan Books)
Alan Moore: *Watchmen* (Titan Books)
Joe Sacco: *Palestine* (Jonathan Cape)
Marjane Satrapi: *Persepolis: The Story of a Childhood vol. 1 & vol. 2* (Jonathan Cape)
Art Spiegelman: *The Complete Maus* (Penguin)
Chris Ware: *Jimmy Corrigan: the Smartest Kid on Earth* (Jonathan Cape)

KS3 Drama texts

Anne Fine: *The Granny Project* (Collins)
Nigel Gray: *Black Harvest* (Collins) – play version of Anne Pilling's novel
Jan Needle: *A Game of Soldiers* (Collins) – play and novel
Paul Whitfield: *Precious* and *A Game of Two Halves* (NATE)
The KS3 Drama Book (English & Media Centre) includes Douglas Maxwell: *Helmet* and scripts/videos
    of a number of other short plays

Fiction and Drama texts frequently taught at KS4

This is not a comprehensive list but features some of the most common titles, some of which have now been taught in schools for many years:

Robert Cormier: *Heroes*
Charles Dickens: *Great Expectations*
Arthur Conan Doyle: stories from *The Adventures of Sherlock Holmes* including 'The Speckled Band',
    'The Red-Headed League' and 'The Five Orange Pips'
Barry Hines: *A Kestrel for a Knave*
Harper Lee: *To Kill a Mocking Bird*
Arthur Miller: *The Crucible; A View from the Bridge*
George Orwell: *Animal Farm; 1984*
J.B. Priestley: *An Inspector Calls*
Willy Russell: *Blood Brothers*
J.D. Salinger: *The Catcher in the Rye*
John Steinbeck: *Of Mice and Men*

KS3 and KS4 Non-Fiction texts

There are a huge variety of texts to select from. The brief selection below will help you to get started. Refer to the non-fiction reading requirements in the National Curriculum for further ideas of authors and look in school stock cupboards for other collections.

Barbara Bleiman (ed.) (2004) *Klondyke Kate Revisited* (English & Media Centre)
Rosy Border (ed.) (2001) *As it Happens* (Collins)
Bill Bryson (2004) *A Short History of Nearly Everything* (Black Swan)
Wendy Cooling (ed.) (2001) *Miles Ahead* (Collins)
Christopher Martin (ed.) (2003) *Lives and Times* (Collins)
John O'Connor (ed.) (2000) *Voices in Time* (Heinemann)
John O'Connor (ed.) (2001) *Eyewitness* (Heinemann)
Joe Simpson (1998) *Touching the Void* (Vintage)
Mike Wilson (2005) *Ice Mountain* (Hodder Murray)

Some recommended poetry texts

This list should help you to begin your exploration of poetry at KS3 level and beyond. It encompasses a range of works from different periods and cultural traditions.

Single Author Collections

Moniza Alvi (2007) *Split World: Poems 1990–2005* (Bloodaxe)
James Berry (1996) *Playing a Dazzler* (Penguin)
James Berry (2002) *A Nest Full of Stars* (Macmillan)
Charles Causley (1996) *Collected Poems for Children* (Macmillan)
Carol Ann Duffy (1999) *Meeting Midnight*; *The Hat* (both Faber & Faber)
T.S. Eliot (illus. Gorey) (1982) *Old Possum's Book of Practical Cats* (Faber & Faber)
Thomas Hardy (1997) *Selected Poems* (Everyman)
Seamus Heaney (1966) *Death of a Naturalist* (Faber & Faber)
Seamus Heaney (1999) *Beowulf* (Faber & Faber)
Miroslav Holub (1987) *The Fly* (Bloodaxe)
Jackie Kay (2007) *Darling* (Bloodaxe)
Jackie Kay (2007) *Red, Cherry Red* (Bloomsbury)
Edward Lear (2001 edition) *The Complete Nonsense of Edward Lear* (Faber & Faber)
Roger McGough (2004) *All the Best: The Selected Poems of Roger McGough* (Puffin)
Ian McMillan (2001) *The Very Best of Ian McMillan* (Macmillan)
Lindsay Macrae (2000) *How to Avoid Kissing Your Parents in Public* (Penguin)
Edwin Morgan (1985) *Selected Poems* (Carcanet)
Grace Nichols (2006) *Everybody Got a Gift* (A & C Black)
Alfred Noyes (illus. Keeping) (1999 edition) *The Highwayman* (OUP)
Gareth Owen (2002, 2nd edition) *The Fox on the Roundabout* (Macmillan)
Brian Patten (2000) *Juggling with Gerbils* (Penguin)
Vasko Popa (1998) *Collected Poems* (Anvil)
Pamela Robertson-Pearce (2008) *In Person: 30 Poets* (DVD-book) (Bloodaxe)
Vernon Scannell (2001) *The Very Best of Vernon Scannell* (Macmillan)
Marin Sorescu (1987) *The Biggest Egg in the World* (Bloodaxe)
Alfred, Lord Tennyson (Keeping's 1996 edition) *The Lady of Shalott* (OUP)

Edward Thomas (1997) *Selected Poems* (Everyman)

Steve Turner (1996) *The day I fell down the toilet* (Lion Publishing)

Benjamin Zephaniah (1994) *Talking Turkeys* (Penguin)

Poetry Anthologies

Many of these are read and used in different ways from KS2 to Post-16 and beyond.

John Agard and Grace Nichols (eds) (1994) *A Caribbean Dozen* (Walker)

Gerard Benson, Judith Chernaik and Cicely Herbert (eds) (1994) *Poems from the Underground* (Cassell)

Gerard Benson (ed.) (1995) *Does W trouble You?* (Puffin)

Michael and Peter Benton (2008) *Touchstones Now* (Hodder)

Madu Bhinda (ed.) (1994) *Jumping Across Worlds* (NATE)

John Burnside and Maurice Riordan (eds) (2004) *Wild Reckoning* (Calouste Gulbenkian Foundation)

Wendy Cope (ed.) (2002) *Is that the New Moon?* (Collins)

Andy Croft and Sue Dymoke (eds) (2006) *Not Just a Game: sporting poetry* (Five Leaves)

Carol Ann Duffy (ed.) (2003) *Overheard on a Saltmarsh* (Young Picador)

John Foster (ed.) (1986) *Spaceways* (OUP)

John Foster (ed.) (1999) *Word Whirls and other shape poems* (OUP)

John Fuller (ed.) (2000) *The Oxford Book of Sonnets* (OUP)

Robert Gent (ed.) (1996) *Poems for the Beekeeper* (Five Leaves)

Michael Harrison (ed.) (2001) *A Book of Very Short Poems* (OUP)

Michael Harrison and Christopher Stuart Clark (eds) (2001) *The Oxford Treasury of Classic Poems* (OUP)

Anne Harvey (ed.) (1996) *Criminal Records* (Penguin)

Seamus Heaney and Ted Hughes (eds) (1982) *The Rattlebag* (Faber & Faber)

Roger McGough (ed.) (1982) *Strictly Private* (Penguin)

Roger McGough (ed.) (1998) *The Ring of Words* (Faber)

Ian McMillan (ed.) (1989) *Against the Grain* (Nelson)

Wes Magee (ed.) (1991) *Madtail, Miniwhale* (Penguin)

Adrian Mitchell (ed.) (1993) *The Orchard Book of Poems* (Orchard)

Brian Moses (ed.) (2002) *Are We Nearly There Yet?* (Macmillan)

Andrew Motion (ed.) (2002) *Here to Eternity* (Faber)

Heather Neill (ed.) (2001) *The TES Book of Young Poets* (Orchard)

Judith Nicholls (ed.) (1993) *Earthways, Earthwise*, OUP

Sean O'Brien (ed.) (1998) *The Firebox: Poetry in Britain and Ireland after 1945* (Picador)

Andrew Fusek Peters (ed.) (1999) *Sheep Don't Go to School* (Bloodaxe)

John Rice (ed.) (2002) *Scottish Poems* (Macmillan)

Michael Rosen (ed.) (1994) *A Different Story* (English and Media Centre)

Morag Styles and Helen Cook (eds) (1990) *Ink-slinger* (A & C Black)

Matthew Sweeney (ed.) (2001) *The New Faber Book of Children's Verse* (Faber & Faber)

John Wain (ed.) (1986) *The Oxford Anthology of English Poetry: Blake to Heaney* (OUP)

Fiona Waters (ed.) (2001) *Poems Then and Now: collection 3* (Evans)

Raymond Wilson (ed.) (1995) *The Nine O' Clock Bell* (Penguin)

If your own knowledge of **poets from different cultures and traditions** needs developing further you should find the following texts enjoyable:

Valerie Bloom (ed.) (2003) *One River Many Creeks* (Macmillan)
Stewart Brown and Mark McWatt (2005) *The Oxford Book of Caribbean Verse* (OUP)
Paula Burnett (ed.) (1986) *The Penguin Book of Caribbean Verse in English* (Penguin)
Debjani Chatterjee (ed.) (2000) *The Redbeck Anthology of British South Asian Poetry* (Redbeck Press)
Bashabi Fraser and Debjani Chatterjee (eds) (2003) *Rainbow World: Poems from Many Cultures* (Hodder Wayland)
Asher and Martin Hoyles (2002) *Moving Voices – Black Performance Poetry* (Hansib Publications)
Jennifer Langer (2005) *The Silver Throat of the Moon: Writing in Exile* (Five Leaves)
E.A. Markham (ed.) (1989) *Hinterland: Caribbean Poetry from the West Indies & Britain* (Bloodaxe)
Lemn Sissay (ed.) (1998) *The Fire People – Black British Poetry* (Payback Press)

Poetry at KS4 and Post-16 level

The range of poets studied for public examinations is considerable and includes poets and poems from many of the anthologies listed in the last section. Poets from Carol Ann Duffy and Emily Dickinson to William Wordsworth and Derek Walcott feature in the specifications. You will find that many schools will use anthologies of GCSE poetry provided by their examination board. These are:

AQA (Specification A) *Anthology*
AQA (Specification B) *Best Words*
Edexcel *Anthology for GCSE English*
OCR *Opening Lines*
WJEC (Specification B) *English Literature Anthology*

You will need to consult examination board websites for precise details of set texts for GCSE, AS/A2 and IB diploma examinations.

Appendix 2

Exploring Citizenship Issues in English Lessons

Some practical teaching ideas from PGCE English and English with Media students

The National Curriculum Programmes of Study for Citizenship at KS3 and KS4 offer many opportunities for cross-curricular links with English and Media. The programmes are underpinned by three key concepts:

- Democracy and justice
- Rights and responsibilities
- Identities and diversity: living together in the UK

and three key processes:

- Critical thinking and enquiry
- Advocacy and representation
- Taking informed and responsible action

For specific details of the 'Range and Content' and the 'Curriculum Opportunities' that students should experience at each Key Stage, consult the National Curriculum website at http://curriculum.qca.org.uk/key-stages-3-and-4/subjects/citizenship/index.aspx (accessed 14 October 2008).

Below are some ideas for potential links with the concepts and key processes. Most of these suggestions have been used very successfully in classrooms by PGCE English and English with Media students at the University of Leicester. I am very grateful to them for their ideas.

Democracy and justice

- Participating in formal debates, balloon debates and school council elections.
- Exploring apartheid through reading 'Nothing's Changed' by Tatamkhulu Afrika or a carefully controlled game of Apartheid Pictionary (modelled on the Milgram classroom experiment in which students were segregated according to hair and eye colour).

- Use of drama strategies such as forum theatre and hot-seating to explore issues emerging from a text.
- Exploring *Let Him Have It* (a film about the wrongful arrest and hanging of Derek Bentley) with GCSE students as a lead-in to discussion of the rights and wrongs of capital punishment and the writing of a persuasive magazine article.
- Using Stanley's experiences at Camp Green lake in *Holes* by Louis Sachar as a starting point for discussion of crime and punishment.

Rights and responsibilities

- Exploring questions of morality and responsibility through study of plays such as Willy Russell's *Blood Brothers* and J.B. Priestley's *An Inspector Calls* or the novels *Of Mice and Men* (John Steinbeck), *Clay* (David Almond) or *Millions* (Frank Cottrell Boyce).
- Collaborative writing of a set of rules for a group (or a fortress as Chas does in *The Machine Gunners* by Robert Westall).
- Students, in role as residents of a small town without laws or law enforcement, have to decide on their priorities for making it a safer place to live.

Identities and diversity: living together in the UK

- Exploring the different ways in which individuals and groups communicate and establish their identities through spoken, written and visual/body language.
- Constructing a sequence of digital images to represent your identity.
- Considering the representation of young people in the Media. Use the BBC North West Tonight report on politician David Cameron's encounter with Ryan Florence and his hooded gang as a starting point (the report is available on YouTube). Other suitable texts on gang culture include the texts *Tribes* by Catherine MacPhail or *The Outsiders* by S.E. Hinton.
- Engaging with many different types of texts set in different cultural contexts, students learn about and reflect on the nature of the multicultural society in which we live. [AQA's *Anthology* for GCSE English/English Literature and OCR's *Opening Worlds* were frequently mentioned in relation to this topic area, especially poems by Tom Leonard and John Agard.]
- Reading and discussion of *The Other Side of Truth* by Beverly Naidoo or Benjamin Zephaniah's *Refugee Boy*.
- Exploring gender roles in societies found in the plays *King Lear* or Aphra Behn's *The Rover*, the children's novel *The Illustrated Mum* by Jacqueline Wilson or the film *My Beautiful Laundrette*.

Critical thinking and enquiry

- Discussion of ideas, opinions, beliefs and values can often be introduced via texts of different kinds that deal with topical issues. For example:
  - cloning – *Frankenstein* by Mary Shelley or *Never Let Me Go* by Kazuo Ishiguro

- animal cruelty – an extract from Hugh Fearnley-Whittingstall's C4 programme *Hugh's Chicken Run* or the poem 'Song of the Battery Hen' by Edwin Brock
- global warming – Al Gore's 2006 film *An Inconvenient Truth*
- healthy eating – Morgan Spurlock's 2004 film *Super Size Me* or Jamie Oliver's manifesto for healthy eating at www.jamieoliver.com
- the abolition of study leave – articles from the *TES* and school Websites
- arranged marriages – *Romeo and Juliet* and *Unarranged Marriage* by Bali Rai
- homelessness – *Stone Cold* by Robert Swindells or extracts from *The Big Issue* magazine.

- Using an opinion line activity to actively explore students' views on a number of linked topics. Students are asked to place themselves on a line marked by various points such as 'strongly agree', 'agree', 'undecided', 'disagree', 'strongly disagree'. The 'undecideds' need to be persuaded by those on each side to move to a more definite location. This activity provides a lively initial stimulus for further in-depth discussion and can also be used at the plenary stage of a lesson to see if opinions have changed.
- Watching the two-minute BBC news summary during morning registration to help students to develop their views on a wide range of topical issues and to wake up their brains for the day!
- Simulations of summit meetings on key national/global issues.

Advocacy and representation

- Taking account of different viewpoints during discussion and interpretation of texts.
- Mock trials for literary characters.
- Learning to use persuasive language to pitch a bid or market a product or an idea to a particular audience.
- Analysis of propaganda posters used in world conflicts.
- Studying and writing protest poetry.

Taking informed and responsible action

- Taking action on a real issue which is affecting the students' lives or that of the wider school community (such as proposed closure of their snack bar, common room or withdrawal of certain privileges) through poster campaigns, scripted presentations, use of vox pop interviews and letter writing.
- Analysing the impact of a character's actions on their community and the wider world, now and in the future (for example as shown in the short story 'A Sound of Thunder' by Ray Bradbury).
- Devising simulations which involve all students in-role in decision-making on issues such as building a new supermarket on the school playing field.

When planning any cross-curricular project it is advisable to involve staff from other subject area(s) from the onset. In this way you can not only capitalize on their own subject expertise but also ensure that the topic is appropriately embedded within schemes of work in the subject areas concerned rather than being a potentially repetitive addition.

Bibliography

Abbs, P. and Richardson, J. (eds) (1990) *The Forms of Poetry: A practical study guide*. Cambridge: Cambridge University Press.

Albery, N. and Ratcliffe, P. (eds) (1994) *Poem for the Day One*. London: Sinclair-Stevenson Ltd.

Alexander, R.J. (2003) 'Talk in teaching and learning: international perspectives', in QCA, *New perspectives on spoken English in the classroom*. London: QCA, pp. 27–37.

Alvi, M. (2000) 'Presents from my Aunts in Pakistan', in *Carrying My Wife*. Newcastle upon Tyne: Bloodaxe.

Amenábar, A. (dir.) (2001) *The Others*. Los Angeles: Cruise/Wagner Productions.

Andrews, R. (1991) *The Problem with Poetry*. Buckingham: Open University Press.

Andrews, R. (2001a) *Teaching and Learning English*. London: Continuum.

Andrews, R. (2001b) 'On Teaching Non-Fiction at GCSE level', *Use of English*, 52, 2, 129–38.

Andrews, R., Beverton, S., Locke, T., Low, G., Robinson, A., Torgerson, C. and Zhu, D. (2004) 'The effect of grammar teaching (syntax) in English on 5 to 16 year olds' accuracy and quality in written composition', in *Research Evidence in Education Library*. London: EPPI-Centre, Social Science Research Unit, Institute of Education.

AQA (2005) *Anthology: GCSE English/English Literature Specification A*. Oxford: Oxford University Press.

Arts Council England (2003) *From looking glass to spyglass: a consultation paper on children's literature*. London: Arts Council. www.artscouncil.org.uk/documents/publications/495.pdf (accessed 10/10/08).

Asimov, I. (1957) 'The Fun They Had', in R. Blatchford (ed.) (1989) *Shorties*. London: Unwin Hyman.

Auden, W.H. (1968) *The Dyer's Hand*. New York: Random House.

Ayres, T. and Dayus, J. (2000) *Reading and Writing Non-Fiction*. Oxford: Heinemann.

Bailey, M., Hall, C. and Gamble, N. (2007) 'Promoting school libraries and schools library services: problems and partnerships', *English in Education*, 41, 2, 71–85.

Bain, E. and Bain, R. (1996/2003) *The Grammar Book* and *The Grammar Book Supplement*. Sheffield: NATE.

Bain, R. (1993) *Exploring Language and Power*. Cambridge: Cambridge University Press.

Baker, N. (2008) 'How I fell in love with Wikipedia', *Guardian*, G2, 10 April, 4–7.

Baldwin, M. (1959) *Poetry without Tears*. London: RKP.

Barrs, M. and Cork. V. (2001) *The Reader in the Writer*. London: CLPE.

Barton, G. (2001) 'How Non-Fiction Can Make Us Better Readers', *Use of English*, 52, 2, 139–51.

Beach, R. and O'Brien, D. (2005) 'Playing texts against each other in the multimodal English classroom', *English in Education*, 39, 2, 44–59.

Beard, A. (2001) *Texts and Contexts*. London: Routledge.

Bearne, E. and Cliff Hodges, G. (2000) 'Reading Rights and Responsibilities', in J. Davison and J. Moss (eds), *Issues in English Teaching*. London: Routledge, pp. 8–22.

Bearne, E., Clark, C., Johnson, A., Manford, P., Mottram, M. and Wolstencroft, H. (2007) *Reading on Screen*. Leicester: UKLA.

Belbin, D. (2001) 'Mystery Train', in D. Hamley (ed.), *The Oxford Book of Train Stories*, pp. 1–11.

Belbin, D. and Brick (2007) 'If Shakespeare were alive today', *Tripod*, 3, 14–15.

Bennett, A. (2005) *Untold Stories*. London: Faber & Faber.

Benton, M. and Fox, G. (1985) *Teaching Literature Nine to Fourteen*. Oxford: Oxford University Press.

Benton, M., Teasey, J., Bell, R. and Hurst, K. (1988) *Young Readers Responding to Poems*. London: Routledge.

Benton, P. (1986) *Pupil, Teacher, Poem*. London: Hodder & Stoughton.

Benton, P. (1995) 'Recipe Fictions . . . Literary Fast Food? Reading Interests in Year 8', *Oxford Review of Education*, 21, 1, 99–111.

Benton, P. (1999) 'Unweaving the Rainbow: poetry teaching in the secondary school I', *Oxford Review of Education*, 25, 4, 521–31.

Benton, P. (2000) 'The Conveyor Belt Curriculum: poetry teaching in the secondary school II', *Oxford Review of Education*, 26, 1, 81–93.

Bereiter, C. and Scardamalia, M. (1987) *The Psychology of Written Composition*. Hillsdale, NJ: Lawrence Erlbaum Associates.

Bigum, C. (2003) 'The knowledge producing school: moving away from the work of finding educational problems for which computers are solutions', *Computers in New Zealand Schools*, 15, 2 (cited in Lankshear and Knobel 2007).

Black, R. (2007) 'Digital Design: English Language Learners and Reader Reviewers in On-line Fiction', in M. Knobel and C. Lankshear (eds), *A New Literacies Sampler*. New York: Peter Lang, pp. 115–38.

Bleiman, B. and Webster, L. (2005) *Studying Blake's Songs*. London: E&MC Publications.

Bourdieu, P. (1986) 'The forms of capital', in J.G. Richardson (ed.), *Handbook of Theory and Research for the Sociology of Education*. Westview, CT: Greenwood Press.

Bradbury, R. (1990) 'A Sound of Thunder', in *The Golden Apples of the Sun* (New Windmills edition). London: Heinemann.

Brautigan, R. (1989) 'The Scarlatti Tilt', in R. Blatchford (ed.) *Shorties*. London: Unwin Hyman.

Brice Heath, S. (1983) *Ways With Words: Language, Life, and Work in Communities and Classrooms*. New York: Cambridge University Press.

British Film Institute (BFI) (2000) *Moving Images in the Classroom*. London: BFI. www.bfi.org.uk/education/teaching/miic (accessed 10/10/08).

Brooks, G. (2003) *Sound sense: the phonics element of the National Literacy Strategy. A report to the Department for Education and Skills*. London: DfES. www.standards.dfes.gov.uk/pdf/literacy/gbrooks_phonics.pdf (accessed 10/10/08).

Brown, L. (ed.) (1993) *The New Shorter Oxford English Dictionary*. Oxford: Clarendon Press.

Brownjohn, S. (1982) *What Rhymes with Secret?* London: Hodder & Stoughton.

Brownjohn, S. (2002) *The Poet's Craft*. London: Hodder.

Bruner, J. (1966) *Toward a Theory of Instruction*. Cambridge, MA: Harvard University Press.

Buckingham, D. (2003) *Media Education: literacy, learning and contemporary culture*. Cambridge: Polity Press.

Burgess, T. (2002) 'Writing, English Teachers and the New Professionalism', in T. Burgess, C. Fox and J. Goody (eds), *When the hurly burly's done: What's worth fighting for in English Education?* Perspectives on English Teaching 1. Sheffield: NATE.

Burn, A. and Durran, J. (2007) *Media Literacy in Schools*. London: Paul Chapman Publishing.

Cajkler, W. and Dymoke, S. (2005) 'Grammar for Reading: why now and what for?', *Changing English*, 12, 1, 125–36.

Cajkler, W. and Hislam, J. (2004) 'Teaching and understanding grammar: how trainee teachers make sense of a new curriculum', in N. Bartels (ed.), *Applied Linguistics in Language Teacher Education*. Dordrecht: Kluwer Academic Publishers.

Carey, J. (ed.) (1987) *The Faber Book of Reportage*. London: Faber & Faber.

Carter, J. (1999) *Talking Books*. London: Routledge.

Carter, R. (ed.) (1990) *Knowledge About Language and the Curriculum: The LINC reader*. Sevenoaks: Hodder & Stoughton.

Carter, R. (2003) *Language and Creativity. The Art of Common Talk*. London: Routledge.

Carter, R. and Nash, W. (1990) *Seeing through Language*. Oxford: Blackwell.

Chambers, A. (1991) *The Reading Environment*. Stroud: Thimble Press.

Chopin, K. (1894) 'The Story of an Hour', www.wsu.edu:8080/~wldciv/world_civ_reader/world_civ_reader_2/chopin.html (accessed 10/10/08).

Clark, J.S. (ed.) (1998–2003) *Children Have Rights, 1* (1998); *Children Have Rights, 2* (1999); *All Children Have Rights, 3* (2000); *Every Child Has Rights, 4* (2001); *Cry Me A River, 5* (2002); *No Secrets, 6* (2003). London: UK Committee for UNICEF.

Cliff Hodges, G. (1998) *Two Poems by John Keats*. Sheffield: NATE.

Coleridge, S.T. (1827) 'Table Talk I', in *Collected Works* (1990 edition). London: Routledge.

Cremin, T., Bearne, E., Mottram, M. and Goodwin, P. (2008) 'Primary teachers as readers', *English in Education*, 42, 1, 8–23.

Croft, A. and Dymoke, S. (eds) (2006) *Not Just a Game: Sporting Poetry*. Nottingham: Five Leaves.

Crossley-Holland, K. (1998) 'Boo' in *Short!: A Book of Very Short Stories*. Oxford: Oxford University Press, p. 56.

Cudd, E. and Roberts, L. (1989) 'Using writing to enhance content area learning in the primary grades', *The Reading Teacher*, 42, 6, cited in Wray and Lewis (1995).

Czerniewska, P. (1992) *Learning about Writing: The Early Years*. Oxford: Blackwell.

D'Arcy, P. (1999) *Two Contrasting Paradigms for the Teaching and Assessment of Writing*. Sheffield: NAAE, NAPE and NATE.

Dahl, R. (1986) *Boy*. London: Puffin.

Dahl, R. (1988) 'Lamb to the Slaughter', in *Tales of the Unexpected*. London: Penguin.

Davies, J. and Merchant, G. (2007) 'Looking from the Inside Out: Academic Blogging as New Literacy', in M. Knobel and C. Lankshear (eds) *A New Literacies Sampler*. New York: Peter Lang, pp. 168–97.

DCSF (2008a) *The Framework for Secondary English*, www.standards.dcsf.gov.uk/secondary/frameworks/ (accessed 10/10/08).

DCSF (2008b) *Identifying Gifted and Talented Learners – getting started*, www.standards.dfes.gov.uk/giftedandtalented/ (accessed 10/10/08).

DES (1975) *A Language for Life* (Bullock Report). London: HMSO.

DES (1984) *English 5–16: Curriculum Matters 1*. London: DES.

DES (1987) *Teaching Poetry in the Secondary School: An HMI view*. London: HMSO.

DES (1988) *Report of the Committee of Enquiry in to the teaching of the English Language* (Kingman Report). London: HMSO.

DES (1989) *English for Ages 5 to 16* (Cox Report). York: National Curriculum Council.

DES (1990a) *English in the National Curriculum* (No. 2). London: HMSO.

DES (1990b) *Language in the National Curriculum (LINC): materials for professional development*. London: HMSO.

DfE (1993) *English for Ages 5–16*. London: HMSO.

DfEE (1998) *The National Literacy Strategy – Framework for Teaching*. London: HMSO.

DfEE (2000) *Grammar for Writing*. London: HMSO.

DfEE (2001) *Framework for Teaching English in Years 7, 8 and 9*. London: DfEE.

DfES (2002) *Access and Engagement in English*, www.standards.dfes.gov.uk/keystage3/all/respub/englishpubs/en_eal (accessed 10/10/08).

DfES (2003) *Drama Objectives Bank*. London: DfES.

DfES (2006a) *The Primary Framework for Literacy and Mathematics*. DfES, www.standards.dfes.gov.uk/ primaryframeworks (accessed 10/10/08).

DfES (2006b) *Independent Review of the Teaching of Early Reading* (Rose Report). London: DfES.

DfES (2006c) *Progression Maps,* http://nationalstrategies.standards.dcsf.gov.uk/node/42856 (accessed 14/1/09).

DfES (2007) *Teaching Speaking and Listening* (DVD). London: DfES.

DfES and NATE (2003) *Group Reading at KS3*. London: DfES.

DfEE/QCA (1999) *The National Curriculum for England: English*. London: DfEE.

Derewianka, B. (1990) *Exploring How Texts Work*. Rozelle, New South Wales: Primary English Teaching Association.

Derewianka, B. (1996) *Exploring the Writing of Genres*. London: UKRA.

Dias, P. and Hayhoe, M. (1988) *Developing Response to Poetry*. Buckingham: Open University Press.

Dymoke, S. (2000) 'The teaching of poetry in secondary schools', unpublished PhD thesis, University of Nottingham.

Dymoke, S. (2002) 'The dead hand of the exam: the impact of the NEAB anthology on GCSE poetry teaching', *Changing English*, 9, 1, 85–93.

Dymoke, S. (2003) *Drafting and Assessing Poetry*. London: Paul Chapman Publishing.

Dymoke, S. (2005) 'Wireless keyboards and mice: could they enhance teaching and learning in the secondary English classroom?', *English in Education*, 39, 5, 62–77.

Dymoke, S. (2007) 'Pre-service poetry teaching: can pursuit of "quality" also embrace creativity?', paper given at American Educational Research Conference, Chicago, April 2007.

Dymoke, S. and Griffiths, R. (2008) 'The Letterbox Club: The social impact of a national project aimed at raising achievements in literacy for children aged 7 to 11 in foster care', paper presented at the ECER conference, Gothenburg, September 2008.

Dymoke, S. and Hughes, J. (2008) 'How can participation in a poetry wiki support beginning teachers in their professional learning about the teaching of poetry?', paper presented at the ECER conference, Gothenburg, September 2008.

Dymoke, S., McMehan, I., Royston, M. and Smith, J. (2008) *Edexcel AS English Literature: student book*. London: Edexcel.

Edwards, J. (2006) *Literature Matters Yorkshire: inspiring cross curricular learning*. Leeds: MLA.

Edexcel (2007) 'Unit 2: Explorations In Drama', *Edexcel GCE in English Literature*. London: Edexcel.

Eide, F. and Eide, B. (2005) 'Brain of the Blogger', http://eideneurolearningblog.blogspot.com/2005/03/brain-of-blogger. html (accessed 10/10/08).

Ellis, V. (2005) 'The Classic Dilemma', *Times Educational Supplement*, 20 May, http://www.tes.co.uk/article. aspx?storycode=2105647 (accessed 27/10/08).

Fairclough, N. (1989) *Language and Power*. Harlow: Longman.

Flaubert, G. (1853) Letter to Louise Colet 14 August 1853, as cited in P. Kemp (ed.) (1997) *The Oxford Dictionary of Literary Quotations*. Oxford: Oxford University Press.

Fleming, M. and Stevens, D. (2004) *English Teaching in the Secondary School* (2nd edition). London: David Fulton.

Flower, L. (1994) *The Construction of Negotiated Meaning: a Social Cognitive Theory of Writing*. Carbondale, IL: Southern Illinois University Press.

Fones, D. (2001) 'Blocking Them in to Free Them to Act: Using Writing Frames to Shape Boys' Responses to Literature in the Secondary School, *English in Education*, 35, 3, 21–30.

Fox, C. (2007) 'History, war and politics: taking "commix" seriously', in V. Ellis, C. Fox and B. Street (eds), *Rethinking English in Schools*. London: Continuum, pp. 88–101.

Freire, P. (1970) *Pedagogy of the Oppressed*. New York: Continuum.

Friel, B. (1979) in P. Coogan (ed.) 'Extracts from a Sporadic Diary', *The Literary Review*. Dublin: Namara Press.

Frost, R. (1930) 'Education by Poetry' in *Collected Poems, Prose and Plays* (1995 edition). New York: Library of America, pp. 712–28.

Furlong, T., Venkatakrishnan, H. and Brown, M. (2001) *Key Stage 3 National Strategy: An Evaluation of the Strategies for Literacy and Mathematics Interim Report*. London: ATL.

Gee, J.P. (2004) *Situated Language and Learning: A Critique of Traditional Schooling*. London: Routledge.

Gee, J.P. (2007) 'Pleasure, Learning, Video Games, and Life: the Projective Stance', in M. Knobel and C. Lankshear (eds) *A New Literacies Sampler*. New York: Peter Lang, pp. 95–114.

Gibbons, S. (2008) 'Can Less Be More? The Renewed Framework for English', *English Drama Media*, 11, 45–8.

Gibson, R. (1998) *Teaching Shakespeare*. Cambridge: Cambridge University Press.

Giuseppi, U. (1990) 'Journey by Night', in P. Abbs and J. Richardson (eds) *The Forms of Narrative*. Cambridge: Cambridge University Press.

Goodwyn, A. (2002) 'Breaking up is hard to do: English teachers and that LOVE of reading', *English Teaching: Practice and Critique*, 1, 6, 66–78.

Goodwyn, A. (2005) 'Literacy versus English: a professional identity crisis', in A. Goodwyn and A. Stables (eds), *Language and Literacy*. London: Sage, pp. 192–204.

Gordimer, N. (1983) 'Enemies', in *Selected Stories*. Harmondsworth: Penguin.

Graham, J. (1990) *Pictures on the Page*. Sheffield: NATE.

Grainger, T., Goouch, K. and Lambirth, A. (2005) *Creativity and Writing*. London: Routledge.

Graves, D. (1983) *Writing: Teachers and Children at Work*. London: Heinemann.

Gygax, G. and Arneson, D. (1974) *Dungeons and Dragons*. Lake Geneva, WI: TSR Inc.

Hall, C. and Coles, M. (1999) *Children's Reading Choices*. London: Routledge.

Hallford, D. and Zaghini, E. (eds) (2006) *Universal Verse: Poetry for children*. London: Barn Owl Books.

Halliday, M.A.K. (1985) *An Introduction to Functional Grammar*. London: Edward Arnold.

Halliday, M.A.K. and Hasan, R. (1989) *Language, Context and Text: Aspects of Language in a Social Semiotic Perspective*. Oxford: Oxford University Press.

Hardy, T. (1966) 'The Grave by the Handpost', in J. Wain (ed.) *Thomas Hardy Selected Stories*. London: Macmillan.

Harrison, B.T. (ed.) (1994) *The Literate Imagination*. London: David Fulton.

Harrison, B.T. and Gordon, H. (1983) 'Metaphor is Thought: does Northtown need Poetry?', *Educational Review*, 35, 3, 265–78.

Harrison, C. (2002) *Key Stage 3 English: Roots and Research*. London: DfES.

Harrison, R. (2008) 'New Technologies and Digital Literacies: Exploring New Approaches to Narrative in Key Stage 3 English', unpublished Masters assignment, University of Leicester.

Heaney, S. (1980) 'Feeling into words', in *Preoccupations – Selected Prose 1968–1978*. London: Faber & Faber.

Heaney, S. (1989) *The Redress of Poetry* (inaugural lecture on 28 October at Oxford University). Oxford: Clarendon Press.

Herbert, W.N. and Hollis, M. (eds) (2000) *Strong Words: Modern poets on modern poetry*. Tarset: Bloodaxe Books.

Hicks, B. (2007) 'Teen poetry: Sonnets from the Underground', *Independent*, 2 August, http://www.independent.co.uk/news/education/schools/teen-poetry-sonnets-from-the-underground-459859.html (accessed 27/10/08).

Hilton, M. (2001) 'Writing process and progress: where do we go from here?' *English in Education*, 35, 1, 4–11.

Hobsbaum, P. (1996) *Metre, Rhythm and Verse Form*. London: Routledge.

Holbrook, D. (1961) *English for Maturity*. Cambridge: Cambridge University Press.

Holub, M. (1987) 'Poem Technology', in *The Fly*. Newcastle upon Tyne: Bloodaxe.

Horner, D. (1999) 'A tough bird is poetry', *Literacy and Learning*, 9, 59.

Hoyles, A. and Hoyles, M. (eds) (2002) *Moving Voices: Black Performance Poetry*. London: Hansib Publications.

Hughes, S. (1998) 'The Art of Not Naming: Riddles and Word-games', in A. Wilson and S. Hughes (eds) *The Poetry Book for Primary Schools*. London: The Poetry Society.

Hughes, T. (1967) *Poetry in the Making*. London: Faber & Faber.

Hull, R. (1988) *Behind the Poem*. London: Routledge.

Hull, R. (2001) 'What hope for children's poetry?', *Books for Keeps*, 126, 10–13.

Iggulden, C. and Iggulden, H. (2007) *The Dangerous Book for Boys*. London: HarperCollins.

Iser, W. (1978) *The Act of Reading*. Baltimore, MD: Johns Hopkins University Press.

Johnston, I. and Mangat, J. (2003) 'Cultural encounters in the liminal spaces of Canadian picture books', *Changing English*, 10, 2, 199–203.

Jones, K. (2003) 'Culture reinvented as management: English in the new urban school', *Changing English*, 10, 2, 143–53.

Kay, J. (1991) *The Adoption Papers*. Newcastle upon Tyne: Bloodaxe.

Keegan, V. (2008) 'Corporate dinosaurs kill sites – in a Flickr', *Technology Guardian,* 17 April, 4.

Kempe, A. and Ashwell, M. (2000) *Progression in Secondary Drama*. Oxford: Heinemann.

Kneale, N. (1986) 'The Pond', in G. Phinn (ed.) *Sweet and Sour*. London: Bell & Hyman.

Knobel, M. and Lankshear, C. (eds) (2007) *A New Literacies Sampler*. New York: Peter Lang.

Kress, G. (1982) *Learning to Write*. London: Routledge.

Kress, G. (2003) *Literacy in the New Media Age*. London: Routledge.

Kress, G. and van Leeuwen, T. (1996) *Reading Images: the Grammar of Visual Design*. London: Routledge (2nd edition 2006).

Kress, G. and van Leeuwen, T. (2001) *Multimodal Discourse*. London: Arnold.

Kress, G., Jewitt, C., Bourne, J., Franks, A., Hardcastle, J., Jones, K. and Reid, E. (2004) *English in Urban Classrooms*. London: RoutledgeFalmer.

Lankshear, C. and Knobel, M. (2003) *New Literacies*. Buckingham: Open University Press.

Lankshear, C. and Knobel, M. (2007) 'New Technologies in Secondary English Classrooms', in A. Adams and S. Brindley (eds) *Teaching Secondary English with ICT*. Maidenhead: Open University Press.

Lawrence, D.H. (1929) Preface to *Chariot of the Sun*, in E. Macdonald (ed.), *Phoenix*. London: Heinemann.

Leach, S. (1992) *Shakespeare in the Classroom*. Buckingham: Open University Press.

Leonard, T. (1975) 'Poetry' in *Intimate Voices: Selected Work 1965–1983*. Newcastle: Galloping Dog Press.

Lewis, C. (2007) 'New Literacies', in M. Knobel and C. Lankshear (eds), *A New Literacies Sampler*. New York: Peter Lang, pp. 229–38.

Lewis, D. (2001) *Reading Contemporary Picture Books*. London: RoutledgeFalmer.

Lewis, M. and Wray, D. (1995) *Developing Children's Non Fiction Writing: working with writing frames*. Leamington Spa: Scholastic.

Lewis, M., Wray, D. and Mitchell, C. (1995) 'Extending Interactions into Texts: theory into practice', *Reading*, 29, 1, 10–15.

Linney, B. (1995) *Pictures, People and Power*. London: Macmillan Education.

Logan, M. (2006) 'The year of the many speaking unto the many', *South China Morning Post*, 28 December, A11.

Lunzer, E. and Gardner, K. (eds) (1979) *The Effective Use of Reading.* London: Schools Council Publications, Heinemann.

Lunzer, E. and Gardner, K. (1984) *Learning from the Written Word.* Edinburgh: Oliver and Boyd.

McEwan, I. (2001) 'Mother Tongue', www.ianmcewan.com/bib/articles/mother-tongue.html (accessed 10/10/08).

McGuinn, N. (2005) 'A place for the personal voice? Gunther Kress and the English Curriculum', *Changing English,* 12, 2, 205–17.

McWilliam, N. (1998) *What's in a Word? Vocabulary Development in Multilingual Classrooms.* Stoke-on-Trent: Trentham Books.

Marsh, G. (1988) *Teaching Through Poetry.* London: Hodder & Stoughton.

Marsh, J. and Millard, E. (2000) *Literacy and Popular Culture.* London: Paul Chapman Publishing.

Marshall, B. (1998) 'English teachers and the third way', in B. Cox (ed.) *Literacy is Not Enough.* Manchester: Manchester University Press.

Marshall, B. (2004) *English Assessed.* Sheffield: NATE.

Martin, J.R. (1984) 'Types of writing in infants and primary school', *Proceedings of Macarthur Institute of Higher Education, Reading Language Symposium 5: Reading, Writing and Spelling,* cited in Czerniewska, P. (1992) *Learning about Writing.* Oxford: Blackwell.

Matthews, S. and Newton, C. (2005). 'Managing Meaning. "Pole to Pole" by Michael Palin', *The Secondary English Magazine,* December, 14–16.

Maybin, J. (1994) 'Teaching writing: process or genre?', in S. Brindley (ed.) *Teaching English.* London: Routledge.

Meek, M. (1990) *On Being Literate.* London: Bodley Head.

Mercer, N. (1995) *The Guided Construction of Knowledge.* Clevedon: Multilingual Matters.

Millard, E. (1997) *Differently Literate.* London: Falmer Press.

Mills, E. (2005) *Cupcakes and Kalashnikovs: 100 Years of the Best Journalism by Women.* London: Constable.

Millum, T. and Warren, C. (2001) *Twenty Things to Do with a Word Processor.* Kegworth: Resource Education.

Misson, R. and Morgan, W. (2006) *Critical Literacy and the Aesthetic: transforming the English Classroom.* Urbana, IL: NCTE.

Morgan, R. (1998) 'Provocations for a media education in small letters', in D. Buckingham, *Teaching Popular Culture: Beyond Radical Pedagogy.* London: UCL.

Morgan, W. (1997) *Critical Literacy in the Classroom.* London: Routledge.

Moss, G. (2007) *Literacy and Gender.* London: Routledge.

Moss, G. and Attar, D. (1999) 'Boys and literacy: Gendering the reading curriculum', in J. Prosser (ed.) *School Culture.* London: Paul Chapman Publishing.

Muir, E. (1962) *The Estate of Poetry.* London: Hogarth Press.

Museum Library Archives (MLA) (2003) 'Literature Matters: background and advocacy document'. London: MLA.

Myhill, D. (2005a) 'Testing times: the impact of prior knowledge on written genres produced in examination settings', *Assessment in Education,* 13, 3, 289–300.

Myhill, D. (2005b) 'The impact of prior knowledge on the sociocultural (re)production of written genres', in T. Koustouli (ed.) *Writing in Context: Research Perspectives and Pedagogical Applications.* New York: Springer, pp. 117–36.

Naidoo, B. (2000) *The Other Side of Truth.* London: Penguin.

NATE (2000) *Cracking Drama.* Sheffield: NATE.

National Year of Reading (2008) 'The cover is blown on teen reading', http://www.yearofreading.org.uk/index.php?id=208 (accessed 10/10/08).

Neelands, J. and Goode, T. (2000) *Structuring Drama Work.* Cambridge: Cambridge University Press.

New London Group (1996) 'A Pedagogy of Multiliteracies: Designing Social Futures', *Harvard Educational Review*, 66, 60–92.

Nicholls, J. (1990) 'Verse and Verbiage', *Times Educational Supplement*, 11 May, B27.

O'Brien, S. (ed.) (1998) *The Deregulated Muse*. Newcastle upon Tyne: Bloodaxe Books.

O'Connor, J. (2003) *The Pocket Guide to the English Language*. Cambridge: Cambridge University Press.

Obied, V. (2007) 'Why did I do nothing? Poetry and the experiences of bilingual pupils in a mainstream inner-city secondary school', *English in Education*, 41, 3, 37–52.

Ofsted (1993) *Boys and English*. London: DfE.

Ofsted (2005) *English 2000–2005, a review of inspection evidence*. London: Ofsted.

Ofsted (2007) *Poetry in schools, a survey of practice 2006/07*. London: Ofsted.

Padel, R. (2004) *52 ways of looking at a poem*. London: Vintage.

Parker, A. (2008) private correspondence.

Pennac, D. (1994) *Reads Like a Novel*. London: Quartet (republished in 2006 in a new translation as *The Rights of the Reader*. London: Walker Books).

Pike, M. (2000) 'Pupils' Poetics', *Changing English*, 7, 1, 45–54.

Pike, M. (2004) *Teaching Secondary English*. London: Paul Chapman Publishing.

Pullman, P. (2002) *Perverse, all monstrous, all prodigous things*. Sheffield: NATE.

Prensky, M. (2001) *Digital Natives, Digital Immigrants*, www.marcprensky.com (accessed 10/10/08).

Protherough, R. and King, P. (1995) *The Challenge of English in the National Curriculum*. London: Routledge.

Prynne, J.H. (1999) *Language and Poetry* (lecture), Cambridge University, 27 October.

QCA (2003) *New Perspectives on spoken English in the classroom*. London: QCA.

QCA (2004) *Grammar for Talk*. London: QCA.

QCA (2005a) *English 21*. London: QCA.

QCA (2005b) *Playback*. London: QCA.

QCA (2005c) *Taking English Forward*. London: QCA.

QCA (2007a) *National Curriculum English KS3 Programme of Study*. London: QCA, http://curriculum.qca.org.uk (accessed 10/10/08).

QCA (2007b) *National Curriculum English KS4 Programme of Study*. London: QCA, http://curriculum.qca.org.uk (accessed 10/10/08).

QCA (2007c) *Cross-curriculum dimensions*. London: QCA, http://curriculum.qca.org.uk/key-stages-3-and-4/cross-curriculum-dimensions/index.aspx (accessed 10/10/08).

Ray, J. (2006) 'Welcome to the Blogosphere: The Educational Use of Blogs (aka Edublogs)', *Kappa Delta Pi Record*, 42, 4, 175–7.

Reid, C. (ed.) (2007) *The Letters of Ted Hughes*. London: Faber & Faber.

Richardson, W. (2006) *Blogs, wikis, podcasts and other powerful web tools for classrooms*. Thousand Oaks, CA: Corwin Press.

Rose, J. and Scafe, R. (1997) 'Interrupting the Literature Lesson', *Changing English*, 4, 1, 123–30.

Rosenblatt, L. (1978) *The Reader, the Text, the Poem*. Carbondale, IL: Southern Illinois University Press.

Rothery, J. (1984) 'The development of genres – primary to junior secondary school', in *Deakin University Course Study Guide: Children Writing*. Melbourne: Deakin University.

Rowling, J.K. (1997) *Harry Potter and the Philosopher's Stone*. London: Bloomsbury.

Sabeti, S. (2002) 'A Language Autobiography', *Changing English*, 9, 2 , 147–50.

Sansom, P. (1994) *Writing Poems*. Newcastle upon Tyne: Bloodaxe Books.

Schmidt, M. (1998) *Lives of the Poets*. London: Phoenix Books.

Simons, J. (1990) *Diaries and Journals of Literary Women from Fanny Burney to Virginia Woolf*. Iowa City: University of Iowa Press.

Smagorinsky, P., Zoss, M. and O'Donnell Allen, C. (2005) 'Mask-making as identity project in a high school English class: a case study', *English in Education*, 39, 2, 60–75.

Snapper, G. (2006) 'Beyond Dead Poets Society: Developing Literary Awareness at A Level', *English Drama Media*, 6, 27–32.

Spiegelman, A. (2003) *The Complete Maus*. London: Penguin.

Spiro, J. (2004) *Creative Poetry Writing*. Oxford: Oxford University Press.

Spufford, F. (2002) *A Child That Books Built*. London: Faber & Faber.

Stafford, W. (1986) 'A Course in Creative Writing', in *You Must Revise Your Life*. Michigan: University of Michigan Press.

Staig, L. (1989) 'Closed Circuit', in *Dark Toys and Consumer Goods*. London: Pan Macmillan.

Steiner, G. (1978) *On Difficulty and Other Essays*. Oxford: Oxford University Press.

Steinkuehler, C. (2005) 'The New Third Place: Massively Multiplayer Online Gaming in American Youth Culture', in *Tidskrift för lärarutbildning och forskning*. Umea, Sweden: Umea Universitet, 3, 12, 17–32.

Steinkuehler, C. (2007) 'Massively multiplayer online gaming as a constellation of literacy practices', *eLearning*, 4, 3, 297–318.

Stevens, D. and McGuinn, N. (2004) *The Art of Secondary English Teaching*. London: RoutledgeFalmer.

Stibbs, A. (1981) 'Teaching Poetry', *Children's Literature in Education*, 12, 1, 39–50.

Stone, J.C. (2007) 'Popular websites in adolescents' out-of -school lives: critical lessons on literacy', in M. Knobel and C. Lankshear (eds) *A New Literacies Sampler*. New York: Peter Lang, pp. 49–65.

Storie, D. (2007) 'Exploring the litblog: how literary blogging can be used to guide readers in the selection of new books', *English in Education*, 41, 1, 37–50.

Street, B. (ed.) (1993) *Cross-cultural Approaches to Literacy*. Cambridge: Cambridge University Press.

Street, B. (1995) *Social Literacies*. New York: Longman.

Styles, M. and Arizipe, E. (2002) *Children reading pictures: interpreting visual texts*. London: RoutledgeFalmer.

Taylor, E. (1990) 'The Fly-Paper', in E. Millard and B. White (eds) *Everyday Use and other stories*. Walton-on-Thames: Thomas Nelson.

Technorati (2007) *The State of the LiveWeb April 2007*, http://technorati.com/weblog/2007/04/328.html (accessed 10/10/08).

Thomas, A. (2007) 'Blurring and Breaking through the Boundaries of Narrative, Literacy and Identity in Adolescent Fan Fiction', in M. Knobel and C. Lankshear (eds) *A New Literacies Sampler*. New York: Peter Lang, pp. 137–67.

Tolkien, J.R.R. (1937) *The Hobbit*. London: Allen & Unwin.

Twining, P. (2007) *The schome-NAGTY Teen Second Life Pilot Final Report*. Open University, http://kn.open.ac.uk/public/document.cfm?docid=9851 (accessed 10/10/08).

Van Riel, R. and Fowler, O. (1996) *Opening the Book: Finding a Good Read*. Bradford: Bradford Libraries.

Vygotsky, L.S. (1978) *Mind and Society: The Development of Higher Psychological Processes*. Cambridge, MA: Harvard University Press.

Wainwright, J. (2004) *Poetry the Basics*. London: Routledge.

Walker, A. (1984) 'The Flowers', in *Love and Trouble*. London: The Women's Press.

Wells, H.G. (1958) 'The Time Machine', in *Selected Short Stories*. London: Penguin.

Westall, R. (1986) 'The Vacancy', in G. Phinn (ed.) *Sweet and Sour*. London: Bell & Hyman.

Whitehead, F., Capey, A.C., Moddren, W. and Wellings, A. (1977) *Children and Their Books*. London: Macmillan.

Wignall, A. (2007) 'I'm in the teachers' hands' (interview with Meera Syal), *Education Guardian*, 13 February, p. 2.

Williams, A. (2007) Introduction to *Riveting Reads plus Boys into Books*. SLA, www.sla.org.uk/boys-into-books-overview.php (accessed 10/10/08).

Wilson, M. (2005) *Ice Mountain*. London: Hodder Murray.

Wood, P. (2008) 'Classroom Management', in S. Dymoke and J. Harrison (eds), *Reflective Teaching and Learning*. London: Sage, pp. 109–54.

Woodhead, C. (1980) 'Getting the Proper Attention', *Times Educational Supplement*, 11 July, p. 42.

Wray, D. and Lewis, M. (1995) 'Extending Interactions with Non-Fiction Texts: An EXIT into Understanding', *Reading*, 29, 1, 2–9.

Wray, D. and Lewis, M. (1996) 'An Approach to Writing Non-Fiction', *Reading*, 30, 2, 7–13.

Wray, D. and Medwell, J. (2001) *Teaching Literacy Effectively*. London: Routledge.

Wyatt-Smith, C. and Kimber, K. (2005) 'Valuing and evaluating student-generated online multimodal texts: rethinking what counts', *English in Education*, 39, 2, 22–43.

Yates, C. (1999) *Jumpstart*. London: The Poetry Society.

Zephaniah, B. (2002) *Refugee Boy*. London: Bloomsbury.

Index